P9-DMQ-088

# CONTEMPORARY IRISH POETRY

New and Revised Edition

The publisher wishes to acknowledge with gratitude the support of the University of Vermont Committee on Research and Scholarship, the assistance of the members of Irish Ethos and the American Irish Historical Society, and the generous contributions provided by the following individuals and institutions:

Kate and Kevin Cahill
Edward Duddy
Mary Ferguson
Pat and Bill Finnegan
Fionnula Flanagan and Garrett O'Connor
Anne Fleming
Don Godson
Grainne W. Hardiman
Connie and Henry Katzenstein
Los Angeles Theater Workspace
Frank McGinity
William Maher
James J. and Anne P. Murphy
John and Kathleen Murphy
Kathleen O'Connor Nielsen
C. Philip O'Carroll, M.D.
Nancy and Carroll O'Connor
Joan Palevsky
Angela Lansbury Shaw
Bernard Towers, M.D., and Carole I. Lieberman, M.D.
Edward Vaughan

# CONTEMPORARY IRISH POETRY

Edited, with Introduction and Notes, by Anthony Bradley

New and Revised Edition

UNIVERSITY OF CALIFORNIA PRESS
BERKELEY LOS ANGELES

University of California Press
Berkeley and Los Angeles, California



LIBRARY OF CONGRESS
Library of Congress Cataloging-in-Publication Data

Contemporary Irish poetry / edited, with introduction and notes, by
Anthony Bradley.—New and rev. ed.
p. cm.
Includes indexes.
ISBN 0-520-05927-1.
ISBN 0-520-05874-7 (pbk.)
1. English poetry—Irish authors. 2. English poetry—20th century. 3. Ireland—Poetry.
I. Bradley, Anthony, 1942–
PR8858.C65 1988
821'.91'08089162—dc19 88-14218
CIP

ISBN 0-520-05927-1 cloth
ISBN 0-520-05874-7 paperback

2 3 4 5 6 7 8 9 10

The paper used in this publication meets the minimum requirements of American National Standard for Information Sciences—Permanence of Paper for Printed Library Materials, ANSI Z39.48–1984. ♾

for PATTY and MARY
and PATRICK JOSEPH

## CONTENTS

CONTENTS

# INTRODUCTION TO THE NEW AND REVISED EDITION

It may be helpful, especially for American readers, to offer by way of preface a very brief sketch of the historical and cultural context in which Irish poetry after William Butler Yeats is rooted. This approach has the incidental advantage of not anticipating the reader's discovery of pleasure in particular poems and poets. It may also be particularly appropriate, in that literature in modern Ireland is more clearly distinguished by its engagement with history and culture than is English or American literature of the same period. Indeed, despite sharing the language of English literature, modern Irish poetry may have more apt parallels in the poetry of other postcolonial cultures.

What sets this body of poetry apart from the Irish poetry that precedes it (that of Yeats and the Irish Literary Revival) is that it reflects (and in part constitutes) the actual social and historical process of modern Ireland more accurately and intimately by far than Yeats's heroic myths and the mysticism of the Revival. Although the poets included in this anthology may follow a Yeatsian agenda in chronicling the life of their country, their collective attitude is closer to that of James Joyce than to that of Yeats; their poems, generally speaking, are contributions to a moral history of Ireland rather than to an aestheticizing of Irish historical events and personages.

The way of life that most of these post-Yeatsian poets reflect is the shared experience of most of the Irish people, which is rooted in Ireland's small farms, the social organization of the rural hinterland, its folkways, pastimes, work, education, and religious faith. These writers, from Patrick Kavanagh and Padraic Fallon to Seamus Heaney and Paul Muldoon, are representative of a still-emerging class with roots in the countryside but also with connections to modern urban life and, generally speaking, aspirations to a broader view of things. In their poetry we have a democratizing but complex version of pastoral that gives us the changing as well as the unchanging countryside; that juxtaposes ways of feeling associated with the city as well as the country; that mingles tradition and loss of tradition, past and present, nature and culture, the community and the isolated individual, faith and disbelief, and all those other antitheses reflective of social process and change. The imaginative topography of this collection of poetry, then, seems close kin to the Hardy country that Raymond Williams describes as "a border country so many of us have been living in: between custom and education, between work and ideas, between love of place and awareness of change."

Partly because of the widespread desire for political stability and the consolidation of workable political entities in both states of Ireland (what are now known as the Republic of Ireland and Northern Ireland) after the island was partitioned in 1920, both states were, in different ways and to different degrees, oppressive places to live in during the subsequent decades. Enervated by a guerrilla war with England and to an even greater extent by a civil war, then by severe and prolonged economic difficulties, the Free State (as the Republic was formerly called) was regrettably inward-looking and intolerant of all but the narrowest definitions of Irishness; it was, in addition, suspicious of literature. Not surprisingly, Ireland's writers were her public conscience, especially in the 1940s and 1950s. At the head of a tradition of verse commentary on social abuses and shortcomings stands the lonely and indomitable figure of Austin Clarke. Clarke's poems, speaking specifically for the dispossessed of his society and generally for human dignity, flay the complacency and bad faith of the times, condemn the collusion of church and state, and imagine another more ample and noble Ireland (based on the Celtic Romanesque era) in which love and art flourish. Clarke, like Thomas Kinsella later, writes out of the urban situation of Joyce, employing a Joycean realism and irony. In this tradition also, Patrick Kavanagh's *The Great Hunger*, as its title suggests, is a savage indictment of the spiritual deprivation that, despite political independence, afflicted rural Ireland in his time, just as physical hunger had racked the country a century earlier. Although social conditions improved greatly in the Republic, especially in the 1960s, and the atmosphere became a lot more congenial for writers, the abuses Clarke, Kavanagh, and others attacked continue to manifest themselves. The mantle of these writers has fallen in more recent times on the shoulders of such poets as Paul Durcan, whose poems puncture the hypocrisies and moral fatuities of life in Ireland today. Contemporary Irish poetry, then, has at least an affiliation with the older poetry in

Gaelic that is marked, especially in the seventeenth and eighteenth centuries, by its tendency to engage social and political matters.

Despite the social dimension of this tradition of verse, it is not written in the service of an abstraction nor is its style a relentlessly grim realism. The poets are invariably concerned with the intersection of the personal and the social, and their poems are quintessentially human documents. To be sure, this verse is characterized by a salutary realism and irony but it also deploys humor, compassion, and a joyful and visionary element—an impulse to praise what is really life and to protect that from the nay-sayers. In Kavanagh, for example, one finds a joyous imaginative repossession of the ordinary countryside of Ireland, as though it had recently been liberated or were being seen for the first time as its unidealized yet radiant self.

The history of Northern Ireland for the whole of its existence has been considerably more oppressive than that of the Republic. A sectarian state dominated for fifty years by what was essentially a one-party system, Northern Ireland was only nominally a democracy. With the advantage of hindsight, the outbreak of violence in 1969 and its apparently intractable continuation down to the present seem inevitable. The poems of John Hewitt and John Montague, before as well as after the outbreak of the present Troubles, are attuned to Ulster's cultural and political schisms. Indeed, even though the Ulster writers have resisted allowing an artistic agenda to be set for them by the present conflict and have been wary of turning into representatives for tribal attitudes in a situation where the feelings of intelligent people are necessarily tangled and ambivalent, they have all inevitably been compelled to write out of their experience of the Troubles.

As one might expect, there are many elegies for victims of the violence, by Seamus Heaney and most of the other poets from the North: at their best, these elegies are not only profoundly moving in their mourning of specific (and indeed of all) human loss but are also profoundly illuminating of the pathology of social relations in the North. Poems by writers like Derek Mahon and Tom Paulin, who come out of the Protestant tradition in the North, are informed by a scathing anger at the Calvinist mixture of theology and politics that pervades Ulster's dominant culture. There are, too, many excellent poems from the Ulster poets that explore the divergent cultural traditions of the North as they are embodied in neighbors from different sides in that ancient quarrel.

Again, it should be stressed that even though these poems emerge from the situation in the North, most are not in any sense a mere documentary reflex to that murderous upheaval. They are written by artists, not spokesmen, and are resonant in their deployment of image, symbol, and myth at the same time that they are shaped by the political predicament in less than obvious or predictable ways. One might take as examples Heaney's "The Tollund Man," Mahon's "Courtyards in Delft," and Muldoon's "Gathering Mushrooms." The connection with Ulster is not simple in any of these poems, which match the cunning passages of history with the complexity, obliquity, and distancing of art in order to achieve their truth. "Courtyards in Delft," for instance, a poem "about" a Dutch painting, manifests the ethos to which Ulster Protestants belong with an exactness, resonance, and power that is inevitably absent from less artful attempts to render the Ulster Protestant mentality.

The obsession with history on the part of the Irish is evident in many of the poems in this collection; not only the contemporary history of the Troubles but the plantation of Ulster, the Famine, the Rebellion of 1798, and even the archaeological past find their way into these poems. This preoccupation is not, however, a peculiarly Irish form of self-indulgence but rather stems from the understanding, gained from experience, that history is personal, that it affects individual lives in the present in urgent ways, and that it needs to be explored, rethought in the light of experience, and understood. So there is for many Irish writers, in George Steiner's phrase in a different context, "a past tense to the grammar of being." But although contemporary Irish poets see the present predicament as the outcome or repetition of a process that has gone on for centuries, they are sharply aware, as the writers of the Revival were not, that our interpretation of history (so Steiner and others have reminded us) depends less on literal facts than on "images of the past." Hence the metahistorical tinge to numerous recent meditations on the Irish past.

Despite their self-consciousness about history, these are not poems about the abstraction "history" but, rather, imaginative structures that make us feel the intimacy of the connection between the personal and the historical. It is the connection in John Montague's *The Rough Field*, for example, between personal and family history on the one hand and the history of Ulster on the other, that validates the sequence imaginatively. The feeling animating that sequence makes "A Grafted Tongue" (for example) not so much a commentary on the loss of a language and culture as an intense, personal enactment and realization of that historical experience.

Religion has always been of obvious and profound significance, spiritually and socially, in Irish life, and it is clearly a dimension of the crisis in the North. What Michael Longley has pointed out about Ulster, that it "must be one of the very few remaining areas in the English speaking world which are still likely to produce poets who write out of a response to religion," is true of all Ireland. Typically that response resists the oppressive aspects of the Catholic church as a social institution in Ireland and the inflexibility of its teaching, especially on social issues. Yet the contemporary poet's sensibility (like that of early Gaelic poets) responds also to the beauty of the liturgy; frequently chooses theme, metaphor, image, and allusion from Catholic belief; and is imprinted with a sense of nature as sacramental, of poetry as a type of prayer, and of the artist as a sacerdotal figure. One can trace the central role of religion, thus understood, in Irish poetry from Clarke to Heaney via numerous points in between. The framework of the pilgrimage to Lough Derg recently employed by Seamus Heaney in *Station Island* and earlier employed by both Denis Devlin and Patrick Kavanagh is one important instance of Irish Catholicism offering a literary structure that is rooted in the experience of the people.

In writers who come out of the Irish Protestant tradition, a comparable process of rejection and transformation of religious orthodoxy can be seen. From Samuel Beckett, Louis MacNeice, and W. R. Rodgers to John Hewitt, Derek Mahon, and Tom Paulin, one finds a sequence of poetic disputes with biblical injunctions, wrestling matches with a Calvinist God or his adherents, essentially attempts to countermand the implacable qualities of that variety of Protestantism. For writers who come out of the Ulster Protestant tradition, in particular, their sense of struggle is intensified by the awareness that this Calvinist belief is the direct source of so much bitterness and violence in the Ulster context, not to mention a more widespread crippling of creative possibilities for the human spirit. At the same time, this strain of poetry, in its Puritan energy, in its capacity for assuming conscience and judgment, and in its self-awareness of being a voice crying in the wilderness, is colored (like the literature of the New England Renaissance) in a compelling and positive way by the belief system it rejects.

Language as well as politics, history, and religion inevitably plays a crucial role in the cultural self-awareness displayed by Irish poetry. Most Irish poets (including those in the North who come from a nationalist background) are haunted by the Gaelic language and have felt bound to come to terms with the literary tradition in Gaelic by creatively translating poems from that tradition. Many of those translations have been included in this collection.

Yet while there is a manifest and pressing need for contemporary Irish poets who write in English to recover Gaelic literature in some measure, there is also an awareness that this heritage is, as a whole, distant and shattered. Of course, there are still poets in Ireland who write in Gaelic (Nuala Ní Dhomhnaill, for example, translations from whose work have been included) and at least one (Michael Hartnett) who started writing in English, later switched to Gaelic, and is now writing in English again. The important thing is that the Gaelic linguistic and literary tradition is a continuous presence and pressure for the Irish writer; moreover the history of Ireland has given the English language in Ireland a distinctive and separate identity. Also, there is in this poetry a more-than-usual self-consciousness about language itself, and a sense of the danger and difficulty of utterance that probably originates in the colonial situation.

Even though Austin Clarke's attempt to import the technique of Gaelic verse into his poems was experimental and resulted at times in oddities, and even though his approach was a bit programmatic, it should be understood that he was trying to create a poetry in the English language that would be distinctively Irish. None of the poets who succeed Clarke are as self-conscious about their indebtedness to Gaelic poetry, but it may be that Clarke's experimentation served to relieve the burden of anxiety of poets who write in English. Poets after Clarke have absorbed elements of technique and form from Gaelic poetry in what now seems like a fairly natural and painless transaction. The Gaelic genre of *dinnseanchas* (the lore of places), for example, is evident in place-poems by Heaney, Montague, and many others: clearly this fascination with place is a major characteristic of Irish literature in English as well as in Gaelic. For the poet who writes in English, the Gaelic place-name is a kind of capsule history that carries him or her back to origins and makes a bridge to a potent aspect of history or myth. Although this type of poem sometimes functions as an intense expression of love for a particular place, most often the place is only the setting for ideas, so that the poem's landscape, rooted in an actual place though it may be, becomes a landscape of the mind.

The cultural self-awareness of these Irish poets does not prevent them from writing many poems that are much less obviously, if at all, dependent on the Irish cultural context—poems about art, the self, childhood, marriage, family, work, and the modern way of life that Ireland, in some respects, now shares with western Europe and America. Indeed, most of these writers would probably argue with considerable justice that their poetry maintains a creative tension between the inner and outer worlds of self and history.

Nonetheless, a large minority of the poets represented in this anthology vigorously dispute, implicitly or explicitly, the Irishness of the agenda—cultural identity, Irish history and society, the rural world, and the Gaelic tradition—set by their fellow poets. For them Irishness and modernity are incompatible. They impatiently dismiss the cultural self-awareness of the others as archaic and provincial, as (at times) dangerously atavistic; they distrust the idea of a national literature, of an Irish poet as opposed to a poet who happens to be Irish. Although there are significant differences between them, one might point to two groups of Irish poets who disclaim Irishness—the European Irish poets led by Beckett and the Ulster poets under the aegis of MacNeice. Beckett categorically rejects the idea of "an accredited theme," proclaiming rather the importance of "self-perception" and "the hegemony of the inner life over the outer life." For MacNeice, the Irish past (the most "accredited" of Irish themes) is "narcotic." Both sets of exiles from Ireland (whether actual exiles or inner exiles) are preoccupied, instead, with the idea of modernity. Their poems reflect an urban or, rather, a cosmopolitan sensibility, and modern feelings of loss and alienation as well as, paradoxically, feelings of being at home in the modern world. They reflect, too, a sense of history based in the convulsions of the two world wars coupled with a sensitivity to humanity's potential for total self-destruction in the nuclear age. For these writers, the literary pantheon is defined by Joyce and European literature. Instead of translations from the Gaelic, they undertake translations from the European languages and the classics. Beckett, Thomas MacGreevy, Brian Coffey, Devlin, MacNeice, Mahon, Longley (and a considerable number of others who do not belong to either the European Irish or the Ulster grouping) reject Irishness for numerous and complex reasons, but those reasons must include a sense that Irish themes and styles are provincial and inadequate for the purpose of expressing the human condition, as well as a need to distance themselves from a political and cultural identity they do not fully share.

Of course, this either/or distinction between Irishness and modernity is too rigid. In practice, those poets who refuse to be identified by Irishness also struggle frequently with Irish history, society, and politics and are fascinated by the landscape, especially of the West of Ireland. By the same token, those poets one might be tempted to identify only in terms of their cultural self-awareness also possess distinctly modern sensibilities.

The technique of contemporary Irish poetry, taken as a whole, varies a great deal but, with certain rather obvious exceptions, is traditional rather than innovative. Most of it is accessible to the general reader, although the experimentalism of Clarke, Kinsella, and Muldoon makes some of their work intriguingly hermetic. There is nonetheless a certain polarity in the matter of form, with classic examples of the well-made poem cherished by the British Movement of the 1950s and much looser and more organic structures akin to the forms of American poetry shaped by Ezra Pound and William Carlos Williams. One might add the observation that certain formal properties of poetry—notably, free verse—no longer seem especially modern or experimental (in fact, may seem by now quite traditional); the corollary process also seems to hold true, that traditional forms such as the sonnet gain new interest from their use in the Irish context by writers such as Kavanagh, Richard Murphy, Heaney, and Muldoon.

The range of accomplishment in contemporary Irish poetry is great, and I have not been tempted to invoke any definition of poetry that might eliminate all but a half-dozen or so of these writers. I have found all the poems enjoyable or, at least, interesting for their attempt on our behalf to make sense of the world that is Ireland and elsewhere. Many of the poems are more than interesting and enjoyable: a considerable number remind us of one test for the truest poetry by giving us the sensation, to paraphrase Emily Dickinson, of having the tops of our heads taken off. My choice of individual poems cannot please everyone, but that is inevitable; I have selected these particular poems deliberately if not dogmatically because they seem to me good poems and because they are in some way typical (or, occasionally, atypical) of the writer's work as a whole. In my inclusion of several generations of poets after Yeats, I have wanted to demonstrate both the rich diversity of that body of poetry as well as its coherence and continuity.

A good deal of critical commentary on this poetry is now available: readers may wish to consult two excellent recent books—Dillon Johnston's *Irish Poetry After Joyce* (University of Notre Dame Press, 1985) and Robert Garratt's *Modern Irish Poetry: Tradition and Continuity from Yeats to Heaney* (University of California Press, 1986). Both books contain extensive and useful bibliographies of criticism.

I am grateful to the University of California Press for offering me the chance to revise this anthology; it is one sign, at least, of the vitality of contemporary Irish poetry that many selections have had to be updated so extensively, and new poets added. With considerable pangs, I have felt compelled to omit a few writers who were featured in the first edition, notably Stewart Parker, whose energies have been channeled away from poetry into theater to make him the significant and accomplished dramatist he now is. That regret is, however, offset by delight that there are so many promising young poets in Ireland today (more of them women than before) who will renew and extend the tradition of Irish poetry in the years to come, as they sing what the great Fionn esteemed the best music in the world—"the music of what happens."

*Anthony Bradley*
The University of Vermont, 1988

# THE POETRY

## THOMAS MacGREEVY

Thomas MacGreevy was born in 1893 in County Kerry. He took degrees at University College, Dublin, and at Trinity College. He was an officer in the British Army during World War I, and was twice wounded at the Battle of the Somme. In 1925 MacGreevy went to London where he worked as a Lecturer at the National Gallery. He moved to Paris in 1927 and held a position as Lecteur at the Ecole Normale Superieure for seven years. During these years he was closely associated with the Irish expatriate writers living in Paris, especially Beckett and Joyce. His poetry and criticism appeared in many journals; critical studies of T. S. Eliot and Richard Aldington were published in 1931 and *Poems* in 1934. MacGreevy returned to London in 1935 when he was reappointed to his position at the National Gallery. In the early 1940s he moved back to Dublin where he established himself as an art critic, and in 1950 he was appointed Director of the National Gallery in Dublin, a position he held until his retirement in 1963. MacGreevy died in 1967. *Collected Poems* appeared in 1971.

## DE CIVITATE HOMINUM

To A. S. F. R.

The morning sky glitters
Winter blue.
The earth is snow-white,
With the gleam snow-white answers to sunlight,
Save where shell-holes are new,
Black spots in the whiteness—

A Matisse ensemble.

The shadows of whitened tree stumps
Are another white.

And there are white bones.

Zillebeke Lake and Hooge,
Ice gray, gleam differently,

Like the silver shoes of the model.

The model is our world,
Our bitch of a world.
Those who live between wars may not know
But we who die between peaces
Whether we die or not.

It is very cold
And, what with my sensations
And my spick and span subaltern's uniform,
I might be the famous brass monkey,
The *nature morte* accessory.

*Morte . . . !*
'Tis still life that lives,
Not quick life—

There are fleece-white flowers of death
That unfold themselves prettily
About an airman

Who, high over Gheluvelt,
Is taking a morning look round,
All silk and silver
Up in the blue.

I hear the drone of an engine
And soft pounding puffs in the air
As the fleece-white flowers unfold.

I cannot tell which flower he has accepted
But suddenly there is a tremor,
A zigzag of lines against the blue
And he streams down
Into the white,
A delicate flame,
A stroke of orange in the morning's dress.

My sergeant says, very low, "Holy God!
'Tis a fearful death."

Holy God makes no reply
Yet.

## AODH RUADH O'DOMHNAILL

To Stiefán MacEnna

Juan de Juni the priest said,
Each J becoming H;

Berruguete, he said,
And the G was aspirate;

Ximenez, he said then
And aspirated first and last.

But he never said
And—it seemed odd—he
Never had heard
The aspirated name
Of the centuries-dead
Bright-haired young man
Whose grave I sought.

All day I passed
In greatly built gloom
From dusty gilt tomb
Marvellously wrought
To tomb
Rubbing
At mouldy inscriptions
With fingers wetted with spit
And asking
Where I might find it
And failing.

Yet when
Unhurried—
    Not as at home
    Where heroes, hanged, are buried
    With non-commissioned officers' bored maledictions
    Quickly in the gaol yard—

They brought
His blackening body
Here
To rest
Princes came
Walking
Behind it

And all Valladolid knew
And out to Simancas all knew
Where they buried Red Hugh.

## RECESSIONAL

In the bright broad Swiss glare I stand listening
To the outrageous roars
Of the Engelbergeraa
As it swirls down the gorge
And I think I am thinking
Of Roderick Hudson.
But, as I stand,
Time closes over sight,
And sound
Is drowned
By a long silvery roar
From the far ends of memory
Of a world I have left
And I find I am thinking:
Supposing I drowned now,
This tired, tiresome body,
Before flesh creases further,
Might, recovered, go, fair,
To be laid in Saint Lachtin's,
Near where once,
In tender, less glaring, island days
And ways
I could hear—
Where listeners still hear—
That far-away, dear
Roar
The long, silvery roar
Of Mal Bay.

## HOMAGE TO MARCEL PROUST

To Jean Thomas

The sea gleamed deep blue in the sunlight
Through the different greens of the trees.
And the talk was of singing.
My mother, dressed in black, recalled a bright image from
a song,
*Those endearing young charms*,
Miss Holly, wearing heliotrope, had a sad line,
*The waves still are singing to the shore.*
Then, as we came out from the edge of the wood,
The island lay dreaming in the sun across the bridge,
Even the white coastguard station had gone quietly to
sleep—it was Sunday,
A chain on a ship at the pier
Rattled to silence,
Cries of children, playing, sounded faintly
And, musically, somewhere,
A young sailor of the island—

He was tall
And slim
And curled, to the moustaches,
And he wore ear-rings
But often he was too ill to be at sea—

Was singing,
*Maid of Athens, ere we part . . .*

Looking suddenly like a goddess
Miss Holly said, half-smiling,
"Listen . . ."
And we stopped
In the sunlight
Listening . . .

The young sailor is dead now.
Miss Holly also is dead.
And Byron . . .
Home they've gone and

And the waves still are singing.

## NOCTURNE OF THE SELF-EVIDENT PRESENCE

Fortunate,
Being inarticulate,
The alps
Rise
In ice
To heights
Of large stars
And little;
To courts
Beneath other courts
With walls of white starlight.
They have stars for pavements,
The valley is an area,
And I a servant,
A servant of servants,
Of metaphysical bereavements,
Staring up
Out of the gloom.

I see no immaculate feet on those pavements,
No winged forms,
Foreshortened,
As by Rubens or Domenichino,
Plashing the silvery air,
Hear no cars,

Elijah's or Apollo's,
Dashing about
Up there.
I see alps, ice, stars and white starlight
In a dry, high silence.

## AUSTIN CLARKE

Austin Clarke was born in 1896 in Dublin. He was educated in Dublin at Belvedere College and University College, where he received his M.A. and was lecturer in English from 1918 to 1922. Clarke was a founding member of the Irish Academy of Letters and served as president from 1952 to 1954. He was married and had three children. During the course of a highly prolific writing career, Clarke produced numerous volumes of poetry, plays, novels, and criticism. His published collections of poetry include *The Vengeance of Fionn* (1917), *The Fires of Baal* (1921), *The Sword of the West* (1921), *The Cattle-drive in Connaught and Other Poems* (1925), *Pilgrimage and Other Poems* (1929), *The Collected Poems of Austin Clarke* (1936), *Night and Morning* (1938), *Ancient Lights* (1955), *Too Great a Vine: Poems and Satires* (1957), *The Horse Eaters: Poems and Satires* (1960), *Collected Later Poems* (1961), *Forget-Me-Not* (1962), *Flight to Africa and Other Poems* (1963), *Mnemosyne Lay in Dust* (1966), *Old Fashioned Pilgrimage and Other Poems* (1967), *The Echo at Coole and Other Poems* (1967), *A Sermon on Swift and Other Poems* (1968), *Orphide* (1970), *Tiresias: A Poem* (1971), *The Wooing of Becfola* (after the Irish, 1973). Clarke died in 1974.

## THE PLANTER'S DAUGHTER

When night stirred at sea
And the fire brought a crowd in,
They say that her beauty
Was music in mouth
And few in the candlelight
Thought her too proud,
For the house of the planter
Is known by the trees.

Men that had seen her
Drank deep and were silent,
The women were speaking
Wherever she went—
As a bell that is rung
Or a wonder told shyly,
And O she was the Sunday
In every week.

## PILGRIMAGE

When the far south glittered
Behind the grey beaded plains,
And cloudier ships were bitted
Along the pale waves,
The showery breeze—that plies
A mile from Ara—stood
And took our boat on sand:
There by dim wells the women tied
A wish on thorn, while rainfall
Was quiet as the turning of books
In the holy schools at dawn.

Grey holdings of rain
Had grown less with the fields,
As we came to that blessed place
Where hail and honey meet.
O Clonmacnoise was crossed
With light: those cloistered scholars,
Whose knowledge of the gospel
Is cast as metal in pure voices,
Were all rejoicing daily,
And cunning hands with cold and jewels
Brought chalices to flame.

Loud above the grassland,
In Cashel of the towers,
We heard with the yellow candles
The chanting of the hours,
White clergy saying High Mass,
A fasting crowd at prayer,
A choir that sang before them;
And in stained glass the holy day
Was sainted as we passed
Beyond that chancel where the dragons
Are carved upon the arch.

Treasured with chasuble,
Sun-braided, rich cloak'd wine-cup,
We saw, there, iron handbells,
Great annals in the shrine
A high-king bore to battle:
Where, from the branch of Adam,
The noble forms of language—
Brighter than green or blue enamels
Burned in white bronze—embodied
The wings and fiery animals
Which veil the chair of God.

Beyond a rocky townland
And that last tower where ocean
Is dim as haze, a sound
Of wild confession rose:
Black congregations moved
Around the booths of prayer
To hear a saint reprove them;
And from his boat he raised a blessing
To souls that had come down
The holy mountain of the west
Or wailed still in the cloud.

Light in the tide of Shannon
May ride at anchor half
The day and, high in spar-top
Or leather sails of their craft,
Wine merchants will have sleep;
But on a barren isle,
Where Paradise is praised
At daycome, smaller than the sea-gulls,
We heard white Culdees pray
Until our hollow ship was kneeling
Over the longer waves.

## NIGHT AND MORNING

I know the injured pride of sleep,
The strippers at the mocking-post,
The insult in the house of Caesar
And every moment that can hold
In brief the miserable act
Of centuries. Thought can but share
Belief—and the tormented soul,
Changing confession to despair,
Must wear a borrowed robe.

Morning has moved the dreadful candle,
Appointed shadows cross the nave;
Unlocked by the secular hand,
The very elements remain
Appearances upon the altar.
Adoring priest has turned his back
Of gold upon the congregation.
All saints have had their day at last,
But thought still lives in pain.

How many councils and decrees
Have perished in the simple prayer
That gave obedience to the knee;
Trampling of rostrum, feathering
Of pens at cock-rise, sum of reason
To elevate a common soul:
Forgotten as the minds that bled
For us, the miracle that raised
A language from the dead.

O when all Europe was astir
With echo of learned controversy,
The voice of logic led the choir.
Such quality was in all being,
The forks of heaven and this earth
Had met, town-walled, in mortal view
And in the pride that we ignore,
The holy rage of argument,
God was made man once more.

## TENEBRAE

This is the hour that we must mourn
With tallows on the black triangle,
Night has a napkin deep in fold
To keep the cup; yet who dare pray
If all in reason should be lost,
The agony of man betrayed
At every station of the cross?

O when the forehead is too young,
Those centuries of mortal anguish,
Dabbed by a consecrated thumb
That crumbles into dust, will bring
Despair with all that we can know;
And there is nothing left to sing,
Remembering our innocence.

I hammer on that common door,
Too frantic in my superstition,
Transfix with nails that I have broken,
The angry notice of the mind.
Close as the thought that suffers him,
The habit every man in time
Must wear beneath his ironed shirt.

An open mind disturbs the soul,
And in disdain I turn my back
Upon the sun that makes a show
Of half the world, yet still deny
The pain that lives within the past,
The flame sinking upon the spike,
Darkness that man must dread at last.

AUSTIN CLARKE

## THE STRAYING STUDENT

On a holy day when sails were blowing southward
A bishop sang the Mass at Inishmore,
Men took one side, their wives were on the other
But I heard the woman coming from the shore:
And wild in despair my parents cried aloud
For they saw the vision draw me to the doorway.

Long had she lived in Rome when Popes were bad,
The wealth of every age she makes her own,
Yet smiled on me in eager admiration
And for a summer taught me all I know,
Banishing shame with her great laugh that rang
As if a pillar caught it back alone.

I learned the prouder counsel of her throat,
My mind was growing bold as light in Greece;
And when in sleep her stirring limbs were shown,
I blessed the noonday rock that knew no tree:
And for an hour the mountain was her throne,
Although her eyes were bright with mockery.

They say I was sent back from Salamanca
And failed in logic, but I wrote her praise
Nine times upon a college wall in France.
She laid her hand at darkfall on my page
That I might read the heavens in a glance
And I knew every star the Moors had named.

Awake or in my sleep, I have no peace now,
Before the ball is struck, my breath is gone,
And yet I tremble lest she may deceive me
And leave me in this land where every woman's son
Must carry his own coffin and believe,
In dread, all that the clergy teach the young.

## THE ENVY OF POOR LOVERS

Pity poor lovers who may not do what they please
With their kisses under a hedge, before a raindrop
Unhouses it; and astir from wretched centuries,
Bramble and briar remind them of the saints.

Her envy is the curtain seen at night-time,
Happy position that could change her name.
His envy—clasp of the married whose thoughts can be
alike,
Whose nature flows without the blame or shame.

Lying in the grass as if it were a sin
To move, they hold each other's breath, tremble,
Ready to share that ancient dread—kisses begin
Again—of Ireland keeping company with them.

Think, children, of institutions mured above
Your ignorance, where every look is veiled,
State-paid to snatch away the folly of poor lovers
For whom, it seems, the sacraments have failed.

## WOLFE TONE

He called a conquered land his own
Although he never bowed at Mass
Behind locked door or knelt on grass.
But we are taught now to disown
Him. Faith needs more than bite and sup.
What may we do but rattle his chains
At College Green, despise cut veins?
We cannot blow his statue up.

AUSTIN CLARKE

# THREE POEMS ABOUT CHILDREN

## I

Better the book against the rock,
The misery of roofless faith,
Than all this mockery of time,
Eternalising of mute souls.
Though offerings increase, increase,
The ancient arms can bring no peace,
When the first breath is unforgiven
And charity, to find a home,
Redeems the baby from the breast.
O, then, at the very font of grace,
Pity, pity—the dumb must cry.
Their tiny tears are in the walls
We build. They turn to dust so soon,
How can we learn upon our knees,
That ironside unropes the bell?

## II

These infants die too quick
For our salvation, caught up
By a fatal sign from Limbo,
Unfathered in our thought
Before they can share the sky
With us. Though faith allow
Obscurity of being
And clay rejoice: flowers
That wither in the heat
Of benediction, one
By one, are thrown away.

## III

Martyr and heretic
Have been the shrieking wick!
But smoke of faith on fire
Can hide us from enquiry
And trust in Providence
Rid us of vain expense.
So why should pity uncage
A burning orphanage
Bar flight to little souls
That set no churchbell tolling?
Cast-iron step and rail
Could but prolong the wailing:
Has not a Bishop declared
That flame-wrapped babes are spared
Our life-time of temptation?
Leap, mind, in consolation
For heart can only lodge
Itself, plucked out by logic.
Those children, charred in Cavan,
Passed straight through Hell to Heaven.

## FORGET ME NOT

*Up the hill,*
*Hurry me not;*
*Down the hill,*
*Worry me not;*
*On the level,*
*Spare me not,*
*In the stable,*
*Forget me not.*

Trochaic dimeter, amphimacer
And choriamb, with hyper catalexis,
Grammatical inversion, springing of double
Rhyme. So we learned to scan all, analyse
Lyric and ode, elegy, anonymous patter,
For what is song itself but substitution?
Let classical terms unroll, with a flourish, the scroll
Of baccalaureate.

Coleridge had picked
That phrase for us—*vergiss-mein-nicht*, emblem
Of love and friendship, delicate sentiments.
Forget-me-nots, forget-me-nots:
Blue, sunny-eyed young hopefuls! He left a nosegay,
A keepsake for Kate Greenaway.

Child climbed
Into the trap; the pony started quick
As fly to a flick and Uncle John began
Our work-a-day, holiday jingle.

*Up the hill,*
*Hurry me not.*

*Down the hill,*
*Worry me not.*

Verse came like that, simple
As join-hands, yet ambiguous, lesson
Implied, a flower-puzzle in final verb
And negative. All was personification
As we drove on: invisibility
Becoming audible. A kindness spoke.
Assumed the god; consensus everywhere
In County Dublin. Place-names, full of Sunday,
Stepaside, Pass-if-you-can Lane, Hole in the Wall.
Such foliage in the Dargle hid Lovers Leap,
We scarcely heard the waters fall-at-all.
Often the open road to Celbridge: we came back
By Lucan Looks Lovely, pulled in at the Strawberry Beds,

Walked up the steep of Knockmaroon. Only
The darkness could complete our rounds. The pony
Helped, took the bit. Coat-buttoned up, well-rugg'd
I drowsed till the clatter of city sets, warning
Of echoes around St. Mary's Place, woke me;
But I was guarded by medal, scapular
And the *Agnus Dei* next my skin, passing
That Protestant Church. Night shirt, warm manger, confusion
Of premise, creed; I sank through mysteries
To our oblivion.
*Ora pro nobis*
*Ora pro me.*
'Gee up,' 'whoa,' 'steady,' 'hike,'
'Hike ow'a that.' Rough street-words, cheerful, impatient:
The hearers knew their own names as well. Horses,
Men, going together to daily work; dairy
Cart, baker's van, slow dray, quick grocery
Deliveries. Street-words, the chaff in them.
Suddenly in Mountjoy Street, at five o'clock
Yes, five in the evening, work rhymed for a minute
with sport.
Church-echoing wheel-rim, roof-beat, tattle of harness
Around the corner of St. Mary's Place:
Cabs, outside cars, the drivers unranked in race
For tips; their horses eager to compete,
With spark and hubbub, greet with their own heat
Galway Express that puffed to Broadstone Station.
They held that Iron Horse in great esteem
Yet dared the metamorphosis of steam.
Soon they were back again. I ran to watch
As Uncle John in elegant light tweeds
Drove smartly by on his outside car, talking
Over his shoulder to a straight-up fare
Or two, coaxing by name his favourite mare;
The best of jarvies, his sarcastic wit
Checked by a bridle rein; and he enlarged
My mind with two Victorian words. Grown-ups

Addressed him as Town Councillor, Cab
And Car Proprietor!

Horse-heads above me,
Below me. Happy on tram top, I looked down
On plaited manes, alighted safely, caught
Sidelong near kerb, perhaps, affectionate glance
As I passed a blinker. Much to offend the pure:
Let-down or drench, the sparrows pecking at fume,
The scavengers with shovel, broom. But, O
When horse fell down, pity was there: we saw
Such helplessness, girth buckled, no knack in knee,
Half-upturned legs—big hands that couldn't unclench.
A parable, pride or the like, rough-shod,
Or goodness put in irons, then, soul uplifted
Bodily; traffic no longer interrupted.
Strength broadened in narrow ways. Champions went by,
Guinness's horses from St. James's Gate:
Their brasses clinked, yoke, collar shone at us:
Light music while they worked. Side-streets, alleys
Beyond St. Patrick's, floats unloading, country
Colt, town hack, hay-cart, coal-bell. Often the whip-crack,
The lash of rein. Hand-stitch in the numb of pain
At school. Religious orders plied the strap
On us, but never on themselves. Each day, too,
Justice tore off her bandage in Mountjoy Street.
The Black Maria passed, van o' the poor.
Weeks, months clung to those bars, cursed, or stared, mute.
Children in rags ran after that absenting,
Did double time to fetlocks. Solemnity
For all; the mournful two or four with plumes,
Hooves blackened to please your crape. The funerals
Go faster now. Our Christianity
Still catching up with All is Vanity.

Nevertheless,
Nature had learned to share our worldliness,

Well-pleased to keep with man the colours in hide,
Dappling much, glossing the chestnut, sunshading the bays,
To grace those carriage wheels, that *vis-à-vis*
In the Park. Let joy cast off a trace, for once,
High-stepping beyond the Phoenix Monument
In the long ago of British Rule, I saw
With my own eyes a white horse that unfabled
The Unicorn.
                    Mechanised vehicles:
Horse-power by handle-turn. My Uncle John
Lost stable companions, drivers, all. Though poor,
He kept his last mare out on grass. They aged
Together. At twenty-one, I thought it right
And proper.

                    How could I know that greed
Spreads quicker than political hate? No need
Of propaganda. Good company, up and down
The ages, gone: the trick of knife left, horse cut
To serve man. All the gentling, custom of mind
And instinct, close affection, done with. The unemployed
Must go. Dead or ghosted by froths, we ship them
Abroad. Foal, filly, farm pony, bred for slaughter:
What are they now but hundredweights of meat?
A double trade. Greed with a new gag of mercy
Grants happy release in our whited abbatoirs.
"Gentlemen, businessmen, kill on the spot! O
That," exclaim the good, "should be your motto.
Combine in a single trade all profits, save
Sensitive animals from channelling wave,
Continental docking, knackering down.
We dread bad weather, zig-zag, tap of Morse."
Well-meaning fools, who only pat the horse
That looks so grand on our Irish half-crown.

I've more to say—

Men of Great Britain
Openly share with us the ploughtail, the field-spoil,
Trucking in Europe what we dare not broil
At home.
Herodotus condemned
Hippophagy.
And Pliny, also.
Beseiged towns
Denied it.
Stare now at Pegasus. The blood
Of the Medusa weakens in him.
Yet all the world
Was hackneyed once—those horses o' the sun,
Apollo's car, centaurs in Thessaly.
Too many staves have splintered the toy
That captured Troy. The Hippocrene is stale.
Dark ages; Latin rotted, came up from night-soil,
New rush of words; thought mounted them. Trappings
Of palfrey, sword-kiss of chivalry, high song
Of grammar. Men pick the ribs of Rosinante
In restaurants now. Horse-shoe weighs in with saddle
Of meat.
Horseman, the pass-word, courage shared
With lace, steel, buff.
Wars regimented
Haunches together. Cities move by in motor
Cars, charging the will. I hear in the lateness of Empires,
A neighing, man's cry in engines. No peace, yet,
Poor draggers of artillery.
The moon
Eclipsed: I stood on the Rock of Cashel, saw dimly
Carved on the royal arch of Cormac's Chapel
Sign of the Sagittary, turned my back
On all that Celtic Romanesque; thinking

Of older story and legend, how Cuchullain,
Half man, half god-son, tamed the elemental
Coursers, dear comrades, how at his death
The Gray of Macha laid her mane upon his breast
And wept.
                    I struggled down
From paleness of limestone.
                                        Too much historied
Land, wrong in policies, armings, hope in prelates
At courts abroad! Rags were your retribution,
Hedge schools, a visionary knowledge in verse
That hid itself. The rain-drip cabin'd the dream
Of foreign aid . . . Democracy at last.
White horses running through the European mind
Of the First Consul. Our heads were cropped like his.
New brow; old imagery. A Gaelic poet,
Pitch-capped in the Rebellion of '98
Called this Republic in an allegory
The Slight Red Steed.
                                        Word-loss is now our gain:
Put mare to stud. Is Ireland any worse
Than countries that fly-blow the map, rattle the sky,
Drop down from it? Tipsters respect our grand sires,
Thorough-breds, jumpers o' the best.
Our grass still makes a noble show, and the roar
Of money cheers us at the winning post.
So pack tradition in the meat-sack, Boys,
Write off the epitaph of Yeats.
                                        I'll turn
To jogtrot, pony bell, say my first lesson:

*Up the hill,*
*Hurry me not;*
*Down the hill,*
*Worry me not;*

*On the level,*
*Spare me not,*
*In the stable,*
*Forget me not.*

*Forget me not.*

## from MNEMOSYNE LAY IN DUST

One night he heard heart-breaking sound.
It was a sigh unworlding its sorrow.
Another followed. Slowly he counted
Four different sighs, one after another.
"My mother," he anguished, "and my sisters
Have passed away. I am alone, now,
Lost in myself in a mysterious
Darkness, the victim in a story."
Far whistle of a train, the voice of steam.
Evil was peering through the peep-hole.

Suddenly heart began to beat
Too quickly, too loudly. It clamoured
As if it were stopping. He left the heat
And stumbled forward, hammered
The door, called out that he was dying.
Key turned. Body was picked up, carried
Beyond the ward, the bedwhite row
Of faces, into a private darkness.
Lock turned. He cried out. All was still.
He stood, limbs shivering in the chill.

He tumbled into half the truth:
Burial alive. His breath was shouting:
"Let, let me out." But words were puny.
Fists hushed on a wall of inward-outness.

Knees crept along a floor that stirred
As softly. All was the same chill.
He knew the wall was circular
And air was catchcry in the stillness
For reason had returned to tell him
That he was in a padded cell.

The key had turned again. Blankets
Were flung into blackness as if to mock
The cringer on the floor. He wrapped
The bedclothes around his limbs, shocked back
To sanity. Lo! in memory yet,
Margaret came in a frail night-dress,
Feet bare, her heavy plaits let down
Between her knees, his pale protectress.
Nightly restraint, unwanted semen
Had ended their romantic dream.

Early next morning, he awakened,
Saw only greyness shining down
From a skylight on the grey walls
Of leather, knew, in anguish, his bowels
Had opened. He turned, shivering, all shent.
Wrapping himself in the filthied blankets,
Fearful of dire punishment,
He waited there until a blankness
Enveloped him . . . When he raised his head up,
Noon-light was gentle in the bedroom.

## INSCRIPTION FOR A HEADSTONE

What Larkin bawled to hungry crowds
Is murmured now in dining-hall
And study. Faith bestirs itself
Lest infidels in their impatience
Leave it behind. Who could have guessed
Batons were blessings in disguise,
When every ambulance was filled
With half-killed men and Sunday trampled
Upon unrest? Such fear can harden
Or soften heart, knowing too clearly
His name endures on our holiest page,
Scrawled in a rage by Dublin's poor.

## MABLE KELLY

    Lucky the husband
Who puts his hand beneath her head.
    They kiss without scandal
Happiest two near feather-bed.
He sees the tumble of brown hair
Unplait, the breasts, pointed and bare
    When nightdress shows
    From dimple to toe-nail,
All Mable glowing in it, here, there, everywhere.

    Music might listen
    To her least whisper,
Learn every note, for all are true.
    While she is speaking,
    Her voice goes sweetly
To charm the herons in their musing.
Her eyes are modest, blue, their darkness

Small rooms of thought, but when they sparkle
    Upon a feast-day,
    Glasses are meeting,
Each raised to Mabel Kelly, our toast and darling.

Gone now are many Irish ladies
Who kissed and fondled, their very pet-names
Forgotten, their tibia degraded.
She takes their sky. Her smile is famed.
Her praise is scored by quill and pencil.
    Harp and spinet
    Are in her debt
And when she plays or sings, melody is content.

    No man who sees her
    Will feel uneasy.
He goes his way, head high, however tired.
    Lamp loses light
    When placed beside her.
She is the pearl and being of all Ireland
Foot, hand, eye, mouth, breast, thigh and instep, all that
        we desire.
Tresses that pass small curls as if to touch the ground;
    So many prizes
    Are not divided.
Her beauty is her own and she is not proud.

*(translation from the Irish)*

## THE SUBJECTION OF WOMEN

Over the hills the loose clouds rambled
From rock to gully where goat or ram
Might shelter. Below, the battering-ram

Broke in more cottages. Hope was gone
Until the legendary Maud Gonne,
For whom a poet lingered, sighed,
Drove out of mist upon a side-car,
Led back the homeless to broken fence,
Potato plot, their one defence,
And, there, despite the threat of Peelers,
With risky shovel, barrow, peeling
Their coats off, eager young men
Jumped over bog-drain, stone, to mend or
Restore the walls of clay; the police
Taking down names without a lease.
O she confronted the evictors
In Donegal, our victory.
When she was old and I was quickened
By syllables, I met her. Quickens
Stirred leafily in Glenmalure
Where story of Tudor battle had lured me.
I looked with wonder at the sheen
Of her golden eyes as though the Sidhe
Had sent a flame-woman up from ground
Where danger went, carbines were grounded.

Old now by luck, I try to count
Those years. I never saw the Countess
Markievicz in her green uniform,
Cock-feathered slouch hat, her Fianna form
Fours. From the railings of Dublin slums,
On the ricketty stairs the ragged slumped
At night. She knew what their poverty meant
In dirty laneway, tenement,
And fought for new conditions, welfare
When all was cruel, all unfair.
With speeches, raging as strong liquor,
Our big employers, bad Catholics,
Incited by Martin Murphy, waged
War on the poorest and unwaged them.

Hundreds of earners were batoned, benighted,
When power and capital united.
Soon Connolly founded the Citizen Army
And taught the workers to drill, to arm.
Half-starving children were brought by ship
To Liverpool from lock-out, hardship.
"Innocent souls are seized by kidnappers,
And proselytisers. Send back our kids!"
Religion guffed.
                    The Countess colled
With death at sandbags in the College
Of Surgeons. How many did she shoot
When she kicked off her satin shoes?

Women rose out after the Rebellion
When smoke of buildings hid the churchbells,
Helena Maloney, Louie Bennett
Unioned the women workers bent
At sewing machines in the by-rooms
Of Dublin, with little money to buy
A meal, dress-makers, milliners,
Tired hands in factories.

                              Mill-girls
In Lancashire were organized,
Employers forced to recognize them:
This was the cause of Eva Gore-Booth,
Who spoke on platform, at polling-booth,
In the campaign for Women's Suffrage,
That put our double beds in a rage,
Disturbed the candle-lighted tonsure.
Here Mrs. Sheehy-Skeffington
And others marched. On a May day
In the Phoenix Park, I watched, amazed,
A lovely woman speak in public
While crowding fellows from office, public
House, jeered. I heard that sweet voice ring

And saw the gleam of wedding ring
As she denounced political craft,
Tall, proud as Mary Wollstonecraft.
Still discontented, our country prays
To private enterprise. Few praise
Now Dr. Kathleen Lynn, who founded
A hospital for sick babes, foundlings,
Saved them with lay hands. How could we
Look down on infants, prattling, cooing,
When wealth had emptied so many cradles?
Better than ours, her simple Credo.

Women, who cast off all we want,
Are now despised, their names unwanted,
For patriots in party statement
And act make worse our Ill-fare State.
The soul is profit. Money claims us.
Heroes are valuable clay.

## MARTHA BLAKE AT FIFTY-ONE

Early, each morning, Martha Blake
    Walked, angeling the road,
To Mass in the Church of the Three Patrons.
    Sanctuary lamp glowed
And the clerk halo'ed the candles
    On the High Altar. She knelt
Illumined. In gold-hemmed alb,
    The priest intoned. Wax melted.

Waiting for daily Communion, bowed head
    At rail, she hears a murmur.
Latin is near. In a sweet cloud
    That cherub'd, all occurred.
The voice went by. To her pure thought,

Body was a distress
And soul, a sigh. Behind her denture,
Love lay, a helplessness.

Then, slowly walking after Mass
Down Rathgar Road, she took out
Her Yale key, put a match to gas-ring,
Half filled a saucepan, cooked
A fresh egg lightly, with tea, brown bread,
Soon, taking off her blouse
And skirt, she rested, pressing the Crown
Of Thorns until she drowsed.

In her black hat, stockings, she passed
Nylons to a nearby shop
And purchased, daily, with downcast eyes,
Fillet of steak or a chop.
She simmered it on a low jet,
Having a poor appetite,
Yet never for an hour felt better
From dilatation, tightness.

She suffered from dropped stomach, heartburn
Scalding, water-brash
And when she brought her wind up, turning
Red with the weight of mashed
Potato, mint could not relieve her.
In vain her many belches,
For all below was swelling, heaving
Wamble, gurgle, squelch.

She lay on the sofa with legs up.
A decade on her lip,
At four o'clock, taking a cup
Of lukewarm water, sip
By sip, but still her daily food
Repeated and the bile

Tormented her. In a blue hood,
    The Virgin sadly smiled.

When she looked up, the Saviour showed
    His Heart, daggered with flame
And, from the mantle-shelf, St. Joseph
    Bent, disapproving. Vainly
She prayed, for in the whatnot corner,
    The new Pope was frowning. Night
And day, dull pain, as in her corns,
    Recounted every bite.

She thought of St. Teresa, floating
    On motes of a sunbeam,
Carmelite with scatterful robes,
    Surrounded by demons,
Small black boys in their skin. She gaped
    At Hell: a muddy passage
That led to nothing, queer in shape,
    A cupboard closely fastened.

Sometimes, the walls of the parlour
    Would fade away. No plod
Of feet, rattle of van, in Garville
    Road. Soul now gone abroad
Where saints, like medieval serfs,
    Had laboured. Great sun-flower shone.
Our Lady's Chapel was borne by seraphs,
    Three leagues beyond Ancona.

High towns of Italy, the plain
    Of France, were known to Martha
As she read in a holy book. The sky-blaze
    Nooned at Padua,
Marble grotto of Bernadette.
    Rose-scatterers. New saints
In tropical Africa where the tsetse

Fly probes, the forest taints.

Teresa had heard the Lutherans
Howling on red-hot spit,
And grill, men who had searched for truth
Alone in Holy Writ.
So Martha, fearful of flame lashing
Those heretics, each instant,
Never dealt in the haberdashery
Shop, owned by two Protestants.

In ambush of night, an angel wounded
The Spaniard to the heart
With iron tip on fire. Swooning
With pain and bliss as a dart
Moved up and down within her bowels
Quicker, quicker, each cell
Sweating as if rubbed up with towels,
Her spirit rose and fell.

St. John of the Cross, her friend, in prison
Awaits the bridal night,
Paler than lilies, his wizened skin
Flowers. In fifths of flight,
Senses beyond seraphic thought,
In that divinest clasp,
Enfolding of kisses that cauterize,
Yield to the soul-spasm.

Cunning in body had come to hate
All this and stirred by mischief
Haled Martha from heaven. Heart palpitates
And terror in her stiffens.
Heart misses one beat, two . . flutters . . stops.
Her ears are full of sound.
Half fainting, she stares at the grandfather clock
As if it were overwound.

The fit had come. Ill-natured flesh
    Despised her soul. No bending
Could ease rib. Around her heart, pressure
    Of wind grew worse. Again,
Again, armchaired without relief,
    She eructated, phlegm
In mouth, forgot the woe, the grief,
    Foretold at Bethlehem.

Tired of the same faces, side-altars,
    She went to the Carmelite Church
At Johnson's Court, confessed her faults,
    There, once a week, purchased
Tea, butter in Chatham St. The pond
    In St. Stephen's Green was grand.
She watched the seagulls, ducks, black swan,
    Went home by the 15 tram.

Her beads in hand, Martha became
    A member of the Third Order,
Saved from long purgatorial pain,
    Brown habit and white cord
Her own when cerges had been lit
    Around her coffin. She got
Ninety-five pounds on loan for her bit
    Of clay in the common plot.

Often she thought of a quiet sick-ward,
    Nuns, with delicious ways,
Consoling the miserable: quick
    Tea, toast on trays. Wishing
To rid themselves of her, kind neighbours
    Sent for the ambulance,
Before her brother and sister could hurry
    To help her. Big gate clanged.

No medical examination
    For the new patient. Doctor
Had gone to Cork on holidays.
    Telephone sprang. Hall-clock
Proclaimed the quarters. Clatter of heels
    On tiles. Corridor, ward,
A-whirr with the electric cleaner,
    The creak of window cord.

She could not sleep at night. Feeble
    And old, two women raved
And cried to God. She held her beads.
    O how could she be saved?
The hospital had this and that rule.
    Day-chill unshuttered. Nun, with
Thermometer in reticule,
    Went by. The women mumbled.

Mother Superior believed
    That she was obstinate, self-willed.
Sisters ignored her, hands-in-sleeves,
    Beside a pantry shelf
Or counting pillow-case, soiled sheet.
    They gave her purgatives.
Soul-less, she tottered to the toilet.
    Only her body lived.

Wasted by colitis, refused
    The daily sacrament
By regulation, forbidden use
    Of bed-pan, when meals were sent up,
Behind a screen, she lay, shivering,
    Unable to eat. The soup
Was greasy, mutton, beef or liver,
    Cold. Kitchen has no scruples.

The Nuns had let the field in front
    As an Amusement Park,
Merry-go-round, a noisy month, all
    Heltering-skeltering at darkfall,
Mechanical music, dipper, hold-tights,
    Rifle-crack, crash of dodgems.
The ward, godless with shadow, lights,
    How could she pray to God?

Unpitied, wasting with diarrhea
    And the constant strain,
Poor Child of Mary with one idea,
    She ruptured a small vein,
Bled inwardly to jazz. No priest
    Came. She had been anointed
Two days before, yet knew no peace:
    Her last breath, disappointed.

## from TIRESIAS

                                        My mother wept loudly,
Crying, "Forgive me, Tiresias, the fault is
Mine alone for when I carried you in my womb, I
Prayed at the local temple that Our Lady Lucina
Might bestow on me a daughter." Tear-in-smile, she
    hugged me,
Kissing my lips and breasts, stood back with little starts of
Admiration, hugged me again, spread out our late supper:
Cake, sweet resin'd wine, put me to bed, whispered:
"Twenty-five years ago, I chose the name of Pyrrha
For you. Now I can use it at last." She tucked me in,
    murmured
"Pyrrha, my latecome Pyrrha, sleep better than I shall."
                                                        Next morning

Gaily she said:
"I must instruct you in domestic
Economy, show you, dear daughter, how to make your own bed, lay
Table, wash up, tidy the house, cook every sort of
Meal, sew, darn, mend, do your hair, then find a well-off
Husband for you. As a young man you have spent too many
Hours in the study of history and science, never frequented
Dance-hall, bull-ring, hurried, I fear, too often to the stews."
Laughter-in-sigh, she handed me a duster.
One fine day
During siesta I gazed in reverence at my naked
Body, slim as a nespoli tree, dared to place my shaving
Mirror of polished silver—a birthday gift from my mother—
Between my legs, inspected this way and that the fleshy
Folds guarding the shortcut, red as my real lips, to Pleasure
Pass. Next day I awoke in alarm, felt a trickle of blood half-
Way down my thigh.
"Mother," I sobbed,
"Our bold Penates
Pricked me during sleep."
"Let me look at it, Pyrrha."
She laughed, then
Said:
"Why it's nothing to worry about, my pet, all women
Suffer this shame every month."
"What does it mean?"
"That you are

Ready for nuptial bliss."
                                    And saying this, she cleansed, bandaged,
Bound my flowers.
                                    When I recovered, a burning sensation
Stayed. Restless at night, lying on my belly, I longed for
Mortal or centaur to surprise me.

## FRANK O'CONNOR

Frank O'Connor (the pseudonym of Michael Francis O'Donovan) was born in 1903 in Cork. He attended St. Patrick's National School where he was a pupil of the writer and critic Daniel Corkery. He left school at the age of fourteen, and shortly afterward joined the First Brigade of the Irish Republican Army; he later fought on the Republican side in the civil war, and was imprisoned in Gormanstown Internment Camp. After he was released in 1924, he became a teacher of Irish in rural schools, and then a librarian in Sligo, Wicklow, Cork, and Dublin. In 1935 he was appointed to the Board of Directors of the Abbey Theatre, and two years later was made Managing Director.

O'Connor wrote two novels, and numerous works of nonfiction, but his short stories—there are many collections—are what made him famous. O'Connor is also highly regarded as a translator of Irish poetry. His translations from the Irish include *The Wild Bird's Nest* (1932), *Lords and Commons* (1938), *The Fountain of Magic* (1939), *A Lament for Art O'Leary* (1940), *The Midnight Court, A Rhythmical Bacchanalia from the Irish of Bryan Merriman* (1946), *Kings, Lords, and Commons* (1959), and *The Little Monasteries* (1963). He published one collection of his own poetry, *Three Old Brothers* (1936). In the 1950s O'Connor lectured at Harvard and the University of Chicago. He died in 1966.

FRANK O'CONNOR

## THE END OF CLONMACNOIS

"Whence are you, learning's son?"
"From Clonmacnois I come.
My course of studies done,
    I'm off to Swords again."
"How are things keeping there?"
"Oh, things are shaping fair—
Foxes round churchyards bare
    Gnawing the guts of men."

*(translation from the Irish)*

## HOPE

Life has conquered, the wind has blown away
Alexander, Caesar and all their power and sway;
Tara and Troy have made no longer stay—
Maybe the English too will have their day.

*(translation from the Irish)*

## THE ANGRY POET

The hound
    Could never be called refined,
So push the tip of his nose
    Up the Master's behind.

The Master,
    May amend his scholarly air
If you screw the tip of his nose
    Up in the lackey's rear.

The lackey
    Will have the chance of his life
If you stuff his nose in turn
    In the tail of the Master's wife.

The wife—
    —Who is always sniffing around—
May sniff for the rest of her days
    Her nose in the tail of the hound.

*(translation from the Irish)*

## ON THE DEATH OF HIS WIFE

I parted from my life last night,
    A woman's body sunk in clay:
The tender bosom that I loved
    Wrapped in a sheet they took away.

The heavy blossom that had lit
    The ancient boughs is tossed and blown;
Hers was the burden of delight
    That long had weighed the old tree down.

And I am left alone tonight
    And desolate is the world I see
For lovely was that woman's weight
    That even last night had lain on me.

Weeping I look upon the place
    Where she used to rest her head—
For yesterday her body's length
    Reposed upon you too, my bed.

Yesterday that smiling face
    Upon one side of you was laid
That could match the hazel bloom
    In its dark delicate sweet shade.

Maelva of the shadowy brows
    Was the mead-cask at my side;
Fairest of all flowers that grow
    Was the beauty that has died.

My body's self deserts me now,
    The half of me that was her own,
Since all I knew of brightness died
    Half of me lingers, half is gone.

The face that was like hawthorn bloom
    Was my right foot and my right side;
And my right hand and my right eye
    Were no more mine than hers who died.

Poor is the share of me that's left
    Since half of me died with my wife;
I shudder at the words I speak;
    Dear God, that girl was half my life.

And our first look was her first love;
    No man had fondled ere I came
The little breasts so small and firm
    And the long body like a flame.

For twenty years we shared a home,
    Our converse milder with each year;
Eleven children in its time
    Did that tall stately body bear.

It was the King of hosts and roads
    Who snatched her from me in her prime:
Little she wished to leave alone
    The man she loved before her time.

Now King of churches and of bells,
    Though never raised to pledge a lie
That woman's hand—can it be true?—
    No more beneath my head will lie.

*(translation from the Irish)*

## PATRICK KAVANAGH

Patrick Kavanagh was born in 1905 in Inniskeen, County Monaghan. He left school at an early age and worked in turn as a hired hand, an apprentice shoemaker, and a farmer. In 1930 Kavanagh left Monaghan and set out on foot for Dublin (though he did not move there permanently until 1939). Kavanagh made a living in Dublin primarily by turning out reviews for the *Irish Times*, the *Irish Independent*, the *Irish Press*, and the *Standard*. He was editor, writer, and publisher (with his brother Peter) of *Kavanagh's Weekly*, a short-lived journal of literature and politics. In 1954, Kavanagh was found to have cancer and had to have one of his lungs surgically removed. He died in 1967, the same year he was married. Kavanagh's major collections of poetry are: *The Ploughman and Other Poems* (1936), *The Great Hunger* (1942), *A Soul for Sale* (1947), *Come Dance with Kitty Stobling* (1960), and *Collected Poems* (1964). *Complete Poems* appeared in 1972.

## INNISKEEN ROAD: JULY EVENING

The bicycles go by in twos and threes—
There's a dance in Billy Brennan's barn to-night,
And there's the half-talk code of mysteries
And the wink-and-elbow language of delight.
Half-past eight and there is not a spot
Upon a mile of road, no shadow thrown
That might turn out a man or woman, not
A footfall tapping secrecies of stone.

I have what every poet hates in spite
Of all the solemn talk of contemplation.
Oh, Alexander Selkirk knew the plight
Of being king and government and nation.
A road, a mile of kingdom, I am king
Of banks and stones and every blooming thing.

## SHANCODUFF

My black hills have never seen the sun rising,
Eternally they look north towards Armagh.
Lot's wife would not be salt if she had been
Incurious as my black hills that are happy
When dawn whitens Glassdrummond chapel.

My hills hoard the bright shillings of March
While the sun searches in every pocket.
They are my Alps and I have climbed the Matterhorn
With a sheaf of hay for three perishing calves
In the field under the Big Forth of Rocksavage.

The sleety winds fondle the rushy beards of Shancoduff
While the cattle-drovers sheltering in the Featherna Bush
Look up and say: "Who owns them hungry hills
That the water-hen and snipe must have forsaken?
A poet? Then by heavens he must be poor."
I hear and is my heart not badly shaken?

# FATHER MAT

## I

In a meadow
Beside the chapel three boys were playing football.
At the forge door an old man was leaning
Viewing a hunter-hoe. A man could hear
If he listened to the breeze the fall of wings—
How wistfully the sin-birds come home!

It was Confession Saturday, the first
Saturday in May; the May Devotions
Were spread like leaves to quieten
The excited armies of conscience.
The knife of penance fell so like a blade
Of grass that no one was afraid.

Father Mat came slowly walking, stopping to
Stare through gaps at ancient Ireland sweeping
In again with all its unbaptized beauty:
The calm evening,
The whitethorn blossoms,
The smell from ditches that were not Christian.
The dancer that dances in the hearts of men cried:
Look! I have shown this to you before—
The rags of living surprised
The joy in things you cannot forget.

His heavy hat was square upon his head,
Like a Christian Brother's;
His eyes were an old man's watery eyes,

Out of his flat nose grew spiky hairs.
He was a part of the place,
Natural as a round stone in a grass field;
He could walk through a cattle fair
And the people would only notice his odd spirit there.

His curate passed on a bicycle—
*He* had the haughty intellectual look
Of the man who never reads in brook or book;
A man designed
To wear a mitre,
To sit on committees—
For will grows strongest in the emptiest mind.

The old priest saw him pass
And, seeing, saw
Himself a mediaeval ghost.
Ahead of him went Power,
One who was not afraid when the sun opened a flower,
Who was never astonished
At a stick carried down a stream
Or at the undying difference in the corner of a field.

## II

The Holy Ghost descends
At random like the muse
On wise man and fool,
And why should poet in the twilight choose?

Within the dim chapel was the grey
Mumble of prayer
To the Queen of May—
The Virgin Mary with the schoolgirl air.

Two guttering candles on a brass shrine
Raised upon the wall
Monsters of despair
To terrify deep into the soul.

Through the open door the hum of rosaries
Came out and blended with the homing bees.
                                        The trees
Heard nothing stranger than the rain or the wind
Or the birds—
But deep in their roots they knew a seed had sinned.

In the graveyard a goat was nibbling at a yew,
The cobbler's chickens with anxious looks
Were straggling home through nettles, over graves.
A young girl down a hill was driving cows
To a corner at the gable-end of a roofless house.

Cows were milked earlier,
The supper hurried,
Hens shut in,
Horses unyoked,
And three men shaving before the same mirror.

## III

The trip of iron tips on tile
Hesitated up the middle aisle,
Heads that were bowed glanced up to see
Who could this last arrival be.

Murmur of women's voices from the porch,
Memories of relations in the graveyard.
On the stem
Of memory imaginations blossom.

In the dim
Corners in the side seats faces gather,
Lit up now and then by a guttering candle
And the ghost of day at the window.
A secret lover is saying
Three Hail Marys that she who knows
The ways of women will bring
Cathleen O'Hara (he names her) home to him.
Ironic fate! Cathleen herself is saying
Three Hail Mary's to her who knows.
The ways of men to bring
Somebody else home to her—
"O may he love me."
What is the Virgin Mary now to do?

## IV

From a confessional
The voice of Father Mat's absolving
Rises and falls like a briar in the breeze.
As the sins pour in the old priest is thinking
His fields of fresh grass, his horses, his cows,
His earth into the fires of Purgatory.
It cools his mind.
"They confess to the fields," he mused,
"They confess to the fields and the air and the sky,"
And forgiveness was the soft grass of his meadow by the river;
His thoughts were walking through it now.

His human lips talked on:
"My son,
Only the poor in spirit shall wear the crown;
Those down
Can creep in the low door
On to Heaven's floor."

The Tempter had another answer ready:
"Ah lad, upon the road of life
'Tis best to dance with Chance's wife
And let the rains that come in time
Erase the footprints of the crime."

The dancer that dances in the hearts of men
Tempted him again:
"Look! I have shown you this before;
From this mountain-top I have tempted Christ
With what you see now
Of beauty—all that's music, poetry, art
In things you can touch every day.
I broke away
And rule all dominions that are rare;
I took with me all the answers to every prayer
That young men and girls pray for: love, happiness, riches—"
O Tempter! O Tempter!

## V

As Father Mat walked home
Venus was in the western sky
And there were voices in the hedges:
"God the Gay is not the Wise."

"Take your choice, take your choice,"
Called the breeze through the bridge's eye.
"The domestic Virgin and Her Child
Or Venus with her ecstasy."

## ART McCOOEY

I recover now the time I drove
Cart-loads of dung to an outlying farm—
My foreign possessions in Shancoduff—
With the enthusiasm of a man who sees life simply.

The steam rising from the load is still
Warm enough to thaw my frosty fingers.
In Donnybrook in Dublin ten years later
I see that empire now and the empire builder.

Sometimes meeting a neighbour
In country love-enchantment,
The old mare pulls over to the bank and leaves us
To fiddle folly where November dances.

We wove our disappointments and successes
To patterns of a town-bred logic:
'She might have been sick. . . . No, never before,
A mystery, Pat, and they all appear so modest.'

We exchanged our fool advices back and forth:
'It easily could be their cow was calving,
And sure the rain was desperate that night . . .'
Somewhere in the mists a light was laughing.

We played with the frilly edges of reality
While we puffed our cigarettes;
And sometimes Owney Martin's splitting yell
Would knife the dreamer that the land begets.

"I'll see you after Second Mass on Sunday."
"Right-o, right-o." The mare moves on again.
A wheel rides over a heap of gravel
And the mare goes skew-ways like a blinded hen.

Down the lane-way of the popular banshees
By Paddy Bradley's; mud to the ankles;
A hare is grazing in Mat Rooney's meadow;
Maggie Byrne is prowling for dead branches.

Ten loads before tea-time. Was that the laughter
Of the evening bursting school?
The sun sinks low and large behind the hills of Cavan,
A stormy-looking sunset. "Brave and cool."

Wash out the cart with a bucket of water and a wangel
Of wheaten straw. Jupiter looks down.
Unlearnedly and unreasonably poetry is shaped
Awkwardly but alive in the unmeasured womb.

## STONY GREY SOIL

O stony grey soil of Monaghan
The laugh from my love you thieved;
You took the gay child of my passion
And gave me your clod-conceived.

You clogged the feet of my boyhood
And I believed that my stumble
Had the poise and stride of Apollo
And his voice my thick-tongued mumble.

You told me the plough was immortal!
O green-life-conquering plough!
Your mandril strained, your coulter blunted
In the smooth lea-field of my brow.

You sang on steaming dunghills
A song of cowards' brood,
You perfumed my clothes with weasel itch,
You fed me on swinish food.

You flung a ditch on my vision
Of beauty, love and truth.
O stony grey soil of Monaghan
You burgled my bank of youth!

Lost the long hours of pleasure
All the women that love young men.
O can I still stroke the monster's back
Or write with unpoisoned pen

His name in these lonely verses
Or mention the dark fields where
The first gay flight of my lyric
Got caught in a peasant's prayer.

Mullahinsha, Drummeril, Black Shanco—
Wherever I turn I see
In the stony grey soil of Monaghan
Dead loves that were born for me.

## TO THE MAN AFTER THE HARROW

Now leave the check-reins slack,
The seed is flying far to-day—
The seed like stars against the black
Eternity of April clay.

This seed is potent as the seed
Of knowledge in the Hebrew Book,
So drive your horses in the creed
Of God the Father as a stook.

Forget the men on Brady's hill.
Forget what Brady's boy may say
For destiny will not fulfil
Unless you let the harrow play.

Forget the worm's opinion too
Of hooves and pointed harrow-pins,
For you are driving your horses through
The mist where Genesis begins.

## from THE GREAT HUNGER

Maguire is not afraid of death, the Church will light him
a candle
To see his way through the vaults and he'll understand the
Quality of the clay that dribbles over his coffin.
He'll know the names of the roots that climb down to
tickle his feet.
And he will feel no different than when he walked
through Donaghmoyne.
If he stretches out a hand— a wet clod,
If he opens his nostrils—a dungy smell;
If he opens his eyes once in a million years—
Through a crack in the crust of the earth he may see a
face nodding in
Or a woman's legs. Shut them again for that sight is sin.

He will hardly remember that life happened to him—
Something was brighter a moment. Somebody sang in the
distance.
A procession passed down a mesmerised street.
He remembers names like Easter and Christmas
By the colour his fields were.

Maybe he will be born again, a bird of an angel's conceit
To sing the gospel of life
To a music as flightily tangent
As a tune on an oboe.
And the serious look of the fields will have changed to the
leer of a hobo
Swaggering celestially home to his three wishes granted.
Will that be? will that be?

Or is the earth right that laughs haw-haw
And does not believe
In an unearthly law.
The earth that says:
Patrick Maguire, the old peasant, can neither be damned
nor glorified:
The graveyard in which he will lie will be just a deep-
drilled potato-field
Where the seed gets no chance to come through
To the fun of the sun.
The tongue in his mouth is the root of a yew.
Silence, silence. The story is done.

He stands in the doorway of his house
A ragged sculpture of the wind,
October creaks the rotted mattress,
The bedposts fall. No hope. No lust.
The hungry fiend
Screams the apocalypse of clay
In every corner of this land.

## TINKER'S WIFE

I saw her amid the dunghill debris
Looking for things
Such as an old pair of shoes or gaiters.

She was a young woman,
A tinker's wife.
Her face had streaks of care
Like wires across it,
But she was supple
As a young goat
On a windy hill.

She searched on the dunghill debris,
Tripping gingerly
Over tin canisters
And sharp-broken
Dinner plates.

## EPIC

I have lived in important places, times
When great events were decided, who owned
That half a rood of rock, a no-man's land
Surrounded by our pitchfork-armed claims.
I heard the Duffys shouting "Damn your soul!"
And old McCabe stripped to the waist, seen
Step the plot defying blue cast-steel—
"Here is the march along these iron stones."
That was the year of the Munich bother. Which
Was more important? I inclined
To lose my faith in Ballyrush and Gortin
Till Homer's ghost came whispering to my mind.
He said: I made the Iliad from such
A local row. Gods make their own importance.

## THE HOSPITAL

A year ago I fell in love with the functional ward
Of a chest hospital: square cubicles in a row,
Plain concrete, wash basins—an art lover's woe,
Not counting how the fellow in the next bed snored.
But nothing whatever is by love debarred,
The common and banal her heat can know.
The corridor led to a stairway and below
Was the inexhaustible adventure of a gravelled yard.

This is what love does to things: the Rialto Bridge,
The main gate that was bent by a heavy lorry,
The seat at the back of a shed that was a suntrap.
Naming these things is the love-act and its pledge;
For we must record love's mystery without claptrap,
Snatch out of time the passionate transitory.

## CANAL BANK WALK

Leafy-with-love banks and the green waters of the canal
Pouring redemption for me, that I do
The will of God, wallow in the habitual, the banal,
Grow with nature again as before I grew.
The bright stick trapped, the breeze adding a third
Party to the couple kissing on an old seat,
And a bird gathering materials for the nest for the Word
Eloquently new and abandoned to its delirious beat.
O unworn world enrapture me, encapture me in a web
Of fabulous grass and eternal voices by a beech,
Feed the gaping need of my senses, give me ad lib
To pray unselfconsciously with overflowing speech
For this soul needs to be honoured with a new dress
    woven
From green and blue things and arguments that cannot be
    proven.

## IN MEMORY OF MY MOTHER

I do not think of you lying in the wet clay
Of a Monaghan graveyard; I see
You walking down a lane among the poplars
On your way to the station, or happily

Going to second Mass on a summer Sunday.
You meet me and you say:
"Don't forget to see about the cattle—"
Among your earthiest words the angels stray.

And I think of you walking along a headland
Of green oats in June,
So full of repose, so rich with life;
And I see us meeting at the end of a town

On a fair day by accident, after
The bargains are all made and we can walk
Together through the shops and stalls and markets
Free in the oriental streets of thought.

O you are not lying in the wet clay,
For it is a harvest evening now and we
Are piling up the ricks against the moonlight
And you smile up at us—eternally.

## OCTOBER

O leafy yellowness you create for me
A world that was and now is poised above time.
I do not need to puzzle out Eternity
As I walk this arboreal street on the edge of a town.
The breeze too, even the temperature
And pattern of movement is precisely the same

As broke my heart for youth passing. Now I am sure
Of something. Something will be mine wherever I am.
I want to throw myself on the public street without caring
For anything but the prayering that the earth offers.
It is October over all my life and the light is staring
As it caught me once in a plantation by the fox coverts.
A man is ploughing ground for winter wheat
And my nineteen years weigh heavily on my feet.

## PADRAIC FALLON

Padraic Fallon was born in 1905 in Athenry, County Galway. He was educated at St. Joseph's College, Roscrea, and worked as a customs official for many years, first in Dublin, then in Wexford (he also worked a small farm outside Wexford). He was married in 1930 and had six sons. Fallon wrote numerous verse plays that were broadcast on Radio Eireann. But while many of his poems were published in journals and periodicals from the early thirties onward, it was not until 1974, the year of Fallon's death, that an extensive collection, *Poems*, was published in book form. A posthumous volume, *Poems and Versions*, edited by Brian Fallon, was published in 1983.

## ODYSSEUS

Last year's decencies
Are the rags and reach-me-downs he'll wear forever,
Knowing one day he'll sober up inside them
Safe in wind and wife and limb,
Respected, of unimpeachable behaviour.

Meanwhile he goes forward
Magniloquently to himself; and, the fit on him,
Pushes his painful hobble to a dance,
Exposing in obscene wounds and dilapidation
The naked metre of the man.

His dog will die at sight of him,
His son want fool-proof, and his lady-wife
Deny his fingerprints; but he
With his talent for rehabilitation
Will be his own man soon, without ecstasy.

## FOR PADDY MAC

### I

Once, so long ago,
You used to probe me gently for the lost
Country, sensing somehow in my airs
The vivid longlipped peasantry of
Last century

And those bronze men pushed
With their diminishing herds far out on
The last ledge of original earth,
Fomorian types
In the big one-eyed sky

All messed up with sundogs and
Too many rainbows, and that wishwashing head of Bran
In the toppling arches seaward sailing and singing
On his weathered maypole from
A caved-in skull.

Ours were the metres
Of early waters, the first argosy hardly home
With new women, orgies
When the moon rode round
Stone circles counting her twelve.

Homer's people.
And wasn't I lucky, born with
Boundaries floating, language still making
Out of the broadlands where my fathers
Tended their clouds of ewes?

Bunkum, Dear P. The thing was gone, or
Never was. And we were the leftovers,
Lord-ridden and pulpit-thumped for all our wild
Cudgels of Gaelic. Ours was Lever's
One-horse country; the bailiff at the bighouse door.

And hags hung all day
In turfsmoke among the fowl where I was licked.
That was a town
Walled and towered as Troy, and never sieged for a
    woman:
Trading bullocks and pennies for glory gone;

And watched from the top of a shilling the homespun
    fellows
Selling their spades on hiring days,
For a year and a day the dear flesh off their bones
From penury to slavery,
The soul thrown in for a spare.

That was my country, beast, sky and anger:
For music a mad piper in the mud;
No poets I knew of; or they mouthed each other's words;
Such low powered gods
They died, as they were born, in byres.

Oh, maybe some rags and tatters did sing.
But poetry, for all your talk, is never that simple,
Coming out of a stone ditch in the broadlands
Newborn, or from
The fitful pibroch of a lonely thorn,

Or old saws at winter fires.
Muted the big words. Love was left
To eloping earls or such
Lest the snake creep up, usurping the ancient timber
And some odd bloom come bursting from the Cross.

## II

And you speak of Raftery, that bold tongue, the tramp
In borrowed bootleather, those rainy eyes
Lifted to empty heaven from a blind man's stick;
I sang like him you say, and praised women,
And I had the true cow's lick;

You who should know how every poet must
Baptize first the font and the very waters,
And have no godfathers but this great thirst
For what is not;
And no mothers;

Who must quote Ambrose crookedly (Nam quid divinius
Isto ut puncto exiguo culpa cadet
Populi), bog Latin for
The bit of earth we tread
Into metaphor

Knowing we're just another civilisation
To be dumped, but go on, say it you,
We've eaten all the Gods yet bow the knee,
And are only really at home
In the larger toleration of the poem.

Carefully, now that you are dead,
I must amend the scribbles of the tribe
Lest sheepman and bullhead
Become a frieze of fathers like stone man,
Hieratic, almost Egyptian,

And from the uncreated, with arms widespread,
From puncto exiguo, beyond the dead
And Lazarus rising, where God is making still
Release the flood
Of living images for good and ill.

Dear P. I'll never know
What you brought over and passed on,
but this seems certain as I grow:
Man lives; Gods die:
It is only the genuflection that survives.

## POT SHOT

I tell words that talk in trees, this hill
Is my vocabulary, and when I lie down
The sky seizes me so very quietly
I reflect the sunset, the river and I are one.
And then the gun goes off. Am I that, too?
Thunder and blast? And when the hooves of the echoes
Have galloped over the grass and the field aloofly
Returns to itself and silence on its toes
Cranes to hear a rabbit squeal, am I
The wound that I give, the hurt I hurt, the shiver
That talks so tall in trees, that is the sky,
That explodes in death, yet walks like the wide river
So calmly through the evening that I tame
The world around me till it names my name.

## WEIR BRIDGE

The lodestoned salmon, hurtling
Always in the right direction, find
The trickle of their birth,
Stand fantailed on the falls
And somersault into the milting weather.

Whole gravels are in rut.
The ocean has come home to melt away
The salt, to lie under
A maybush and almost tenderly
Suck from the lazy heavens a blue-green fly.

On love's seething house,
Rocking the thousand cradles the first fresh
Will fall and the spent bulls
Drop with it down the slow river spirals;
Aching for space now the once rampant males;

Caught here in their bored
Congregations, while the wandering nerve
Twitches towards Norway. How many years
Since I first saw the stones waver,
The river paving turn to fins and tails?

Loafing a lunch hour in the sun,
And here's the wheel come round again;
So much to do, so little done;
The tiny trickle of my birth
Dwindling back into the earth.

PADRAIC FALLON

## THE HEAD

### I

The day after decapitation
Was no wound yet. Noon found the head
Excited still and still singing
The visionary woman, still exalting
The woman in measures to which no words came
Off the black tongue. The river flies
Were busy on specks of blood, in clouds upon the hair;
But where her praise was fixed upon his face
No one had died, the flesh was adequate;
And on a mouth that seemed alive
Only the smile was anti-clockwise;
But no wound yet.

That night it drifted on
Through stars that buzzed no brighter, inches
Of radiance before it and around
That felt no wound;
And this was dyed with a flutter of vague moths,
And overhead where a curious white owl
Dilated, there was some reflection too;
And down below
More of it and stranger for the eels
Had scented blood and wavered under the wicker;
This was a head that trickled down many tails
Into the deeps, eddying without end;
And still was felt no wound.

The slow morning came
Back to the eyes and brought the labouring crow
(Corvus corax corax) who discharged himself
Upon the skull unskilfully and cawed
Once, twice, and there for long was still.

The gulls disturbed him when the eyes were gone
And over the bloody mess rose such confusion
Three salmon fishers rowed out from a draft
Only to retch their morning stirabout:
That noon the skull gaped
And still was felt no wound.

The second afternoon it rained;

Rinsing the ruin the nozzled drops removed
Sundry strips, tissues, barber's clippings,
Odds of nerves, bits, leaving such scrags, jags
And rags as still clung and dripped
To shine strangely when the sun came out.
The waters steamed a little before night
And from the skull where little pools remained
There oozed a smoke, a vagrant and hairlike smoke;
And in the hollow eyes the rain
Was bright as sight, and so it seemed
The nose put forth its bridge again,
And from the earholes arched two tufts of fawn,
Two gilded wisps, the ears. The face had dreamed
Itself right back again.
And still no pain;
Still the exultant thing was fixed, and dawn
Found the bare teeth beautiful.

## II

The third day repeated as before
Washed out the skullhouse and refurnished it
With the changeable midsummer weather:
The head alone at last
Was bonebare and beaming; and where it floated
Down the broad vowel of the river, once
Its song was heard;

Snatches only, faint upon the ripple
And weirs of the water-word: A thin
Piping.

The reeds heavytopped tipped to it
As to a breeze.

So it was the wind
That used the tattered wizen of the throat
As well as the sockets of the eyes, the earholes
And the pit behind the nose for hollow music,
Not overlooking the jewels of the mouth
That still smiled
For yet no wound was felt.

So time stopped
Outwardly, but there was still this woman
In the weather of the head
Who was all time to it no longer human.
And in that time the head came

By stages of water world
From green granaries, tilled, from fat uddered
Cow-lawns by river houses, woods that spoke in oak
And heavy roots and clumped along the banks,
To a country narrow low and cold
And very thin like a wire,
Where the head sang all day.

There the seas fell inland almost vacantly
Over a sieve of sand;
There the head lay
While the coracle under it of sally withes
Dried, withered in sunlight, salt sealight,
Rotted till the ashen thwart that held the head
Rigid and singing, sprung the spent lashings,
Tipping over;

This, one day when the set from the southwest
Piled up an equinoctial on the coast;
On the white shore with no one to notice
The head fell.

And broke

In a separation of its major and distinct parts.
Two.

And from the still centre where was the true
Bubble or heartbeat, came the tiny whimper
Of some unhouselled thing;
The head's first cry
At last and never heard

By gull, gale, sandpiping bird
Or gannet in the tall and touselled blue,
Nor the wader on two pins nearby,
Though the cry was human,
The pain spreading greatly, going
Towards blood in every direction

But never arriving
Near and away where the woman was
Doing the usual things to men and clothes
Afraid of the glass,
Groundswell and undertows,
What happens and the happening
That will never come to pass.

## A HEDGE SCHOOLMASTER

Any niche is my college.
In wayside ditch roofed by a bramble
I light the small rush candle
Of knowledge in numbskulls.

No mouth-open fledglings sit
Around this Socrates on the turf
But Pat's famished son, the lout
And his daughter, scrapings of the pot.

Thankless the task, to create
Fine manners on salt and potatoes,
To hatch out the morrow's priest
From father's old waistcoat;

Spelling out for the shockhaired
The wars of Caesar,
Hannibal in the Alps or
The Emperor Nero on the fiddle;

To construct with a slate pencil the town of Troy,
Thumbnailing; the geography of heroes;
All history from Adam down
To hobble home on bare toes;

With profit and loss and mensuration
Goes towering Agamemnon
And Arius with his heresy
Of Three-in-one and Homousion,

To be lost in little walls and ricks of turf,
Dwindle down at peasant fires,
Huge ghosts in hungry fields
Wandering without memories.

No profit in it, or credit. Boors thrive
But I eat afield with the crows;
No goose gravy for Tom Euclid;
The master feasts on the hedgerows;

Yet, Pallas Athene, your true legionary
In the last earthworks, the lone garrison, still
Arrays himself in the delicate dactyls to
Decline you to the barbarian.

## DARDANELLES 1916

Last night in stomped
Our Connaught Ranger, Private Patrick Carty
On his way:
                    fully accoutred now, a ramp
Of belts and bandoliers, a bayonet
Wags at his side with no wound yet, the heavy
Haversack sits high:

                    filling the back kitchen, squinting
Down from the roofbeams, shyly
Shaking hands all round the family, smiling;
Me he picks up and by God kisses me.

                                        Up there under
The brown-white plaster an unknown soldier's face
Is weeping.

                    Do I remember more? The urchin daughters
Bold for once and peeping
Washed and ribboned through the door to wave
Him off on the Mail, the 4:15, and away
Where muted now in a long sand he lies, if not
Entirely melted into
The steadfast bony glare of Asia Minor.

## BRIAN COFFEY

Brian Coffey was born near Dublin in 1905. He attended Clongowes Wood College, then University College, Dublin, where his father was president. His poems appeared first in student publications, then in *Poems* (1930) which was co-authored by his friend Denis Devlin. Coffey graduated from University College, Dublin, with an M.Sc., and did research in Paris in the early thirties in physical chemistry. Later he completed his doctoral studies at Paris in philosophy. He continued to write poetry during his studies, encouraged by Beckett, Devlin, and MacGreevy. He married in 1938, the year his collection *Third Person* was published. He spent the war years in England. After the war he taught philosophy for five years at St. Louis University, Missouri, then returned to England with his family. He taught mathematics in London schools until 1972. His translation of Mallarmé's *Coup de Dés* was published in 1965, and of Neruda's love poems in 1973. Coffey's *Selected Poems* was published in 1971; his long poem *Advent* was published in the *Irish University Review* in 1975. *Death of Hektor*, a poem with illustrations by S. W. Hayter, was published in 1978 and *Chanterelles: Short Poems 1971–1983* in 1985.

## from MISSOURI SEQUENCE

### Nightfall, Midwinter, Missouri

To Thomas MacGreevy

Our children have eaten supper,
play Follow-my-Leader,
make songs from room to room
around and around;
once each minute
past my desk they go.

Inside the house is warm.
Winter outside blows from Canada
freezing rain to ice our trees
branch by branch, leaf by leaf.
The mare shelters in the barn.

On the impassable road no movement.
Nothing stirs in the sky against the black.
If memory were an ice-field
quiet as all outside!
Tonight the poetry is in the children's game:
I am distracted by comparisons,
Ireland across the grey ocean,
here, across the wide river.

*

We live far from where
my mother grows very old.
Five miles away, at Byrnesville,
the cemetery is filled with Irish graves,
the priest an old man born near Cork,
his bloss like the day he left the land.

People drifted in here from the river,
Irish, German, Bohemians,
more than one hundred years ago,
come to make homes.

Many Irish souls have gone back to God from Byrnesville,

many are Irish here today
where cedars stand like milestones
on worn Ozark hills
and houses white on bluegrass lawns
house people honest, practical and kind.

All shows to a long love
yet I am charmed
by the hills behind Dublin,
those white stone cottages,
grass green as no other green is green,
my mother's people, their ways.

France one loves with a love apart
like the love of wisdom;
Of England everyday love is the true love;
there is a love of Ireland
withering for Irishmen.

Does it matter where one dies,
supposing one knows how?

Dear Tom, in Ireland,
you have known
the pain between
its fruiting and the early dream
and you will hear me out.

*

Our children have ended play,
have gone to bed,
left me to face
what I had rather not.

They know nothing of Ireland,
they grow American.
They have chased snakes through the couch-grass
in summer, caught butterflies and beetles
we did not know existed,
fished for the catfish,
slept on an open porch
when Whip-poor-Will and tree-frog
work all night,
observed the pupa of the shrill cicada
surface on dry clay,
disrobe for the short ruinous day.
The older ones have helped a neighbour, farmer,
raise his field of ripe corn
in heat that hurt us to the bone,
paid homage to dead men
with fire-crackers in July,
eaten the turkey in November.
Here now they make their friendships,
learn to love God.

Yet we must leave America,
bitter necessity no monopoly
of Irish soil.
It was pain once to come,
it is pain now to go.

How the will shifts from goal to goal
for who does not freely choose.
Some choose, some are chosen
to go their separate paths.
I would choose, I suppose, yet would be chosen

in some equation between God's will and mine,
rejecting prudence to make of conflict
a monument to celtic self-importance.

The truth is, where the cross is not
the Christian does not go.

*

Return home takes on while I dream it
the fictive form of heaven on earth,
the child's return to motherly arms
for fright at frogs disturbed among iris leaves.

One poet I admire has written:
*wherever the soul gives in to flesh*
*without a struggle is home.*
Would one want home like that,
rest, supine surrender
to oneself alone,
flight from where one is?

There is no heaven on earth,
no facile choice for one
charged with care of others,
none for one like me
for whom no prospect opens
fairly on clear skies.

It grows late and winter
lays its numbing pall.
Doubts restless like what you see
when you lift a flat damp stone
exasperate my warring wishes
until wrenched apart by desperate extremes
I am back where I started.

Pain it was to come,
Pain it will be to go.

*

Not just to go,
not just to stay,
but the act done in wisdom's way—
not impossible
if one is wise.

Our William Butler Yeats
made island flowers grow
that need as much
the local rain
as wind from overseas
to reach their prime.
He struggled towards the exact muse
through a sunless day.

No servant, the muse
abides in truth,
permits the use of protest
as a second best
to make clean fields,
exults only in the actual
expression of a love,
love all problem,
wisdom lacking.

*

How near the surface of the pool
sunfish play, distract
us from where down deep
real reasons impose their rule.

The room is filled with children's lives
that fill my cares who turn again
to sudden starting words
like birds in cages.
Without all is silent,
within I have no peace at all,
having failed to choose
with loving-wise choice.

Midnight now.
Deepest winter perfect now.
Tomorrow early we shall make lunches
for the children to take to school,
forgetting while working out the week
our wrestling with the sad flesh
and the only Ireland we love
where in Achill still
the poor praise Christ aloud
when the priest elevates
the Saviour of the world.

## H E A D R O C K

IpsofactopaperAnswerallquesti
onstakingallyourtimeONEWhatha
veyouforgottenAreyoubeyonddou
btingyourmotives'honestyWhomd
idyousupposeinwhoseskinlastti
meyoumadeitTWOIsyourmotherath
omedearieordoyoumentallyreser
ve/prudentlydissimulateWho'sl
yingnowTHREECandamnationbeama
tterofroutineadminCouldyouorg
aniseandmaintainaninquisition
wouldyouAreyouthatstrongreall

yFOURAreyoupushedfortimeyetDi
dyoutakeyourpillAndhaveyoufou
ndaplacetohideintohidefromFIV
EWhataboutyourmotherDoyoudrin
kunusallymuchwaterthesedaysS
IXWhenyouwerebeatingyourwifed
idshesmileandifsowhySEVENWhoa
reyouWhereareyouWhenareyouWha
tdidthenthGadareneswinesaytot
he(n+1)thonthewaydownEIGHTWas
yourMaagoodchapyourfatherwors
hippedwhenhechasedyourlittles
istertothetoolshedNINEActuall
yAkchelliFranklyspeakingManto
man/WomantowomandidyoueverIov
eanyonedeadEverownedabodTENDo
youagreethatitisfaircommenton
FUZZ'Sviewoftheevilthatisabro
adinourlandthatManthereisMant
hereisabsolutelyManManthereis

N O E S C A P E

## from ADVENT

Awakening like return to Earth from Moon
Splashdown to difference

Point-light-studded velvet-black
to sapphire sea
Start into conjecture

One had been programmed for any case whatever
naught unmanageable assumed
Like ballet-dancer each step as if remembered
Cave cave      All in the bag      Cave cave

## BRIAN COFFEY

Never the unforeseen
Even on rocking yielding water
a destined helping hand is awaited

Victor in the now no longer
could one fail in the not yet now

Home base and
how behind summer heat-veil
Earth could give one pause     Earth strange
like the stranger grown from one's child

From Northleigh to Southleigh
from the Flats to Farwood
wide one stretched one's arms
in standing greeting
across mocking plains of contentment

A day so perfect one found oneself
asking     of whom     for a cloud in the sky

Beyond concrete apron trees summerly
branches supple green with crowding leaves
How their quietude does arrest movement
as when one remembers
what one had not failed to forget

Trees grasses carpet and shelter earthly home
stretch fingers in turned soil soil welcomes warm

What sky-blue pollen-haze slight-swallows-high
feel and touch intensified by wind out of nowhere
One remembers from Samothrace fields of butterflies
scattered like scraps by screech-wind from sea

As if uncounted years of waiting had fruited
for Earth in unrepeatable day and pang of longing
to show her very best her fields of ripest corn

We had forgotten Earth Earth's muted murmur anguished
Earth since early savannahs ours all ours

## COLD

*Martyr witnesseth*
*how malice chilleth*
*the whole man*

Look
There
The smiling infant
wrapped in light and noise
it could be sun and sea
all future all perhaps
his maccabean deed
not yet achieved
gone
in a flash
where cloud of dust and steel
battens on torn flesh

Late in history
"How it was" we ask
They say "Our chosen god
favoured our side"
And men men's sons
held the coast farms
framed friendly law
worked commonweal
to Selves Alone

Pleasant the trampling
helots to clay
Helots How dare they
heave ground and slay
Helots see how it is
with staring eyes
centuries
pain and woe

Helots stage
no sun to rise
ken foe
cry he tribute
cry he justice at last
trust none
hope never
patient endure
oppression the devil known
deliverance
but change in devil kind
and boot fails not
bruising the naked face

When cold men come
gaze pitiless
at broken frames
Old tyrants out means
new tyrants in

But mothers
chilled through they are
pray
"Cold men
who right no wrongs
go where you came from
What can you give back now
Go Dust to dust"

## SAMUEL BECKETT

Samuel Beckett was born in 1906 near Dublin. He was educated at Portora Royal School, County Fermanagh, and at Trinity College, Dublin, where he received his B.A. in French and Italian in 1927 and his M.A. in 1931. He was Lecturer in English at the Ecole Normale Superieure in Paris from 1928 to 1930, during which time he met and became friends with Joyce. He then was Lecturer in French at Trinity for several years. After wandering over the continent for five years, he settled in Paris in 1937, renewing his earlier friendship with Joyce. In 1938 he narrowly escaped death when he was stabbed on a Paris street by a complete stranger. In 1940 he joined the Resistance and had to flee Paris in 1942 to avoid arrest by the Gestapo. Beckett received the Nobel Prize for Literature in 1969; his international reputation rests chiefly on his plays, particularly on *Waiting for Godot*. Beckett has also written numerous novels and volumes of short stories. Of his collections of poems, the most complete to date is *Collected Poems 1930–1978* (1984).

## MALACODA

thrice he came
the undertaker's man
impassible behind his scutal bowler
to measure
is he not paid to measure
this incorruptible in the vestibule
this malebranca knee-deep in the lilies
Malacoda knee-deep in the lilies

Malacoda for all the expert awe
that felts his perineum mutes his signal
sighing up through the heavy air
must it be it must be it must be
find the weeds engage them in the garden
hear she may see she need not

to coffin
with assistant ungulata
find the weeds engage their attention
hear she must see she need not

to cover
to be sure cover cover all over
your targe allow me hold your sulphur
divine dogday glass set fair
stay Scarmilion stay stay
lay this Huysum on the box
mind the imago it is he
hear she must see she must
all aboard all souls
half-mast aye aye

nay

## ENUEG I

Exeo in a spasm
tired of my darling's red sputum
from the Portobello Private Nursing Home
its secret things
and toil to the crest of the surge of the steep
    perilous bridge
and lapse down blankly under the scream of the
    hoarding

round the bright stiff banner of the hoarding
into a black west
throttled with clouds.

Above the mansions the algum-trees
the mountains
my skull sullenly
clot of anger
skewered aloft strangled in the cang of the wind
bites like a dog against its chastisement.

I trundle along rapidly now on my ruined feet
flush with the livid canal;
at Parnell Bridge a dying barge
carrying a cargo of nails and timber
rocks itself softly in the foaming cloister of the
    lock;
on the far bank a gang of down and outs would
    seem to be mending a beam.

Then for miles only wind
and the weals creeping alongside on the water
and the world opening up to the south
across a travesty of champaign to the mountains
and the stillborn evening turning a filthy green
manuring the night fungus
and the mind annulled
wrecked in wind.

I splashed past a little wearish old man,
Democritus,
scuttling along between a crutch and a stick,
his stump caught up horribly, like a claw, under
    his breech, smoking.
Then because a field on the left went up in a
    sudden blaze

of shouting and urgent whistling and scarlet
    and blue ganzies
I stopped and climbed the bank to see the game.
A child fidgeting at the gate called up:
"Would we be let in Mister?"
"Certainly" I said "you would."
But, afraid, he set off down the road.
"Well" I called after him "why wouldn't you
    go on in?"
"Oh" he said, knowingly,
"I was in that field before and I got put out."
So on,
derelict,
as from a bush of gorse on fire in the mountain
    after dark,
or, in Sumatra, the jungle hymen,
the still flagrant rafflesia.

Next:
a lamentable family of grey verminous hens,
perishing out in the sunk field,
trembling, half asleep, against the closed door
    of a shed,
with no means of roosting.
The great mushy toadstool,
green-black,
oozing up after me,
soaking up the tattered sky like an ink of
    pestilence,
in my skull the wind going fetid,
the water . . .

Next:
on the hill down from the Fox and Geese into
    Chapelizod
a small malevolent goat, exiled on the road,

remotely pucking the gate of his field;
the Isolde Stores a great perturbation of sweaty
    heroes,
in their Sunday best,
come hastening down for a pint of nepenthe or
    moly or half and half
from watching the hurlers above in Kilmain ham.

Blotches of doomed yellow in the pit of the
    Liffey;
the fingers of the ladders hooked over the
    parapet,
soliciting;
a slush of vigilant gulls in the grey spew of the
    sewer.

Ah the banner
the banner of meat bleeding
on the silk of the seas and the arctic flowers
that do not exist.

## I WOULD LIKE MY LOVE TO DIE

I would like my love to die
and the rain to be falling on the graveyard
and on me walking the streets
mourning the first and last to love me

*(translated from the French)*

## JOHN HEWITT

John Hewitt was born in 1907 in Belfast. He was educated at Methodist College and at Queen's University, Belfast, where he received his B.A. and M.A. From 1930 to 1957 he was assistant and then deputy director of the Belfast Museum and Art Gallery. For the next fifteen years he was director of the Herbert Art Gallery and Museum in Coventry, England. Hewitt was a member of the Irish Academy of Letters, associate editor of the magazine *Lagan*, and poetry editor of *Threshold*. He was Queen's University's first writer-in-residence (1976–1979) and was awarded the Gregory Medal by the Irish Academy of Letters in 1984. His major collections of poetry are *Collected Poems 1932–1967* (1968), *An Ulster Reckoning* (1971), *Out of My Time* (1974), *Time Enough: Poems New and Revised* (1976), *The Rain Dance* (1978), *Kites in Spring* (1980), *The Selected John Hewitt* (1981), *Mosaic* (1982), *Loose Ends* (1983), *Freehold and Other Poems* (1986). Hewitt died in 1987.

### IRELAND

We Irish pride ourselves as patriots
and tell the beadroll of the valiant ones
since Clontarf's sunset saw the Norsemen broken . . .
Aye, and before that too we had our heroes:
but they were mighty fighters and victorious.
The later men got nothing save defeat,
hard transatlantic sidewalks or the scaffold . . .

We Irish, vainer than tense Lucifer,
are yet content with half-a-dozen turf,
and cry our adoration for a bog,
rejoicing in the rain that never ceases,
and happy to stride over the sterile acres,
or stony hills that scarcely feed a sheep.
But we are fools, I say, are ignorant fools
to waste the spirit's warmth in this cold air,
to spend our wit and love and poetry
on half-a-dozen peat and a black bog.

We are not native here or anywhere.
We were the keltic wave that broke over Europe,
and ran up this bleak beach among these stones:
but when the tide ebbed, were left stranded here
in crevices, and ledge-protected pools
that have grown salter with the drying up
of the great common flow that kept us sweet
with fresh cold draughts from deep down in the ocean.

So we are bitter, and are dying out
in terrible harshness in this lonely place,
and what we think is love for usual rock,
or old affection for our customary ledge,
is but forgotten longing for the sea
that cries far out and calls us to partake
in his great tidal movements round the earth.

## BECAUSE I PACED MY THOUGHT

Because I paced my thought by the natural world,
the earth organic, renewed with the palpable seasons,
rather than the city falling ruinous, slowly
by weather and use, swiftly by bomb and argument,

I found myself alone who had hoped for attention.
If one listened a moment he murmured his dissent:
this is an idle game for a cowardly mind.
The day is urgent. The sun is not on the agenda.

And some who hated the city and man's unreasoning acts
remarked: He is no ally, he does not say that
Power and Hate are the engines of human treason.
There is no answering love in the yellowing leaf.

I should have made it plain that I stake my future
on birds flying in and out of the schoolroom window,
on the council of sunburnt comrades in the sun
and the picture carried with singing into the temple.

## AN IRISHMAN IN COVENTRY

A full year since, I took this eager city,
the tolerance that laced its blatant roar,
its famous steeples and its web of girders,
as image of the state hope argued for,
and scarcely flung a bitter thought behind me
on all that flaws the glory and the grace
which ribbons through the sick, guilt-clotted legend
of my creed-haunted, Godforsaken race.
My rhetoric swung round from steel's high promise
to the precision of the well-gauged tool,
tracing the logic in the vast glass headlands,
the clockwork horse, the comprehensive school.

Then, sudden, by occasion's chance concerted,
in enclave of my nation, but apart,
the jigging dances and the lilting fiddle
stirred the old rage and pity in my heart.
The faces and the voices blurring round me,

the strong hands long familiar with the spade,
the whiskey-tinctured breath, the pious buttons,
called up a people endlessly betrayed
by our own weakness, by the wrongs we suffered
in that long twilight over bog and glen,
by force, by famine and by glittering fables
which gave us martyrs when we needed men,
by faith which had no charity to offer,
by poisoned memory and by ready wit,
with poverty corroded into malice
to hit and run and howl when it is hit.

This is our fate: eight hundred years' disaster
crazily tangled as the Book of Kells,
the dream's distortion and the land's division,
the midnight raiders and the prison cells.
Yet like Lir's children banished to the waters
our hearts still listen for the landward bells.

## ONCE ALIEN HERE

Once alien here my fathers built their house,
claimed, drained, and gave the land the shapes of use,
and for their urgent labour grudged no more
than shuffled pennies from the hoarded store
of well rubbed words that had left their overtones
in the ripe England of the mounded downs.

The sullen Irish limping to the hills
bore with them the enchantments and the spells
that in the clans' free days hung gay and rich
on every twig of every thorny hedge,
and gave the rain-pocked stone a meaning past
the blurred engraving of the fibrous frost.

So, I, because of all the buried men
in Ulster clay, because of rock and glen
and mist and cloud and quality of air
as native in my thought as any here,
who now would seek a native mode to tell
our stubborn wisdom individual,
yet lacking skill in either scale of song,
the graver English, lyric Irish tongue,
must let this rich earth so enhance the blood
with steady pulse where now is plunging mood
till thought and image may, identified
find easy voice to utter each aright.

## THE SCAR

for Padraic Fiacc

There's not a chance now that I might recover
one syllable of what that sick man said,
tapping upon my great-grandmother's shutter,
and begging, I was told, a piece of bread;
for on his tainted breath there hung infection
rank from the cabins of the stricken west,
the spores from black potato-stalks, the spittle
mottled with poison in his rattling chest;
but she who, by her nature, quickly answered,
accepted in return the famine-fever;
and that chance meeting, that brief confrontation,
conscribed me of the Irishry forever.

Though much I cherish lies outside their vision,
and much they prize I have no claim to share,
yet in that woman's death I found my nation;
the old wound aches and shews its fellow-scar.

## ST. STEPHEN'S DAY

St. Stephen's Day, the air is warm,
fair, early prelude to the spring,
though finches pick at withered haws
and stiff-necked swans beat leaden wing.

The old men bundled in their coats
creep out to greet the peeping sun,
as if, like jewel-headed toads,
they'd splintered winter's flinty stone.

## CALLING ON PEADAR O'DONNELL AT DUNGLOE

I remember striding through the August twilight
along a narrow lane from house to house;
a crowd of lads were hurling loud and shouting,
and once a black calf gave a mournful cry.

It seemed the long track round that we had taken
over a rough ground higher than the bog.
Three fields away foam topped the distant breakers.
Storm's opposition flogged us both dog-tired.

Then darkness dropped, and window after window
offered no trace of colour. We went on,
slow pacing now, and painfully admonished
by plaintive gulls above the ocean's din.

We reached the three small houses and the gate
which faced the place the drive swung to the right.
Now far too late to make our call we argued.
There was no blink of light in any room.

But halfway up the drive we glimpsed the writer
still working in the garden with his wife;
I shouted and he straightened up to answer,
and in the gloom his fine head glimmered white.

## LOUIS MACNEICE

Louis MacNeice was born in Belfast in 1907 and educated in England at Marlborough and at Oxford, where he received a B.A. degree. Before the outbreak of World War II, he lectured in Classics at the University of Birmingham, the University of London, and Cornell University. On his return to England in 1940, he became a producer for the BBC. Besides his radio plays, translations, critical and autobiographical prose, he published sixteen collections of poetry. His *Collected Poems* appeared in 1966, three years after his death in London.

---

### DUBLIN

Grey brick upon brick,
Declamatory bronze
On sombre pedestals—
O'Connell, Grattan, Moore—
And the brewery tugs and the swans
On the balustraded stream
And the bare bones of a fanlight
Over a hungry door
And the air soft on the cheek
And porter running from the taps
With a head of yellow cream
And Nelson on his pillar
Watching his world collapse.

This was never my town,
I was not born nor bred
Nor schooled here and she will not
Have me alive or dead
But yet she holds my mind
With her seedy elegance,
With her gentle veils of rain
And all her ghosts that walk
And all that hide behind
Her Georgian façades—
The catcalls and the pain,
The glamour of her squalor,
The bravado of her talk.

The lights jig in the river
With a concertina movement
And the sun comes up in the morning
Like barley-sugar on the water
And the mist on the Wicklow hills
Is close, as close
As the peasantry were to the landlord,
As the Irish to the Anglo-Irish,
As the killer is close one moment
To the man he kills,
Or as the moment itself
Is close to the next moment.

She is not an Irish town
And she is not English,
Historic with guns and vermin
And the cold renown
Of a fragment of Church latin,
Of an oratorical phrase.
But oh the days are soft,
Soft enough to forget
The lesson better learnt,
The bullet on the wet

Streets, the crooked deal,
The steel behind the laugh,
The Four Courts burnt.

Fort of the Dane,
Garrison of the Saxon,
Augustan capital
Of a Gaelic nation,
Appropriating all
The alien brought,
You give me time for thought
And by a juggler's trick
You poise the toppling hour—
O greyness run to flower,
Grey stone, grey water,
And brick upon grey brick.

## SNOW

The room was suddenly rich and the great bay-window
  was
Spawning snow and pink roses against it
Soundlessly collateral and incompatible:
World is suddener than we fancy it.

World is crazier and more of it than we think,
Incorrigibly plural. I peel and portion
A tangerine and spit the pips and feel
The drunkenness of things being various.

And the fire flames with a bubbling sound for world
Is more spiteful and gay than one supposes—
On the tongue on the eyes on the ears in the palms of
  one's hands—
There is more than glass between the snow and the huge
  roses.

## from TRILOGY FOR X

And love hung still as crystal over the bed
    And filled the corners of the enormous room;
The boom of dawn that left her sleeping, showing
    The flowers mirrored in the mahogany table.

O my love, if only I were able
    To protract this hour of quiet after passion,
Not ration happiness but keep this door for ever
    Closed on the world, its own world closed within it.

But dawn's waves trouble with the bubbling minute,
    The names of books come clear upon their shelves,
The reason delves for duty and you will wake
    With a start and go on living on your own.

The first train passes and the windows groan,
    Voices will hector and your voice become
A drum in tune with theirs, which all last night
    Like sap that fingered through a hungry tree
Asserted our one night's identity.

## from AUTUMN JOURNAL

### XVI

Nightmare leaves fatigue:
    We envy men of action
Who sleep and wake, murder and intrigue
    Without being doubtful, without being haunted.
And I envy the intransigence of my own
    Countrymen who shoot to kill and never
See the victim's face become their own
    Or find his motive sabotage their motives.

So reading the memoirs of Maud Gonne,
    Daughter of an English mother and a soldier father,
I note how a single purpose can be founded on
    A jumble of opposites:
Dublin Castle, the vice-regal ball,
    The embassies of Europe,
Hatred scribbled on a wall,
    Gaols and revolvers.
And I remember, when I was little, the fear
    Bandied among the servants
That Casement would land at the pier
    With a sword and a horde of rebels;
And how we used to expect, at a later date,
    When the wind blew from the west, the noise of shooting
Starting in the evening at eight
    In Belfast in the York Street district;
And the voodoo of the Orange bands
    Drawing an iron net through darkest Ulster,
Flailing the limbo lands—
    The linen mills, the long wet grass, the ragged hawthorn.
And one read black where the other read white, his hope
    The other man's damnation:
Up the Rebels, To Hell with the Pope,
    And God Save—as you prefer—the King or Ireland.
The land of scholars and saints:
    Scholars and saints my eye, the land of ambush,
Purblind manifestoes, never-ending complaints,
    The born martyr and the gallant ninny;
The grocer drunk with the drum,
    The land-owner shot in his bed, the angry voices
Piercing the broken fanlight in the slum,
    The shawled woman weeping at the garish altar.
Kathleen ni Houlihan! Why
    Must a country, like a ship or a car, be always female,
Mother or sweetheart? A woman passing by,
    We did but see her passing.
Passing like a patch of sun on the rainy hill

And yet we love her for ever and hate our neighbour
And each one in his will
Binds his heirs to continuance of hatred.
Drums on the haycock, drums on the harvest, black
Drums in the night shaking the windows:
King William is riding his white horse back
To the Boyne on a banner.
Thousands of banners, thousands of white
Horses, thousands of Williams
Waving thousands of swords and ready to fight
Till the blue sea turns to orange.
Such was my country and I thought I was well
Out of it, educated and domiciled in England,
Though yet her name keeps ringing like a bell
In an under-water belfry.
Why do we like being Irish? Partly because
It gives us a hold on the sentimental English
As members of a world that never was,
Baptised with fairy water;
And partly because Ireland is small enough
To be still thought of with a family feeling,
And because the waves are rough
That split her from a more commercial culture;
And because one feels that here at least one can
Do local work which is not at the world's mercy
And that on this tiny stage with luck a man
Might see the end of one particular action.
It is self-deception of course;
There is no immunity in this island either;
A cart that is drawn by somebody else's horse
And carrying goods to somebody else's market.
The bombs in the turnip sack, the sniper from the roof,
Griffith, Connolly, Collins, where have they brought us?
Ourselves alone! Let the round tower stand aloof
In a world of bursting mortar!
Let the school-children fumble their sums
In a half-dead language;

Let the censor be busy on the books; pull down the Georgian
        slums;
    Let the games be played in Gaelic.
Let them grow beet-sugar; let them build
    A factory in every hamlet;
Let them pigeon-hole the souls of the killed
    Into sheep and goats, patriots and traitors.
And the North, where I was a boy,
    Is still the North, veneered with the grime of Glasgow,
Thousands of men whom nobody will employ
    Standing at the corners, coughing.
And the street-children play on the wet
    Pavement—hopscotch or marbles;
And each rich family boasts a sagging tennis-net
    On a spongy lawn beside a dripping shrubbery.
The smoking chimneys hint
    At prosperity round the corner
But they make their Ulster linen from foreign lint
    And the money that comes in goes out to make more
        money.
A city built upon mud;
    A culture built upon profit;
Free speech nipped in the bud,
    The minority always guilty.
Why should I want to go back
    To you, Ireland, my Ireland?
The blots on the page are so black
    That they cannot be covered with shamrock.
I hate your grandiose airs,
    Your sob-stuff, your laugh and your swagger,
Your assumption that everyone cares
    Who is the king of your castle.
Castles are out of date,
    The tide flows round the children's sandy fancy;
Put up what flag you like, it is too late
    To save your soul with bunting.

*Odi atque amo:*
    Shall we cut this name on trees with a rusty dagger?
Her mountains are still blue, her rivers flow
    Bubbling over the boulders.
She is both a bore and a bitch;
    Better close the horizon,
Send her no more fantasy, no more longings which
    Are under a fatal tariff.
For common sense is the vogue
    And she gives her children neither sense nor money
Who slouch around the world with a gesture and a brogue
    And a faggot of useless memories.

## DENIS DEVLIN

Denis Devlin was born of Irish parents in 1908 in Greenock, Scotland. He grew up in Dublin and was educated at Belvedere and University College, Dublin, where he took his M.A. in 1930. Devlin continued his studies in Munich and Paris before teaching in the English department at University College, Dublin (1933–1935). Devlin then joined the Irish Foreign Service, in which he had a very distinguished career. He held important diplomatic posts in the United States, was minister plenipotentiary to Italy, then to Turkey, and ambassador to Italy. Devlin published three collections of translations of the French poet St. John Perse: *Rains* (1945), *Snows* (1945), and *Exile and Other Poems* (1949). His own published collections of poetry include *Poems* (with Brian Coffey, 1930), *Intercessions* (1937), *Lough Derg and Other Poems* (1946), and the posthumous *Selected Poems* (1963), *Collected Poems* (1964), and *The Heavenly Foreigner* (1967). When Devlin died in Dublin in 1959, an award for poetry was inaugurated to commemorate him.

---

### LOUGH DERG

The poor in spirit on their rosary rounds,
The jobbers with their whiskey-angered eyes,
The pink bank clerks, the tip-hat papal counts,
And drab, kind women their tonsured mockery tries,
Glad invalids on penitential feet
Walk the Lord's majesty like their village street.

With mullioned Europe shattered, this Northwest,
Rude-sainted isle would pray it whole again:
(Peasant Apollo! Troy is worn to rest.)
Europe that humanized the sacred bane
Of God's chance who yet laughed in his mind
And balanced thief and saint: were they this kind?

Low rocks, a few weasels, lake
Like a field of burnt gorse; the rooks caw;
Ours, passive, for man's gradual wisdom take
Firefly instinct dreamed out into law;
The prophets' jeweled kingdom down at heel
Fires no Augustine here. Inert, they kneel;

All is simple and symbol in their world,
The incomprehended rendered fabulous.
Sin teases life whose natural fruits withheld
Sour the deprived nor bloom for timely loss:
Clan Jansen! less what magnanimity leavens
Man's wept-out, fitful, magniloquent heavens

Where prayer was praise, O Lord! the Temple trumpets
Cascaded down Thy sunny pavilions of air,
The scroll-tongued priests, the galvanic strumpets,
All clash and stridency gloomed upon Thy stair;
The pharisees, the exalted boy their power
Sensually psalmed in Thee, their coming hour!

And to the sun, earth turned her flower of sex,
Acanthus in the architects' limpid angles;
Close priests allegorized the Orphic egg's
Brood, and from the Academy, tolerant wranglers
Could hear the contemplatives of the Tragic Choir
Drain off man's sanguine, pastoral death-desire.

It was said stone dreams and animal sleeps and man
Is awake; but sleep with its drama on us bred
Animal articulate, only somnambulist can
Conscience like Cawdor give the blood its head
For the dim moors to reign through druids again.
O first geometer! tangent-feelered brain

Clearing by inches the encircled eyes,
Bolder than the peasant tiger whose autumn beauty
Sags in the expletive kill, or the sacrifice
Of dearth puffed positive in the stance of duty
With which these pilgrims would propitiate
Their fears; no leafy, medieval state

Of paschal cathedrals backed on earthy hooves
Against the craftsmen's primary-colored skies
Whose gold was Gabriel on the patient roofs,
The parabled windows taught the dead to rise,
And Christ the Centaur, in two natures whole,
With fable and proverb joinered body and soul.

Water withers from the oars. The pilgrims blacken
Out of the boats to masticate their sin
Where Dante smelled among the stones and bracken
The door to Hell (O harder Hell where pain
Is earthed, a casuist sanctuary of guilt!).
Spirit bureaucracy on a bet built

Part by this race when monks in convents of coracles
For the Merovingian centuries left their land,
Belled, fragrant; and honest in their oracles
Bespoke the grace to give without demand,
Martyrs Heaven winged nor tempted with reward.
And not ours, doughed in dogma, who never have dared

Will with surrogate palm distribute hope:
No better nor worse than I who, in my books,
Have angered at the stake with Bruno and, by the rope
Watt Tyler swung from, leagued with shifty looks
To fuse the next rebellion with the desperate
Serfs in the sane need to eat and get;

Have praised, on its thunderous canvas, the Florentine
smile
As man took to wearing his death, his own,
Sapped crisis through cathedral branches (while
Flesh groped loud round dissenting skeleton)
In soul, reborn as body's appetite:
Now languisht back in body's amber light,

Now is consumed. O earthly paradise!
Hell is to know our natural empire used
Wrong, by mind's molting, brute divinities.
The vanishing tiger's saved, his blood transfused.
Kent is for Jutes again and Glasgow town
Burns high enough to screen the stars and moon.

Well may they cry who have been robbed, their wasting
Shares in justice legally lowered until
Man his own actor, matrix, mold and casting,
Or man, God's image, sees his idol spill.
Say it was pride that did it, or virtue's brief:
To them that suffer it is no relief.

All indiscriminate, man, stone, animal
Are woken up in nightmare. What John the Blind
From Patmos saw works and we speak it. Not all
The men of God nor the priests of mankind
Can mend or explain the good and broke, not one
Generous with love prove communion;

Behind the eyes the winged ascension flags,
For want of spirit by the market blurbed,
And if hands touch, such fraternity sags
Frightened this side the dikes of death disturbed
Like Aran Islands' bibulous, unclean seas:
*Pietà*: but the limbs ache; it is not peace.

Then to see less, look little, let hearts' hunger
Feed on water and berries. The pilgrims sing:
Life will fare well from elder to younger,
Though courage fail in a world-end, rosary ring.
Courage kills its practitioners and we live,
Nothing forgotten, nothing to forgive,

We pray to ourself. The metal moon, unspent
Virgin eternity sleeping in the mind,
Excites the form of prayer without content;
Whitethorn lightens, delicate and blind,
The negro mountain, and so, knelt on her sod,
This woman beside me murmuring *My God! My God!*

## ANK'HOR VAT

The antlered forests
Move down to the sea.
Here the dung-filled jungle pauses

Buddha has covered the walls of the great temple
With the vegetative speed of his imagery
Let us wait, hand in hand

No Western god or saint
Ever smiled with the lissome fury of this god
Who holds in doubt
The wooden stare of Apollo
Our Christian crown of thorns:

There is no mystery in the luminous lines
Of that high, animal face
The smile, sad, humoring and equal
Blesses without obliging
Loves without condescension;
The god, clear as spring-water
Sees through everything, while everything
Flows through him

A fling of flowers here
Whose names I do not know
Downy, scarlet gullets
Green legs yielding and closing

While, at my mental distance from passion,
The prolific divinity of the temple
Is a quiet lettering on vellum.

Let us lie down before him
His look will flow like oil over us.

## WISHES FOR HER

Against Minoan sunlight
Slight-boned head,
Buildings with the thin climb of larks
Trilling off whetstone brilliants,
Slight head, nor petal nor marble
Night-shell
Two, one and separate.

Love in loving, all
A fledgling, hard-billed April,
Soil's gaudy chemistry in fission and fuse.
And she

Lit out of fire and glass
Lightning
The blue flowers of vacant thunder.

In the riverlands
Stained with old battlefields, old armor
In which their child, rust, sighs,
Strangers lost in the courtyard,
I lie awake.
The ice recedes, on black silk
Rocks the seals sway their heads.

No prophet deaths
In the webbed tensions of memory,
No harm
Night lean with hunters.
I wish you well, wish
Tall angels whose rib-freezing
Beauty attend you.

## DAPHNE STILLORGAN

The stationmaster is garrulous in
The modest station set in the glen
Bushes wink with brown birdwings
The benches spread their knees, present
Drowsy laps to the sun.
A white cat sacred dangerous within
Egyptian memories considers
Like a marksman a celluloid ball on a water-jet
A tigermoth's fatal rise and fall
On her rank breath.

One shadow makes the whole sky shake
But I flick with instantaneous eyes
The next quick change before the change begins.
The water spouts are dried
Laurel leaves
Shine in the waxen summer.

The clean metronome of horses' feet on the road
Made anguish with clocks and rules which now
Silence beyond measure floods again
Through the trees' green bazaar and patches
Of light like muslin girls in forest lost.
And lost, but after noisy pebble wrinkling
This scene became a pool in air limpid
Restoring to the inimitable Images
Reflections paled but smooth as smooth as smooth.

Fuchsias revive and breathe through scarlet mouths
Rumors on wind
Far-off the humid pounding of a train
Wind-cylinders boom along
Steel wires, the rails drone,
Far-off thudding, trampling, thud
Of thousand pink-soled apes, no humorous family god!

Southward, storm
Smashes the flimsy sky.

Vines, virgins, guard your red wine
Cross branching arms frail on breasts
Small showers will fall before the rain crowds:
Use them to cool your rind-stiffening flesh
Writhing with blood for sap
To suck the insect-pointed air, the first threat
Of eager ravishers.

Scared faces lifted up
Is the menace bestial or a brusque pleiad
Of gods of fire vagabond?
Quick just in time quick just in time; ah!
Trees in light dryad dresses
Birds (O unreal whitewashed station!)
Compose no more that invisible architecture.

## ANTEROOM: GENEVA

The General Secretary's feet whispered over the red carpet
And stopped, a demure pair, beside the demure
Cadet, poor but correct,
Devoted menial of well-mannered Power.
"A word with you." "Yes, your Excellency."
Excellency smiled. "Your silk shirt is nice, Scriptor.
But listen. Better not let these private letters
Reach the President. He gets worried, you know,
About the personal misfortunes of the people;
And really, the Minister is due to arrive.
It is surely most unseemly
To keep the State in the waiting-room
For God knows what beggars,
For totally unnecessary people."

Their mutual shirtfronts gleamed in a white smile
The electorate at breakfast approved of the war for peace
And the private detective idly deflowered a rose.

DENIS DEVLIN

## RENEWAL BY HER ELEMENT

The hawthorn morning moving
Above the battlements,
Breast from breast of lover
Tears, reminds of difference
And body's raggedness.

Immune from resolution
Into common clay
Because I have not known you;
Self-content as birdsong
Scornful at night-breakage
You seem to me. I am
Fresh from a long absence.

O suave through surf lifting
My smile upon your mouth;
Limbs according to rhythm
Separating, closing;
Scarcely using my name,
Traveller through troubling gestures,
Only for rare embraces
Of prepared texture.
Your lips amused harden
My arms round you defiant,
You shirk my enwreathing
Language, and you smile,
Turning aside my hand
Through your breath's light leafage,
Preferring yourself reflected
In my body to me,
Preferring my image of you
To you whom I achieved.
Noise is curbed attentive,
The sea hangs on your lips:
What would I do less?

It is over now but once
Our fees were nothing more,
Each for use of the other
In mortgage, than a glance.
I knew the secret movements
Of the blood under your throat
And when we lay love-proven
Whispering legends to sleep
Braceleted in embrace
Your hands pouring on me
Fresh water of their caresses,
Breasts, nests of my tenderness,
All night was laced with praise.

Now my image faded
In the lucid fields
Of your eyes. Never again
Surprise for years, years.

My landscape is grey rain
Aslant on bent seas.

## from THE HEAVENLY FOREIGNER

### Chartres

The spires, firm on their monster feet rose light and thin
  and trembling in the tracery of bird-motion and
  bell-echo;
A woodshaving sailed on the calm, vernal water.
Now, fixing our secret in my eyes, that's what is there,
That's what is there, she said, all this is more
Beautiful than Chartres.
Again, again protesting
Like those who will not surrender a small liberty

Which they cannot cultivate in any case.
Rebellion is imperfection, like all matter:
Mirror without reflection, I am helpless,
As if I were watching a wooden beam pushing up through
  the soil
As if I were the soft-voiced people forever against the
  people with hard voices.

Whereas, O my term, my unavoidable turnstile
In the cathedral porch, I call you these things,
Term itself, apse itself, had you but come,
Our absolute Lord had not been me, not me or you,
But an instant preconising eternity
Borne between our open eyes,
With no perceptible bank of land between,
Nor oblique eyesight deciding other objects were there.

## Ile-St-Louis

It goes on all night, the sorceresses whispering
Wind in the wood, and when you listen
Vanishing like a whistle downriver. Then, Oh, cling
Close to the world and her; she crowns
This moment with the diadem of her Time, and waves
The floral barge into a frame of trees;
Her eyes darken with the music,
Darkness lies against her mouth,
There is a sharp wind between laugh and cry.

Last night on the gilded Bourbon bridge
The doom of Adam brought me down to earth
While the houses with their ruined freight
Filed down the soft, erotic river.
I was not guilty, had I but known it!
For now and then the royal pall of peace
Can fall without prayer, without need,
Love's earnest gift being frivolously given;

And as the lucid, pagan music
Blows with brown leaves over the asphalt,
Guilt slips off like a wet coat in the hall.

. . . And past her ivory head
Stream the pebble notes like a run of deer;
A shy god moves across the terrace,
A being born among the flowers of her mind
Beautiful, loving and beloved.

In all these one-room flats, while the street-lamps,
    unseasonably awake all night long,
Mutter their proverbs—that it's not worth it, it makes no
    difference—
How many white-collar clerks sit alone over a thin drink
Singing ballads out of anthologies,
Reading, in a spurt and laze, the provincial eyebrow
    raised,
The Essays of Sorel, the novels of Maxim Gorky! and
    brush their teeth,
Take two aspirins and fall between the soiled sheets,
Thinking of the good brother and sister who have stayed
    at home
In the country where the trucks are loading now
With greens and tuberose and cackle;
And fall asleep and resume the dream
Of the fern and roses altar in childhood,
Of the campaigns of childhood
Against the fortress of the Snow Princess.

## W. R. RODGERS

W. R. Rodgers was born in 1909 in Belfast and educated at Queen's University, Belfast. From 1934 to 1946 Rodgers was a Presbyterian minister in County Armagh. He worked as a BBC producer and scriptwriter from 1946 to 1952, during which time he produced a number of lively radio discussions of the major literary figures of modern Ireland. Rodgers was elected to the Irish Academy of Letters in 1951. His first wife died in 1953, and in that year he remarried; there are two children from his first marriage and one from his second. In 1966 Rodgers moved to Claremont, California, to become writer-in-residence at Pitzer College, and in 1968 he worked at the California State Polytechnic College. He died the following year in Los Angeles. His published collections of poetry are *Awake and Other Poems* (1941), *Europa and the Bull* (1952), and *Collected Poems* (1971).

### THE NET

Quick, woman, in your net
Catch the silver I fling!
O I am deep in your debt,
Draw tight, skin-tight, the string
And rake the silver in.
No fisher ever yet
Drew such a cunning ring.

Ah, shifty as the fin
Of any fish this flesh
That, shaken to the shin,
Now shoals into your mesh,
Bursting to be held in;
Purse-proud and pebble-hard,
Its pence like shingle showered.

Open the haul, and shake
The fill of shillings free,
Let all the satchels break
And leap about the knee
In shoals of ecstasy.
Guineas and gills will flake
At each gull-plunge of me.

Though all the Angels, and
Saint Michael at their head,
Nightly contrive to stand
On guard about your bed,
Yet none dare take a hand,
But each can only spread
His eagle-eye instead.

But I, being man, can kiss
And bed-spread-eagle too;
All flesh shall come to this,
Being less than angel is,
Yet higher far in bliss
As it entwines with you.
Come, make no sound, my sweet;
Turn down the candid lamp
And draw the equal quilt
Over our naked guilt.

## PAIRED LIVES

Though to strangers' approach
(Like swing doors cheek to cheek)
Presenting one smooth front
Of summed resistance and
Aligned resentment, yet,
On nearer view note how,
At the deflecting touch
Of intervening hand,
Each in its lonely arc
Reaches and rocks inward
(Retires and returns
Immediately to join
The other moiety).
Each singly yields to thrust,
Is hung on its own hinge
Of fear and hope, and in
Its own reticence rests.

## SCAPEGOAT

God broke into my house last night
With his flying-squad, narks, batmen, bully-boys,
Proctors, bailiffs, aiders and abettors—
Call them what you will—hard-mouthed, bowler-hatted.
Hearing a lack of noise I had gone downstairs
To let the dog out.
The tall figure with his obedient shadows
Pushed past me into the light and turned
With the accusing document; all my fears.
It seemed I had for years out of mind
Owed him a sum of money and had paid
Nothing. "Lord," I said reluctantly, looking

Into his implacably-forgiving face,
"I would have called it a lie, but if you
Say so, it must be so."
I do not know—
It being a dream of sorts—I do not know
If it were His son or my son
The doomsmen laid upon the floor then,
The knife to his throat.
I saw no more. But the dog of the house
Fled howling through the open door.

## DONAGH MacDONAGH

Donagh MacDonagh, the son of Thomas MacDonagh, poet and leader of the Easter Rising, was born in 1912 in Dublin. He was educated at University College, Dublin, and was admitted to the Irish Bar in 1936. He pursued a legal as well as a literary career, becoming a justice of the district courts. MacDonagh wrote several successful plays. His published collections of poetry are *Veterans and Other Poems* (1941), *The Hungry Grass* (1947), and *A Warning to Conquerors* (1968). MacDonagh died in 1968.

### THE VETERANS

Strict hairshirt of circumstance tears the flesh
Off most delicate bones;
Years of counter and office, the warped mesh
Of social living, dropping on stones,
Wear down all that was rough and worthy
To a common denominator of dull tones.

So these, who in the sixteenth year of the century
Saw their city, a Phoenix upturned,
Settle under her ashes and bury
Hearts and brains that more frantically burned
Than the town they destroyed, have with the corrosion of
time

Spent more than they earned;
And with their youth has shrunk their singular mystery
Which for one week set them in the pulse of the age,
Their spring adventure petrified in history,
A line on a page,
Betrayed into the hands of students who question
Oppressed and oppressor's rage.

Only the dead beneath their granite signatures
Are untroubled by the touch of day and day,
Only in them the first rich vision endures;
Those over clay
Retouch in memory, with sentiment relive,
April and May.

## from CHARLES DONNELLY

Dead in Spain 1937

Of what a quality is courage made
That he who gently walked our city streets
Talking of poetry or philosophy,
Spinoza, Keats,
Should lie like any martyred soldier
His brave and fertile brain dried quite away
And the limbs that carried him from cradle to death's
    outpost
Growing down into a foreign clay.

Gone from amongst us and his life not half begun
Who had followed Jack-o'-Lantern truth and liberty
Where it led wavering from park-bed to prison-cell
Into a strange land, dry misery;
And then into Spain's slaughter, sniper's aim
And his last shocked embrace of earth's lineaments.

Can I picture truly that swift end
Who see him dead with eye that still repents?

What end, what quietus can I see for him,
Who had the quality of life in every vein?
Life with its passion and poetry and its proud
Ignorance of eventual loss or gain . . .
This first fruit of our harvest, willing sacrifice
Upon the altar of his integrity,
Lost to us. Somewhere his death is charted,
A signature affixed to his brief history.

*

They gave him a gun,
A trigger to pull that any peasant finger
Could have pulled as well, a barrel to keep sweet
That any eye from Valencia to Madrid
Could have looked through.
His body stopped a bullet and little else,
Stopped no tank or French 75
From crunching over roads of human bones.
His brain might have done that
But it has melted into Spanish soil,

But speaks into my brain in parody
Of the voice that was its servant,
And speaks only what it spoke before.
The intricate cells, the labyrinthine ways,
The multicoloured images that lurked and shone,
The dreams betrayed into expression,
Melted into a red earth, richer for olive crop.
And through the pleasant European landscapes
The legions march; theodolite and map
Plan out the tactical approach, the gun emplacement,
The unencumbered field for cemetery.

## JUST AN OLD SWEET SONG

The pale, drooping girl and the swaggering soldier
The row-dow-dow-dow of the stuttering drum,
The bugles, the charges, the swords are romantic
For those who survive when the bugles are dumb.

The lice of the trenches, the mortars, machine-guns,
The prisoners exchanged and the Christmas Day lull,
The no-man's-land raid and the swagger-stick rally
Are stirring, for when was a finished war dull?

The road-block, the ambush, the scrap on the mountain,
The slouch-hat, the trench-coat, the raid in the night,
The hand-grenade hefted, police-barracks burning
Ah, that was the life, and who's hurt in a fight?

The blitzkrieg, the landings, the victories, the losses,
The eyes blind with sand, the retreat, the alert,
Commando and D-Day, H-Hour and Block-buster
Have filed through the glass, and was anyone hurt?

A flash and a mushroom, a hole in the planet,
Strange growth in the flora, less fauna to feed.
Peace enters, the silence returns and the waters
Advance on the earth as the war tides recede.

## CHARLES DONNELLY

Charles Donnelly was born in 1914 in County Tyrone, and raised in Dublin. Donnelly received his education at University College, Dublin, where he was a contemporary of Flann O'Brien, Denis Devlin, and Donagh MacDonagh. Donnelly left home when his Marxist political activities involved him in difficulties with the authorities. He lived and worked for some time in London, then, in 1936, joined the Republican forces in Spain as a volunteer in the James Connolly centuria attached to the Abraham Lincoln Brigade. He was killed on the Jarama Front in Spain on February 27, 1937. Charles Donnelly's poems and a brief biography are published in Joseph Donnelly's *Charlie Donnelly: The Life and Poems* (1987).

### POEM

Between rebellion as a private study and the public
Defiance is simple action only which will flicker
Catlike, for spring. Whether at nerve-roots is secret
Iron, there's no diviner can tell, only the moment can
show.
Simple and unclear moment, on a morning utterly
different
And under circumstances different from what you'd
expected.

Your flag is public over granite. Gulls fly above it.
Whatever the issue of the battle is, your memory
Is public, for them to pull awry with crooked hands,
Moist eyes. And villages' reputations will be built on
Inaccurate accounts of your campaigns. You're name for
orators,
Figure stone-struck beneath damp Dublin sky.

In a delaying action, perhaps, on hillside in remote parish,
Outposts correctly placed, retreat secured to wood, bridge
mined
Against pursuit, sniper may sight you carelessly
contoured.
Or death may follow years in strait confinement, where
diet
Is uniform as ceremony, lacking only fruit
Or on the barracks square before the sun casts shadow.

Name, subject of all considered words, praise and blame
Irrelevant, the public talk which sounds the same on
hollow
Tongue as true, you'll be with Parnell and with Pearse.
Name alderman will raise a cheer with, teacher make
reference
Oblique in class, and boys and women spin gum of
sentiment
On qualities attributed in error.

Man, dweller in mountain huts, possessor of colored mice,
Skilful in minor manual turns, patron of obscure subjects,
of
Gaelic swordsmanship and medieval armory,
The technique of the public man, the masked servilities
are
Not for you, Master of military trade, you give
Like Raleigh, Lawrence, Childers, your services but not
yourself.

## THE TOLERANCE OF CROWS

Death comes in quantity from solved
Problems on maps, well-ordered dispositions,
Angles of elevation and direction;

Comes innocent from tools children might
Love, retaining under pillows
Innocently impales on any flesh.

And with flesh falls apart the mind
That trails thought from the mind that cuts
Thought clearly for a waiting purpose.

Progress of poison in the nerves and
Discipline's collapse is halted.
Body awaits the tolerance of crows.

## THE FLOWERING BARS

After sharp words from the fine mind,
protest in court,
the intimate high head constrained,
straight lines of prison, empty walls,
a subtle beauty in a simple place.

There to strain thought through the tightened brain,
there weave
the slender cords of thought, in calm,
until routine in prospect bound
joy into security,
and among strictness sweetness grew,
mystery of flowering bars.

## VALENTIN IREMONGER

Valentin Iremonger was born in 1918 in Dublin. He was educated at Synge St. Christian Brothers School, at Colaiste Mhuire, and at the Abbey Theatre School of Acting (1938–1940). He was associated with the Abbey and the Gate theaters as actor and producer until 1946, when he entered the Irish Foreign Service. Iremonger has had an impressive career in the Foreign Service: he was Irish ambassador to Sweden, Norway, and Finland (1964–1968), then ambassador to India (1968–1973), and since 1973 ambassador to Luxembourg. Iremonger has also managed to pursue the vocation of man of letters: he was poetry editor of *Envoy* magazine in Dublin from 1949 to 1951, and is author of many articles and reviews in Irish and British journals. He received the AE Memorial Award in 1945. His poems are collected in *On the Barricades* (1944), *Reservations* (1950), and *Horan's Field and Other Reservations* (1972). Iremonger has translated two novels from the Irish; *Beatha Mhuire* (1955) is his translation into Irish of Rilke's *Das Marienleben*.

### HECTOR

Talking to her, he knew it was the end,
The last time he'd speed her into sleep with kisses:
Achilles had it in for him and was fighting mad.
The roads of his longing she again wandered,
A girl desirable as midsummer's day.

He was a marked man and he knew it,
Being no match for Achilles whom the gods were backing.
Sadly he spoke to her for hours, his heart
Snapping like sticks, she on his shoulder crying.
Yet, sorry only that the meaning eluded him.

He slept well all night, having caressed
Andromache like a flower, though in a dream he saw
A body lying on the sands, huddled and bleeding,
Near the feet a sword in bits and by the head
An upturned, dented helmet.

## ICARUS

As, even to-day, the airman, feeling the plane sweat
Suddenly, seeing the horizon tilt up gravely, the wings
    shiver,
Knows that, for once, Daedalus has slipped up badly,
Drunk on the job, perhaps, more likely dreaming, high-
    flier Icarus,
Head butting down, skidding along the light-shafts
Back, over the tones of the sea-waves and the slip-stream,
    heard
The gravel-voiced, stuttering trumpets of his heart
Sennet among the crumbling court-yards of his brain the
    mistake
Of trusting somebody else on an important affair like this;
And, while the flat sea, approaching, buckled into oh!
    avenues
Of acclamation, he saw the wrong story fan out into
    history.
Truth, undefined, lost in his own neglect. On the hills,
The summer-shackled hills, the sun spanged all day;
Love and the world were young and there was no ending:

But star-chaser, big-time-going, chancer Icarus
Like a dog on the sea lay and the girls forgot him,
And Daedalus, too busy hammering another job,
Remembered him only in pubs. No bugler at all
Sobbed taps for the young fool then, reported missing,
Presumed drowned, wing-bones and feathers on the tide
Drifting in casually, one by one.

## THIS HOURE HER VIGILL

Elizabeth, frigidly stretched,
On a spring day surprised us
With her starched dignity and the quietness
Of her hands clasping a black cross.

With book and candle and holy water dish
She received us in the room with the blind down.
Her eyes were peculiarly closed and we knelt shyly
Noticing the blot of her hair on the white pillow.

We met that evening by the crumbling wall
In the field behind the house where I lived
And talked it over, but could find no reason
Why she had left us whom she had liked so much.

Death, yes, we understood: something to do
With age and decay, decrepit bodies;
But here was this vigorous one, aloof and prim,
Who would not answer our furtive whispers.

Next morning, hearing the priest call her name,
I fled outside, being full of certainty,
And cried my seven years against the church's stone wall.
For eighteen years I did not speak her name

Until this autumn day when, in a gale,
A sapling fell outside my window, its branches
Rebelliously blotting the lawn's green. Suddenly, I thought
Of Elizabeth, frigidly stretched.

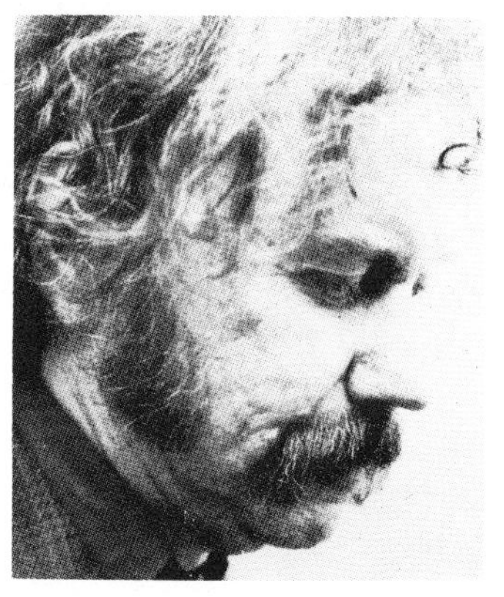

## PADRAIC FIACC

Padraic Fiacc (the pseudonym of Patrick Joseph O'Connor) was born in 1924 in Belfast. His father emigrated in 1930 to New York City and Fiacc was educated at St. Joseph's Seminary in Calicoon, New York. He returned to Belfast in 1946. In 1957 he won the AE Memorial Award for poetry, in 1980 a bursary from the Arts Council of Northern Ireland, and in 1981 a Poetry Ireland Award. He has edited an anthology of contemporary Ulster poetry, *The Wearing of the Black* (1974), and has published several collections of his own poetry: *By the Black Stream* (1969), *Odour of Blood* (1973), *Nights in the Bad Place* (1977), *The Selected Padraic Fiacc* (1979), and *Missa Terribilis* (1986).

### HAEMORRHAGE

I bleed by the black stream
for my torn bough.
*James Joyce*

Entries patent leather with sleet
Mirror gas and neon light.

A boy with a husky voice picks
And kicks a tin down home in

To tram rattle and ship horn
In a fog from where fevers come

In at an East Wind's
Icy burst of black rain . . .

Here I was good and got and born
Cold, lost, not predictable

Poor, bare crossed in grain
With a shudder no one can still

In the damp down by the half-dried river
Slimy at night on the mudflats in

The moon light gets an un-
earthly white Belfast man.

## THE POET

I am the chaunt-rann of a Singer
Who has sung to heart at night
How the rust-loch's hazel waters
Mirror the stars all right:
*Christ on a tree for you and me*
*And the moon-dark worlds between!*

I am the chaunt-rann of a Singer
Who has sung to heart by day
How the grey rain on the wet street
Washes our lives away:
*Christ on a tree for you and me*
*And the sun-bright worlds between!*

I am the chaunt-rann of a Singer
Who does not cease chaunt with loam
As the crouched lime of the good earth
Eats us away on home:
*Christ on a tree for you and me*
*And none of the worlds between!*

## GLOSS

Nor truth nor good did they know
But beauty burning away.
They were the dark earth people of old
Restive in the clay.

Deirdre watched Naisi die
And great King Conor of himself said
"Did you ever see a bottomless bucket
In the muck discarded?"

And comradely Dermot was destroyed by Fionn
Because of the beauty of a girl.
Because of the beauty of a girl
The sky went raging on fire

And the sea was pushed out into rage.
They were the dark earth people of old
And Deirdre pitched herself into the sea.
*Turn the page. Turn the page.*

## INTROIT

It raindrops on the cold
Silver windowpanes
Of evening, starting to stare

With innumerable eyes over
The Military, white
-faced as young girls . . .

"We're all going to be blown
To Hell's gates" cries
The Welsh one: "The bomb is

Going off at the gasworks!"
A sudden ball of orange
Spurts over the black

-board sky of chalk
Houses, and old ladies and
Soldiers shake like flowers

Crying "Christ!" and "Fuck!"

## GOODBYE TO BRIGID / AN *AGNUS DEI*

I take you by the hand. Your eyes,
Mirroring the traffic lights,
Are green and orange and red.

The Military lorries by our side
Drown out your child-heart
Thumping tired under the soot

-black thorn trees these
Exhaust-fumed greasy mornings.

My little girl, my Lamb of God,
I'd like to set you free from
Bitch Belfast as we pass the armed

-to-the-back-teeth barracks and
Descend the road into the school
Grounds of broken windows from

A spate of car-bombs, but
Don't forgive me for not.

## ANTHONY CRONIN

Anthony Cronin was born in 1925 in County Wexford. He was educated at University College, Dublin, and later lived for some years in London and in Spain. Cronin has been editor of the important Irish magazine *The Bell*, literary editor of the London weekly review *Time and Tide*, and a columnist for the *Irish Times*. A fairly perceptive literary critic, he has published two collections of critical essays. Cronin's collections of poetry include *Poems* (1958), *Collected Poems 1950–1973* (1973), and *New and Selected Poems* (1982).

### APOLOGY

It was proper for them, awaking in ordered houses,
Among russet walls where fruit grew ripe to the hand,
Walking on lawns where fountains arched in the summer,
To praise through their gentle days the dwelling virtues
And architect epics to honour the good and the brave.
And easy perhaps for the desert-maddened preacher,
With his withered loins and the dirt hard in his pores,
To lash with his locust-tongue the uncertainly happy
And call on the townsmen to shrive and to shrivel for
  God.
But we who have climbed to the top of tall houses in
  winter
And heard in the gathering silence the limp of the clock,

Who dunned by our need through the days are unfailingly
traitors
In sad and undignified ways to each circle of friends,
How can we praise in our poems the simplified heroes,
Or urge to the truth we can never be true to ourselves?
O love that forgives because needing forgiveness also
Forgive us that we have not lived through a virtuous day,
That we ask to be judged in the end by our own
compassion,
Thief calling to thief from his cross with no Christ in
between.

## THE MAN WHO WENT ABSENT FROM THE NATIVE LITERATURE

He did not come of a long line of stone-cutters,
Wise but silent men who had learned silence from the stone,
Or seamen, whose eyes reflected distance,
Though there isn't much distance in the alleyways and
man-cupboards of a modern ship;
His lot were not even Dubliners with the desperate
generosity of the Dublin slums,
Expressed through drink in the grimy man-traps where the
generosity of working class men found its profitable-to-
others outlet,
Nor were they doctors whose hands had calmed heartbeats
and children in the womb
As well as dealing cards nightly in the bridge club,
Or savants, careless of advancement and intent only on
learning,
Unlike any savants you might have the misfortune to meet
today.
And they were certainly not aristocrats whose blood had
darkened the dim banners in the village church like
wine-stains

And ran in the veins of the village children as proof of
everybody's careless virility.

His mother was not the sort who put other people, but
especially sentimental men, in mind of the Great Earth
Goddess, Everybody's Mother.
She was a neurotic woman, much given to dyspepsia and
novenas, especially the Nine Fridays,
And so far from being careless and bountiful and
all-embracing like nature,
Spewing out children and other creations like a volcano
giving out rocks,
When he knew her anyway she emanated mostly anxiety,
And the only things she seemed to want to take in were
money, priests' opinions and stories about girls who
were in trouble.
Nor were his grandmas, so far as he knew, any more
outgoing or disdainful of consequence.
At the times he met them he never heard anything but
words of caution about knocking over ornaments and
not getting wet on the way to school from them,
Expressed in stale musty clichés in musty stale parlours,
Where, in any case any ideas about saving the world might
have been generated over the odd drop of sherry,
Several representations of a mauled, battered, eviscerated
and totally dispirited saviour and his broken-hearted
mother were exhibited to dispel them,
Even Parnell, even Robert Emmet being absent from those
walls.

You couldn't say either that such and such a landscape had
helped to mould him or his ancestors.
His forebears were not gaunt upland people, slow of speech
but unshakable once decided,
Some of them might have been of course, but the reasons
for the slowness of speech if any in the more proximate
cases of his da and ma

Were the obvious dangers of small-town life;
And his daddy as a matter of fact kept decisions to a minimum and was easily dissuaded from anything except a drink.
Nor were they mountainy men whose feuds and lovings became legends in the peaceful valleys.
Any family scandal he sniffed in the wind was of a different order.
Nor yet, not to make a meal of it, secretive canny folk from the back of the hill.
They were secretive all right, and canny in their way, but there was no known hill that had anything to do with them.
And he came in any case from what you might call mixed and migrant stock,
Who in the era of petty officialdom and jobs for the more educated
Had been stationed here, transferred there, married somewhere else,
And so the town he was born in was an accident for his parents,
And a much more serious, nearly fatal, to the spirit anyway, one for him.
When he thought of it afterwards he did not think of colourful characters,
Ne'er-do-wells with a turn of phrase, charming rapscallions with a gleam in their eyes and the arse nearly out of their breeches,
Idling down by the river where the chestnut trees cast their nets,
Friends of his father or otherwise.
As a matter of fact his father had no friends.
He did not see it all as picturesque.
Wherever the picturesque was it was not there.
And the local colour the place had was the colour of shame,
For him anyway,
His memories memories of idiotic burgeonings and

incoherent mistakes,
The mistakes of an ignorant outsider with the wrong
enthusiasms
Whose first loves were based on false premises.

And so, granted that in his heart there was a sort of void,
Unfilled by images of the Greyhound Racing Track, the
Arcadia Dance Hall and the Cattle Dealers' Cathedral
of his native place,
Or the memory of companions who had sometimes
diverted him,
While he undoubtedly diverted them,
That the tendrils that would root had found no soil
Comparable to the rich ploughlands and pastures of
pastoral epic
In the asphalt of the school playground or the ashy soil of
the backyard,
And you could say that he was a man without a tribe,
Pariah wandering on the outskirts, by woods and streams
not his;
And though for years he felt that these lackings of
stonecutter ancestors and comic, picturesque characters
among his father's friends
Made him somehow inferior in blood and in bone to those
who had them
Or said they had,
Nevertheless:
He did not bang a local drum.
He did not give a hoot who won the tribal conflicts.
He didn't want anybody to win.
Nor did he think that your ancestors' creations, folk-songs
and folk-lore,
Or come-all-ye's and war-cries,
Made you somehow creative yourself if you made enough
fuss about them
And got money from the radio by doing it.
Neither did he flog a line in identity whether real or false,

Nor in the picturesque,
Whatever that is.
He did not think that the local hero was more real than the
unlocal one.
When he walked through cities he was not always yearning
for the soft pints and softer options of the pubs where
his playmates drank.
He thought that *du sang, de la volupté et de la mort*
He would learn as much on his travels as in his native
province.
He did not think that the cabin where the rain came in
under the door was free from sordidity;
And thought in any case that the sordid we had always
with us;
But that when it came to the sordid
Metropolitan sordidity was richer and more fecund.
And that when it came to freedom,
Which it would come to in the end,
The metropolis if it was a real metropolis would have free-
doms which would astonish any peasant who ever lived,
Or any picturesque character from our world of misfortune
either.
And that when there were free men on this earth
They would strike a balance with their ancestors
Which would not begin in regret,
Or in nostalgia,
Or in lies.

## THE MIDDLE YEARS

These are the middle years,
The years of aggrandisement, when
The big philosophical question
Seems not to need any answer.
This is what it's about,

Youth's gaucheries survived,
The missus and he in accord,
The new Jag in the garage,
The odd bit on the side.
Now life justifies itself,
The strong grip on the racquet,
A firm hand on the gears,
Confidence worn like a suit,
The memorable week-end
With that real wild Danish piece.
The kids making eager choices
Are nearly enough to provide
Sufficient purpose in living:
By God, that's a clever lad!
An actuary! Think of that!
If you can stretch them out,
Still fit and trim enough,
A secretary's dream,
The bugbear what's it about
Is successfully postponed
Even for those who, well . . .
Still go to mass of course.
Stretch them out further still
It might even seem to vanish.

## PEARSE HUTCHINSON

Pearse Hutchinson was born in 1927 in Glasgow, Scotland. He was educated in Dublin at the Christian Brothers School and at University College. From 1951 to 1953 Hutchinson worked as a translator for the International Labor Organization in Geneva, Switzerland. He was drama critic for Radio Eireann from 1957 to 1961, and for Telefis Eireann in 1968. Hutchinson lived in Spain for seven years. He was a Gregory Fellow in Poetry at the University of Leeds from 1971 to 1973, and received the Butler Award for Gaelic writing in 1969. He has published two collections of translations: *Josep Carner: 30 Poems* (from Catalan, 1962) and *Friend Songs: Medieval Love-Poems* (from Galaico-Portuguese, 1970). His collections of poetry are *Tongue Without Hands* (1963), *Faoistin Bhacach (Imperfect Confession)* (1968), *Expansions* (1969), *Watching the Morning Grow* (1972), *The Frost Is All Over* (1975), *Selected Poems* (1982), and *Climbing the Light* (1985).

---

## INTO THEIR TRUE GENTLENESS

For Katherine Kavanagh

If love is the greatest reality,
and I believe it is,
the gentle are more real
than the violent or than
those like me who
hate violence,

long for gentleness,
but never in our own act
achieve true gentleness.
We fall in love with people
we consider gentle,
we love them violently
for their gentleness,
so violently we drive
them to violence,
for our gentleness
is less real
than their breaking patience,
so falsely we accuse
them of being false.

But with any luck,
time half-opens our eyes
to at least a hundredth
part of our absurdity,
and lets them travel back
released from us,
into their true gentleness,
even with us.

## BOXING THE FOX

We rode the canals
    we steered the locks
we may have caught scabies
    but never the pox
we were happy just cruising
    and boxing the fox
cruising the rivers of Dublin and
    foxing the cops

some of the *time*
*some* of the time
cruising the rivers and
boxing the fox

Across the orchards of custom,
over the high wall of law,
over hatred's broken glass,
past fear's envious claw,
we reached our own true rivers,
the rivers of your hair,
and peace as brief as man's contempt
came through and healed us there.
And who's to know but some small stream
from the rivers of your care
may break their broken glass
and be their cure and care.

We rode the canals
we steered the locks
we may have caught scabies
but never the pox
we were happy just cruising
and boxing the fox
cruising the rivers of Dublin and
foxing the cops
some of the *time*
*some* of the time
cruising the rivers and
boxing the fox

We dodged around begrudgers,
stuck in many a weary craw,
for snobs and hypocrites became
the antepenultimate straw.
But we boxed the fox of jealousy,

and slept in the glens of your hair,
and pleasure as long as man's contempt
came down and kept us there.
And who's to know but a lucky drop
from the beauty of your sweat
could melt their batons of hatred,
and be their saviour yet.

We rode the canals
we steered the locks
we may have caught scabies
but never the pox
we were happy just cruising
and boxing the fox
cruising the rivers of Dublin and
foxing the cops
some of the *time*
*some* of the time
cruising the rivers and
boxing the fox

## MANIFEST DESTINY

That every county in this developed state
sprout its very own
Ballyporeen: stone-crop, small potato, jackstone.
That's a must, a summit priority.
The tourist bounty, the NATO fall-out,
could solve—dissolve—the Border overnight.

With small-potato-lounges in every single county,
wouldn't the tyrant be proud of us?
He wouldn't even have to murder us.
Next time he calls
let's all

crawl
on naked knees and one hand—the other
tugging green plastic forelocks (there's a thought
for the IDA)—to as near as we can get to the Dáil,
our Dáil,
our, the people's, parliament,
and beg his majesty, this highest king,
via petitions clampt in our gums or green plastic teeth,
signed by all five thousand million
inhabitants of this developed state,
to let us become the fifty-second
state of the union—if any uppity rainbow
dares to show itself higher than this most ardest rí,
why shucks we'll shoot it down,
lower than a snake in a waggon-track,
with missiles the milk-thief lent us—

And speaking of her, we might as well while we're at it
petition for re-admission to the Empire—
no not the commonwealth or common poverty
the old Empire itself, for nothing less
can satisfy
our plastic forelocks.
We thus could be
ruled by three
which is much better
than one-and-a-half.

But for all this glory to come to pass
we must work night and day
might and main
*to ensure*
that every future incumbent of the White House
can, with cross-channel help,
trace his glorious descent back
to one or other manifest destiny village in the ould sod.
It is of course just possible

that some Chicano, Black, or Jew
might throw a bleeding-heart spanner in the works,
paint the white house black or even rainbow-coloured.
The danger is remote; but should it happen,
after the button's pressed, and we're all born again,
that need not faze us, we can always find,
even for black or jew or nicaragüense,
a touch o' the shamrock, a drop a the oul' crater,
the ever-new volcano—the Limerick pogrom
and the Sack of Baltimore might yield
some helpful hints. . . .

## RICHARD MURPHY

Richard Murphy was born in 1927 in County Galway, Ireland, and educated in England; he received his B.A. and M.A. degrees in English language and literature from Oxford. Before returning to Ireland in 1956, he worked for Lloyds of London, taught at the English School in Crete, and studied at the Sorbonne. In 1961 he settled in Cleggan, County Galway, where he skippered a fishing boat for seven years during the summers. He now lives in Dublin. He has won numerous awards for his poetry and taught at several English and American universities. His collections of poetry include *Sailing to an Island* (1963), *The Battle of Aughrim* (1968), *High Island* (1974), and *The Price of Stone* (1985).

## THE PHILOSOPHER AND THE BIRDS

In memory of Wittgenstein at Rossroe

A solitary invalid in a fuchsia garden
Where time's rain eroded the root since Eden,
He became for a tenebrous epoch the stone.

Here wisdom surrendered the don's gown
Choosing, for Cambridge, two deck chairs,
A kitchen table, undiluted sun.

He clipped with February shears the dead
Metaphysical foliage. Old, in fieldfares
Fantasies rebelled though annihilated.

He was haunted by gulls beyond omega shade,
His nerve tormented by terrified knots
In pin-feathered flesh. But all folly repeats

Is worth one snared robin his fingers untied.
He broke prisons, beginning with words,
And at last tamed, by talking, wild birds.

Through accident of place, now by belief
I follow his love which bird-handled thoughts
To grasp growth's terror or death's leaf.

He last on this savage promontory shored
His logical weapon. Genius stirred
A soaring intolerance to teach a blackbird.

So before alpha you may still hear sing
In the leaf-dark dusk some descended young
Who exalt the evening to a wordless song.

His wisdom widens: he becomes worlds
Where thoughts are wings. But at Rossroe hordes
Of village cats have massacred his birds.

## THE POET ON THE ISLAND

To Theodore Roethke

On a wet night, laden with books for luggage,
And stumbling under the burden of himself,
He reached the pier, looking for a refuge.

Darkly he crossed to the island six miles off:
The engine pulsed, the sails invented rhythm,
While the sea expanded and the rain drummed softly.

Safety on water, he rocked with a new theme:
And in the warmth of his mind's greenhouse bloomed
A poem as graceful as a chrysanthemum.

His forehead, a Prussian helmet, moody, domed,
Relaxed in the sun: a lyric was his lance.
To be loved by the people, he, a stranger, hummed

In the herring-store on Sunday crammed with drunks
Ballads of bawdry with a speakeasy stress.
Yet lonely they left him, "one of the Yanks."

The children understood. This was not madness.
How many orphans had he fathered in words
Robust and cunning, but never heartless.

He watched the harbour scouted by sea-birds:
His fate was like fish under poetry's beaks:
Words began weirdly to take off inwards.

Time that they calendar in seasons not in clocks,
In gardens dug over and houses roofed,
Was to him a see-saw of joys and shocks,

Where his body withered but his style improved.
A storm shot up, his glass cracked in a gale:
An abstract thunder of darkness deafened

The listeners he'd once given roses, now hail.
He'd burst the lyric barrier: logic ended.
Doctors were called, and he agreed to sail.

## from THE BATTLE OF AUGHRIM

### Legend

The story I have to tell
Was told me by a teacher
Who read it in a poem
Written in a language that has died.
Two hundred and fifty years ago
The poet recalled
Meeting a soldier who had heard
From veterans of the war
The story I have to tell.

Deep red bogs divided
Aughrim, the horse's ridge
Of garland hedgerows and the summer dance,
Ireland's defence
From the colonists' advance:
Twenty thousand soldiers on each side,
Between them a morass
Of godly bigotry and pride of race,
With a causeway two abreast could cross.

In opposite camps our ancestors
Ten marriages ago,
Caught in a feud of absent kings
Who used war like a basset table
Gambling to settle verbal things,
Decide if bread be God
Or God a parable,
Lit matches, foddered horses, thirsted, marched,
Halted, and marched to battle.

## Mercenary

"They pick us for our looks
To line up with matchlocks,
Face shot like sandbags,
Fall, and manure the grass
Where we wouldn't be let trespass
Alive, but to do their work
Till we dropped in muck.

"Who cares which foreign king
Governs, we'll still fork dung,
No one lets *us* grab soil:
Roman or English school
Insists it is God
Who must lighten our burden
Digging someone else's garden."

## God's Dilemma

God was eaten in secret places among the rocks
His mother stood in a cleft with roses at her feet
And the priests were whipped or hunted like stags.

God was spoken to at table with wine and bread
The soul needed no heavenly guide to intercede
And heretics were burnt at stakes for what they said.

God was fallen into ruins on the shores of lakes
Peasants went on milking cows or delving dikes
And landlords corresponded with landlords across bogs.

## SEALS AT HIGH ISLAND

The calamity of seals begins with jaws.
Born in caverns that reverberate
With endless malice of the sea's tongue
Clacking on shingle, they learn to bark back
In fear and sadness and celebration.
The ocean's mouth opens forty feet wide
And closes on a morsel of their rock.

Swayed by the thrust and backfall of the tide,
A dappled grey bull and a brindled cow
Copulate in the green water of a cove.
I watch from a cliff-top, trying not to move.
Sometimes they sink and merge into black shoals;
Then rise for air, his muzzle on her neck,
Their winged feet intertwined as a fish tail.

She opens her fierce mouth like a scarlet flower
Full of white seeds; she holds it open long
At the sunburst in the music of their loving;
And cries a little. But I must remember
How far their feelings are from mine marooned.
If there are tears at this holy ceremony
Theirs are caused by brine and mine by breeze.

When the great bull withdraws his rod, it glows
Like a carnelian candle set in jade.
The cow ripples ashore to feed her calf;
While an old rival, eyeing the deed with hate,
Swims to attack the tired triumphant god.
They rear their heads above the boiling surf,
Their terrible jaws open, jetting blood.

At nightfall they haul out, and mourn the drowned,
Playing to the sea sadly their last quartet,
An improvised requiem that ravishes

Reason, while ripping scale up like a net:
Brings pity trembling down the rocky spine
Of headlands, till the bitter ocean's tongue
Swells in their cove, and smothers their sweet song.

## HIGH ISLAND

A shoulder of rock
Sticks high up out of the sea,
A fisherman's mark
For lobster and blue-shark.

Fissile and stark
The crust is flaking off,
Seal-rock, gull-rock,
Cove and cliff.

Dark mounds of mica schist,
A lake, mill and chapel,
Roofless, one gable smashed,
Lie ringed with rubble.

An older calm,
The kiss of rock and grass,
Pink thrift and white sea-campion,
Flowers in the dead place.

Day keeps lit a flare
Round the north pole all night.
Like brushing long wavy hair
Petrels quiver in flight.

Quietly as the rustle
Of an arm entering a sleeve,
They slip down to nest
Under altar-stone or grave.

Round the wrecked laura
Needles flicker
Tacking air, quicker and quicker
To rock, sea and star.

## A NEST IN A WALL

Smoky as peat your lank hair on my pillow
Burns like a tinker's fire in a mossy ditch.
Before I suffocate, let me slowly suck
From your mouth a tincture of mountain ash,
A red infusion of summer going to seed.
Ivy-clumps loosen the stonework of my heart.
Come like a wood-pigeon gliding there to roost!

I float a moment on a gust sighing for ever
Gently over your face where two swans swim.
Let me kiss your eyes in the slate-blue calm
Before their Connemara clouds return.
A spancelled goat bleats in our pleasure ground.
A whippet snarls on its chain. The fire dies out.
Litter of rags and bottles in the normal rain.

Your country and mine, love, can it still exist?
The unsignposted hawthorn lane of your body
Leads to my lichenous walls and gutted house.
Your kind of beauty earth has almost lost.
Although we have no home in the time that's come,
Coming together we live in our own time.
Make your nest of moss like a wren in my skull.

## BEEHIVE CELL

There's no comfort inside me, only a small
Hart's-tongue sprouting square, with pyramidal headroom
For one man alone kneeling down: a smell
Of peregrine mutes and eremitical boredom.

Once, in my thirteen hundred years on this barren
Island, have I felt a woman giving birth,
On her own in my spinal cerebellic souterrain,
To a living child, as she knelt on earth.

She crawled under my lintel that purgatorial night
Her menfolk marooned her out of their coracle
To pick dillisk and sloke. What hand brought a light
With angelica root for the pain of her miracle?

Three days she throve in me, suckling the child,
Doing all she had to do, the sea going wild.

## THOMAS KINSELLA

Thomas Kinsella was born in 1928 in Dublin. He was educated at University College, Dublin, and worked from 1948 to 1965 in the Irish civil service. In 1965 he moved to the United States, where he became first writer-in-residence and then professor of English at Southern Illinois University. He has been professor of English at Temple University in Philadelphia since 1970, and now divides his time between living in Ireland, where he has his own press (Peppercanister), and the United States. Kinsella is one of the most widely acclaimed of modern Irish poets. He has received numerous awards, including the Guinness Award (1958), the Irish Arts Council Triennial Book Award (1961), the Denis Devlin Memorial Award (1967 and 1970), and Guggenheim Fellowships (1968 and 1971). In 1965 he became a member of the Irish Academy of Letters. He is married and has three children. Kinsella has translated a substantial amount of material from the Irish, including the epic of the Ulster cycle, *The Tain* (1969), and with Sean O'Tuama, *An Duanaire 1600–1900: Poems of the Dispossessed* (1981). Kinsella's major collections of poetry include *Poems and Translations* (1961), *Nightwalker and Other Poems* (1968), *Notes from the Land of the Dead and Other Poems* (1973), *New Poems* (1973), *Poems 1956–1973* (1979), and *Peppercanister Poems 1972–1978* (1979). His most recent collections are *Songs of the Psyche* (1985) and *Her Vertical Smile* (1985). Kinsella is editor of *The New Oxford Book of Irish Verse* (1986).

## BAGGOT STREET DESERTA

Lulled, at silence, the spent attack.
The will to work is laid aside.
The breaking-cry, the strain of the rack,
Yield, are at peace. The window is wide
On a crawling arch of stars, and the night
Reacts faintly to the mathematic
Passion of a cello suite
Plotting the quiet of my attic.
A mile away the river toils
Its buttressed fathoms out to sea;
Tucked in the mountains, many miles
Away from its roaring outcome, a shy
Gasp of waters in the gorse
Is sonnetting origins. Dreamers' heads
Lie mesmerised in Dublin's beds
Flashing with images, Adam's morse.

A cigarette, the moon, a sigh
Of educated boredom, greet
A curlew's lingering threadbare cry
Of common loss. Compassionate,
I add my call of exile, half-
Buried longing, half-serious
Anger and the rueful laugh.
We fly into our risk, the spurious.

Versing, like an exile, makes
A virtuoso of the heart,
Interpreting the old mistakes
And discords in a work of Art
For the One, a private masterpiece
Of doctored recollections. Truth
Concedes, before the dew, its place
In the spray of dried forgettings Youth

Collected when they were a single
Furious undissected bloom.
A voice clarifies when the tingle
Dies out of the nerves of time:
*Endure and let the present punish.*
Looking backward, all is lost;
The Past becomes a fairy bog
Alive with fancies, double crossed
By pad of owl and hoot of dog,
Where shaven, serious-minded men
Appear with lucid theses, after
Which they don the mists again
With trackless, cotton-silly laughter;
Secretly a swollen Burke
Assists a decomposing Hare
To cart a body of good work
With midnight mutterings off somewhere;
The goddess who had light for thighs
Grows feet of dung and takes to bed,
Affronting horror-stricken eyes,
The marsh bird that children dread.

I nonetheless inflict, endure,
Tedium, intracordal hurt,
The sting of memory's quick, the drear
Uprooting, burying, prising apart
Of loves a strident adolescent
Spent in doubt and vanity.
All feed a single stream, impassioned
Now with obsessed honesty,
A tugging scruple that can keep
Clear eyes staring down the mile,
The thousand fathoms, into sleep.
Fingers cold against the sill
Feel, below the stress of flight,
The slow implosion of my pulse
In a wrist with poet's cramp, a tight

Beat tapping out endless calls
Into the dark, as the alien
Garrison in my own blood
Keeps constant contact with the main
Mystery, not to be understood.
Out where imagination arches
Chilly points of light transact
The business of the border-marches
Of the Real, and I—a fact
That may be countered or may not—
Find their privacy complete.

My quarter-inch of cigarette
Goes flaring down to Baggot Street.

## ANOTHER SEPTEMBER

Dreams fled away, this country bedroom, raw
With the touch of the dawn, wrapped in a minor peace,
Hears through an open window the garden draw
Long pitch black breaths, lay bare its apple trees,
Ripe pear trees, brambles, windfall-sweetened soil,
Exhale rough sweetness against the starry slates.
Nearer the river sleeps St. John's, all toil
Locked fast inside a dream with iron gates.

Domestic Autumn, like an animal
Long used to handling by those countrymen,
Rubs her kind hide against the bedroom wall
Sensing a fragrant child come back again
—Not this half-tolerated consciousness,
Its own cold season never done,
But that unspeaking daughter, growing less
Familiar where we fell asleep as one.
Wakeful moth-wings blunder near a chair,

Toss their light shell at the glass, and go
To inhabit the living starlight. Stranded hair
Stirs on the still linen. It is as though
The black breathing that billows her sleep, her name,
Drugged under judgment, waned and—bearing daggers
And balances—down the lampless darkness they came,
Moving like women: Justice, Truth, such figures.

## CLARENCE MANGAN

Sometimes, childishly watching a beetle, thrush or trout,
Or charting the heroes and animals of night-time, sudden
    unhappiness
Would bewilder me, strayed in the long void of youth
Where nothing is understood.

Later, locked in a frantic pose, all mankind calling,
I, being anxious, eager to please, shouted my fear
That something was wrong.

Back to a wall, facing tumultuous talking faces,
Once I lost the reason for speech. My heart was taken,
Stretched with terror by only a word a mouth had
    uttered,
Clipped to a different, faceless destroyer.

Long I waited to know what naked meeting would come
With what was moving behind my eyes and desolating
What I touched.

Over a glass, or caught in lamplight, caught on the edge
Of act, my hand is suddenly stopped and fills with waiting.
Out of the shadows behind my laughter surgical fingers
Come and I am strapped to a table.

Ultimate, pitiless, again I ply the knife.

## COVER HER FACE

*She has died suddenly, aged twenty-nine years, in Dublin. Some of her family travel from the country to bring her body home. Having driven all morning through a storm*

### I

They dither softly at her bedroom door
In soaking overcoats, and words forsake
Even their comforters. The bass of prayer
Haunts the chilly landing while they take
Their places in a murmur of heartbreak.

Shabby with sudden tears, they know their part,
Mother and brother, resigning all that ends
At these drab walls. For here, with panicked heart,
A virgin broke the seal; who understands
The sheet pulled white and Maura's locked blue hands?

Later her frown will melt, when by degrees
They flinch from grief; a girl they have never seen,
Sunk now in love and horror to her knees,
The black official giving discipline
To shapeless sorrow, these are more their kin,

By grace of breath, than that grave derelict
Whose blood and feature, like a sleepy host,
Agreed a while with theirs. Her body's tact
Swapped child for woman, woman for a ghost,
Until its buried sleep lay uppermost;

And Maura, come to terms at last with pain,
Rests in her ruptured mind, her temples tight,
Patiently weightless as her time burns down.
Soon her few glories will be shut from sight:
Her slightness, the fine metal of her hair spread out,

Her cracked, sweet laugh. Such gossamers as hold
Friends, family—all fortuitous conjunction—
Sever with bitter whispers; with untold
Peace shrivel to their anchors in extinction.
There, newly trembling, others grope for function.

## II

Standing by the door, effaced in self,
I cannot deny her death, protest, nor grieve,
Dogged by a scrap of memory: some tossed shelf
Holds, a secret shared, that photograph,
Her arm tucked tiredly into mine; her laugh,

As though she also knew a single day
Would serve to bleed us to a diagram,
Sighs and confides; she waived validity
The night she drank the furnace of the Lamb,
Draining one image of its faint *I am*.

I watch her drift, in doubt whether dead or born
—Not with Ophelia's strewn virginity
But with a pale unmarriage—out of the worn
Bulk of day, under its sightless eye,
And close her dream in hunger. So we die.

Monday, without regret, darkens the pane
And sheds on the shaded living, the crystal soul,
A gloomy lustre of the pouring rain.
Nuns have prepared her for the holy soil
And round her bed the faded roses peel

That the fruit of justice may be sown in peace
To them that make peace, and bite its ashen bread.
Mother, brother, when our questions cease
Such peace may come, consenting to the good,
Chaste, biddable, out of all likelihood.

## A COUNTRY WALK

Sick of the piercing company of women
I swung the gate shut with a furious sigh,
Rammed trembling hands in pockets and drew in
A breath of river air. A rook's wet wing
Cuffed abruptly upward through the drizzle.

On either hand dead trunks in drapes of creeper,
Strangled softly by horse-mushroom, writhed
In vanished passion, broken down like sponge.
I walked their hushed stations, passion dying,
Each slow footfall a drop of peace returning.

I clapped my gloves. Three cattle turned aside
Their fragrant bodies from a corner gate
And down the sucking chaos of a hedge
Churned land to liquid in their dreamy passage.
Briefly through the beaded grass a path
Led to the holy stillness of a well
And there in the smell of water, stone and leaf
I knelt, baring my hand, and scooped and drank,
Shivering, and inch by inch rejoiced:
Ferocity became intensity.

Or so it seemed as with a lighter step
I turned an ivied corner to confront
The littered fields where summer broke and fled.
Below me, right and left, the valley floor
Tilted, in a silence full of storms;
A ruined aqueduct in delicate rigor
Clenched cat-backed, rooted to one horizon;
A vast asylum reared its potent calm
Up from the other through the sodden air,
Tall towers ochre where the gutters dripped;
A steeple; the long yielding of a railway turn
Through thorn and willow; a town endured its place . . .

Joining the two slopes, blocking an ancient way
With crumbled barracks, castle and brewery
It took the running river, wrinkling and pouring,
Into its blunt embrace. A line of roofs
Fused in veils of rain and steely light
As the dying sun struck it huge glancing blows.
A strand of idle smoke mounted until
An idler current combed it slowly west,
A hook of shadow dividing the still sky . . .
Mated, like a fall of rock, with time,
The place endured its burden: as a froth
Locked in a swirl of turbulence, a shape
That forms and fructifies and dies, a wisp
That hugs the bridge, an omphalos of scraps.

I moved, my glove-backs glistening, over flesh-
And forest-fed earth; till, skirting a marshy field
Where melancholy brambles scored the mud
By the gapped glitter of a speckled ford,
I shuddered with a visual sweet excitement.

Those murmuring shallows made a trampling place
Apt for death-combat, as the tales agree:
There, the day that Christ hung dying, twin
Brothers armed in hate on either side;
The day darkened but they moved to meet
With crossed swords under a dread eclipse
And mingled their bowels at the saga's end.
There the first Normans massacred my fathers,
Then stroked their armoured horses' necks, disposed
In ceremony, sable on green sward.
Twice more the reeds grew red, the stones obscured:
When knot-necked Cromwell and his fervent sword
Dispatched a convent shrieking to their Lover;
And when in peasant fear a rebel host,
Through long retreat grown half hysterical
—Methodical, ludicrous—piked in groups of three

Cromwell's puritan brood, their harmless neighbours,
Forked them half living to the sharp water
And melted into the martyred countryside,
Root eaters, strange as badgers. Pulses calmed;
The racked heroic nerved itself for peace;
Then came harsh winters, motionless waterbirds,
And generations that let welcome fail.

Road and river parted. Now my path
Lay gleaming through the greasy dusk, uphill
Into the final turn. A concrete cross
Low in the ditch grew to the memory
Of one who answered latest the phantom hag,
Tireless Rebellion, when with mouth awry
She hammered at the door, disrupting harvest.
There he bled to death, his line of sight
Blocked by the corner-stone, and did not see
His town ablaze with joy, the grinning foe
Driven in heavy lorries from the field;
And he lay cold in the Hill Cemetery
When freedom burned his comrades' itchy palms,
Too much for flesh and blood, and—armed in hate—
Brother met brother in a modern light.
They turned the bloody corner, knelt and killed,
Who gather still at Easter round his grave,
Our watchful elders. Deep in his crumbled heart
He takes their soil, and chatting they return
To take their town again, that have exchanged
A trenchcoat playground for a gombeen jungle.

Around the corner, in an open square,
I came upon the sombre monuments
That bear their names: MacDonagh & McBride,
Merchants; Connolly's Commercial Arms . . .
Their windows gave me back my stolid self
In attitudes of staring as I paced
Their otherworldly gloom, reflected light

Playing on lens and raincoat stonily.
I turned away. Down the sloping square
A lamp switched on above the urinal;
Across the silent handball alley, eyes
That never looked on lover measured mine
Over the Christian Brothers' frosted glass
And turned away. Out of the neighbouring shades
A car plunged soundlessly and disappeared
Pitching downward steeply to the bridge.
I too descended. Naked sycamores,
Gathered dripping near the quay, stood still
And dropped from their combining arms a single
Word upon my upturned face. I trod
The river underfoot; the parapet
Above the central arch received my hands.

Under a darkening and clearing heaven
The hastening river streamed in a slate sheen,
Its face a-swarm. Across the swollen water
(Delicate myriads vanishing in a breath)
Faint ripples winked; a thousand currents broke,
Kissing, dismembering, in threads of foam
Or poured intact over the stony bed
Glass-green and chill; their shallow, shifting world
Slid on in troubled union, forging together
Surfaces that gave and swallowed light;
And grimly the flood divided where it swept
An endless debris through the failing dusk
Under the thudding span beneath my feet.

*Venit Hesperus;*
In green and golden light; bringing sweet trade.
The inert stirred. Heart and tongue were loosed:
"The waters hurtle through the flooded night . . ."

## MIRROR IN FEBRUARY

The day dawns, with scent of must and rain,
Of opened soil, dark trees, dry bedroom air.
Under the fading lamp, half dressed—my brain
Idling on some compulsive fantasy—
I towel my shaven jaw and stop, and stare,
Riveted by a dark exhausted eye,
A dry downturning mouth.

It seems again that it is time to learn,
In this untiring, crumbling place of growth
To which, for the time being, I return.
Now plainly in the mirror of my soul
I read that I have looked my last on youth
And little more; for they are not made whole
That reach the age of Christ.

Below my window the awakening trees,
Hacked clean for better bearing, stand defaced
Suffering their brute necessities;
And how should the flesh not quail, that span for span
Is mutilated more? In slow distaste
I fold my towel with what grace I can,
Not young, and not renewable, but man.

## WORMWOOD

I have dreamt it again: standing suddenly still
In a thicket, among wet trees, stunned, minutely
Shuddering, hearing a wooden echo escape.

A mossy floor, almost colourless, disappears
In depths of rain among the tree shapes.
I am straining, tasting that echo a second longer.

If I can hold it . . . familiar if I can hold it . . .
A black tree with a double trunk—two trees
Grown into one—throws up its blurred branches.

The two trunks in their infinitesimal dance of growth
Have turned completely about one another, their join
A slowly twisted scar, that I recognise . . .

A quick arc flashes sidewise in the air,
A heavy blade in flight. A wooden stroke:
Iron sinks in the gasping core.

I will dream it again.

## RITUAL OF DEPARTURE

A man at the moment of departure, turning
To leave, treasures some stick of furniture
With slowly blazing eyes, or the very door
Broodingly with his hand as it falls shut.

*

Open the soft string that clasps in series
A dozen silver spoons, and spread them out,
Matched perfectly, one maker and to the year:
brilliance in use that fell
Open before the first inheritor.

A stag crest stares from the soft solid silver
And grimaces, with fat cud-lips but jaws
That could crack bones.
The stag heart stumbles.
He rears at bay, slavering silver; rattles
A trophied head among my gothic rocks.

*

Stones of a century and a half ago.
The same city distinct in the same air,
More open in an earlier evening light.
Dublin under the Georges . . .
stripped of Parliament,
Lying powerless in sweet-breathing death-ease
after forced Union.
Under a theatre of swift-moving cloud
Domes, pillared, in the afterglow—
A portico, beggars moving on the steps—
A horserider locked in soundless greeting,
Bowed among dogs and dung; the panelled vista
Closing on pleasant smoke-blue far-off hills.

*

The ground opens. Pale wet potatoes
Break into light. The black soil falls from their flesh,
From the hands that tear them up and spread them out
In fresh disorder, perishable roots to eat.
The fields vanish in rain
Among white rock and red bog—saturated
High places traversed by spring sleet
Or thrust up in summer through the thin wind
Into pounding silence. Farther south: cattle,
Wheat, salmon glistening, the sea.
Landscape with ancestral figures . . . names
Settling and intermixing on the earth,
The seed in slow retreat, through time and blood,
Into bestial silence.
Faces sharpen and grow blank,
With eyes for nothing.
And their children's children
Venturing to disperse, some came to Dublin
To vanish in the city lanes.
I saw the light

Enter from the laneway, through the scullery
To the foot of the stairs, creep across grey floorboards,
Sink in plush in the staleness of an inner room.

I scoop at the earth, and sense famine, a first
Sourness in the clay. The roots tear softly.

## HEN WOMAN

The noon heat in the yard
smelled of stillness and coming thunder.
A hen scratched and picked at the shore.
It stopped, its body crouched and puffed out.
The brooding silence seemed to say "Hush . . ."

The cottage door opened,
a black hole
in a whitewashed wall so bright
the eyes narrowed.
Inside, a clock murmured "Gong . . ."

(I had felt all this before . . .)

She hurried out in her slippers
muttering, her face dark with anger,
and gathered the hen up jerking
languidly. Her hand fumbled.
Too late. Too late.

It fixed me with its pebble eyes
(seeing what mad blur?).
A white egg showed in the sphincter;
mouth and beak opened together;
and time stood still.

Nothing moved: bird or woman,

fumbled or fumbling—locked there
(as I must have been) gaping.

*

There was a tiny movement at my feet,
tiny and mechanical; I looked down.
A beetle like a bronze leaf
was inching across the cement,
clasping with small tarsi
a ball of dung bigger than its body.
The serrated brow pressed the ground humbly,
lifted in a short stare, bowed again;
the dung-ball advanced minutely,
losing a few fragments,
specks of staleness and freshness.

*

A mutter of thunder far off
—time not quite stopped.
I saw the egg had moved a fraction:
a tender blank brain
under torsion, a clean new world.

As I watched, the mystery completed.
The black zero of the orifice
closed to a point
and the white zero of the egg hung free,
flecked with greenish brown oils.

It slowly turned and fell.
Dreamlike, fussed by her splayed fingers,
it floated outward, moon-white,
leaving no trace in the air,
and began its drop to the shore.

*

I feed upon it still as you see;
there is no end to that which,
not understood, may yet be noted
and hoarded in the imagination,
in the yolk of one's being, so to speak,
there to undergo its (quite animal) growth,
dividing blindly,
twitching, packed with will,
searching in its own tissue
for the structure
in which it may wake.
Something that had—clenched
in its cave—not been
now was: an egg of being.
Through what seemed a whole year it fell
—as it still falls, for me,
solid and light, the red gold beating
in its silvery womb,
alive as the yolk and white
of my eye; as it will continue
to fall, probably, until I die,
through the vast indifferent spaces
with which I am empty.

*

It smashed against the grating
and slipped down quickly out of sight.
It was over in a comical flash.
The soft mucous shell clung a little longer,
then drained down.

She stood staring, in blank anger.
Then her eyes came to life, and she laughed
and let the bird flap away.
"It's all the one.

There's plenty more where that came from!"
Hen to pan!
It was a simple world.

## A HAND OF SOLO

Lips and tongue
wrestle the delicious
    life out of you.

A last drop.
Wonderful.
    A moment's rest.

In the firelight glow
the flickering
    shadows softly

come and go up on the shelf:
red heart and black spade
    hid in the kitchen dark.

Woman throat song
help my head
    back to you sweet.

*

Hushed, buried green baize.
Slide and stop. Black spades. Tray. Still.
Red deuce. Two hearts. Blood-clean. Still.

Black flash. Jack Rat grins.
She drops down. Silent. Face disk blank. Queen.

The Boss spat in the kitchen fire.
His head shook.

Angus's fat hand brushed in all the pennies.
His waistcoat pressed the table.

Uncle Matty slithered the cards together
and knocked them. Their edges melted. Soft gold.

Angus picked up a bright penny and put it
in my hand: satiny, dream-new disk of light . . .

"Go on out in the shop and get yourself something."
"Now, Angus . . ."
"Now, now, Jack. He's my luck."
"Tell your grandmother we're waiting for her."

She was settling the lamp.
Two yellow tongues rose and brightened.
The shop brightened.

Her eyes glittered.
A tin ghost beamed, Mick McQuaid
nailed across the fireplace.

"Shut the kitchen door, child of grace.
Come here to me.
Come here to your old grandmother."

Strings of jet beads wreathed her neck
and hissed on the black taffeta
and crept on my hair.

". . . You'd think I had three heads!"
My eyes were squeezed shut against the key
in the pocket of her apron. Her stale abyss . . .

Old knuckles pressed on the counter,
then were snatched away. She sat down at the till
on her high stool, chewing nothing.

The box of Indian apples
was over in the corner
by the can of oil.

I picked out one of the fruit,
a rose-red hard wax
turning toward gold, light like wood,

and went at it with little bites,
peeling off bits of skin
and tasting the first traces of the blood.

When it was half peeled,
with the glassy pulp exposed like cells,
I sank my teeth in it

loosening the packed mass of dryish beads
from their indigo darkness.
I drove my tongue among them

and took a mouthful, and slowly
bolted them. My throat filled
with a rank, Arab bloodstain.

## DEATH BED

Motionless—his sons—
we watched his brows draw together with strain.
The wind tore at the leather walls of our tent;
two grease lamps fluttered
at the head and foot of the bed.
Our shadows sprang here and there.

At that moment our sign might
have coursed across the heavens,
and we had spared no one to watch.

*

Our people are most vulnerable to loss
when we gather like this to one side,
around some death,

and try to weave it into our lives
—who can weave nothing but our ragged
routes across the desert.

And it is those among us
who most make the heavens their business
who go most deeply into this death-weaving.

As if the star might
spring from the dying mouth
or shoot from the agony of the eyes.

"We must not miss it,
however it comes."
—If it comes.

He stretched out his feet
and seemed to sink deeper in the bed,
and was still.
                    Sons no longer,
we pulled down his eyelids
and pushed the chin up gently to close his mouth,
and stood under the flapping roof.
Our shelter sheltered under the night.

*

Hides, furs and skins,
are our shelter and our garments.

We can weave nothing.

## from A TECHNICAL SUPPLEMENT

### XIX

It is hard to beat a good meal
and a turn on the terrace,
or a picnic on the beach at evening,
watching the breakers blur and gleam
as the brain skews softly.
Or an enjoyable rest, with a whodunit
under a flowering chestnut, an essay or two
on a park bench, a romance devoured
at one stroke on a grassy slope.

But for real pleasure there is nothing to equal
sitting down to a *serious* read,
getting settled down comfortably for the night
with a demanding book on your knee
and your head intent over it,
eyes bridging the gap, closing a circuit.

Except that it is not a closed circuit,
more a mingling of lives, worlds simmering
in the entranced interval: all that you are
and have come to be
—or as much as can be brought to bear—
"putting on" the fixed outcome of another's
encounter with what he was
and had come to be
impelled him to stop in flux, living,

and hold that encounter out from
the streaming away of lifeblood, timeblood,
a nexus a nexus a nexus
wriggling with life not of our kind.

Until one day as I was . . .

I met a fair maid all shining
with hair all over her cheeks
and pearly tongue
who spoke to me and sighed
as if my own nervous nakedness
spoke to me and said:

*My heart is a black fruit.*
*It is a piece of black coal.*
*When I laugh a black thing hovers.*

## XXIII

That day when I woke
a great private blade
was planted in me from bowels to brain.
I lay there alive round it. When I moved
it moved with me, and there was no hurt.
I knew it was not going to go away.
I got up carefully, transfixed.

From that day forth I knew
what it was to taste reality
and not to; to suffer tedium or pain
and not to; to eat, swallowing with pleasure,
and not to; to yield and fail,
to note this or that withering in me,
and not to; to anticipate
the Breath, the Bite, with cowering arms,
and not to . . .

(Tiny delicate dawn-antelope that go without water
getting all they need in vegetation and the dew.
Night-staring jerboa.
The snapping of their slender bones,
rosy flesh bursting in small sweet screams
against the palate fine. Just a quick
note. Lest we forget.)

Meanwhile, with enormous care,
to the split id—delicate
as a flintflake—the knifed nous . . .

## from THE MESSENGER

Inside, it is bare but dimly alive.
Such light as there is comes in overcast
through a grey lace curtain across the window,

diffuses in the dust above the bench
and shows him stooped over his last
in a cobbler's shop. He is almost still a boy:

his hands are awkwardly readying something,
his face and shoulders are soft-handsome,
pale silver, ill at ease

in the odour-bearing light. The rest is obscure,
swallowed back in man-smells
of leather and oily metal, and the faintest

musk. Beside him, his father's leaden skull
is inclined, gentle and deaf,
above the work on his apron.

The old lion-shoulders expand in the Guinness jersey,
the jaws work in his cheeks
as the quivering awl

pierces the last hole in a sole with a grunt.
He wheezes and pulls it out, and straightens.
The tide is rising and the river runs fast

into the middle span of the last bridge.
He touches the funnel on a nerve at the base
and doffs it on its hinge at the last instant

—the smoke occluding—and hauls it up again
gleaming and pluming in open water.
Here and there along the Liffey wall

he is acclaimed in friendly mockery,
humbly, saturninely, returned . . .
He reaches for needle and thread

patiently, as his son
struggles at the blank iron foot
in his father's den.

He will not stick at this . . . The knife-blades,
the hammers and pincers, the rasps and punches,
the sprigs in their wooden pits,

catching the light on the plank bench
among uppers and tongues and leather scraps
and black stumps of heelball.

He reaches for a hammer,
his jaw jutting as best it can
with Marx, Engels, Larkin

howling with upstretched arms into the teeth
of Martin Murphy and the Church
and a flourish of police batons,

Connolly strapped in a chair
regarding the guns

that shall pronounce his name for ever.

Baton struck,
                    gun spat,
and Martin Murphy shall change his hat.

Son and father, upright, right arms raised.
Stretching a thread.
Trying to strike right.

## MODEL SCHOOL, INCHICORE

Miss Carney handed us out blank paper and marla,
old plasticine with the colours
all rolled together into brown.

You started with a ball of it
and rolled it into a snake curling
around your hand, and kept rolling it
in one place until it wore down into two
with a stain on the paper.

We always tittered at each other
when we said the adding-up table in Irish
and came to her name.

*

In the second school we had Mr. Browne.
He had white teeth in his brown man's face.

He stood in front of the black board
and chalked a white dot.

                "We are going to start
                        decimals."

I am going to know
everything.

*

One day he said:
"Out into the sun!"
We settled his chair under a tree
and sat ourselves down delighted
in two rows in the greeny gold shade.

A fat bee floated around
shining amongst us
and the flickering sun
warmed our folded coats
and he said: "History . . . !"

*

When the Autumn came
and the big chestnut leaves
fell all over the playground
we piled them in heaps
between the wall and the tree trunks
and the boys ran races
jumping over the heaps
and tumbled into them shouting.

*

I sat by myself in the shed
and watched the draught
blowing the papers
around the wheels of the bicycles.

Will God judge
    our most secret thoughts and actions?
God will judge
    our most secret thoughts and actions
and every idle word that man shall speak
he shall render an account of it
on the Day of Judgment.

*

The taste
of ink off
the nib shrank your
mouth.

## JOHN MONTAGUE

John Montague was born in Brooklyn, New York, in 1929, but his family returned to County Tyrone, Northern Ireland, a few years later. He was educated at University College, Dublin, where he received his B.A. and M.A. degrees. In 1955 he received a M.F.A. degree from the University of Iowa. From 1956 to 1959 he worked for Bord Failte, the Irish tourist agency, and then as Paris correspondent for the *Irish Times*. He was visiting lecturer at the University of California, Berkeley, in 1961 and has taught since then at universities in France, Ireland, Canada, and the United States. In 1976 Montague received the award for Irish writers from the Irish-American Cultural Institute, and in 1977 the Martin Toonder Award for Literature. He has also been awarded a Guggenheim Fellowship and the Alice Hunt-Bartlett Award of the Poetry Society. He is presently a member of the English Department at University College, Cork; he lives with his wife and daughters in Cork. In addition to his translations, critical articles, and short stories, he has edited *The Faber Book of Irish Verse* (1974) and published eight major collections of poetry, *Poisoned Lands* (1961—reissued 1976), *A Chosen Light* (1967), *Tides* (1970), *The Rough Field* (1972), *A Slow Dance* (1975), *The Great Cloak* (1978), *Selected Poems* (1982), and *The Dead Kingdom* (1984).

JOHN MONTAGUE

## A BRIGHT DAY

for John McGahern

At times I see it, present
    As a bright day, or a hill,
The only way of saying something
    Luminously as possible.

Not the accumulated richness
    Of an old historical language—
That musk-deep odour!
    But a slow exactness

Which recreates experience
    By ritualizing its details—
Pale web of curtain, width
    Of deal table, till all

Takes on a witch-bright glow
    And even the clock on the mantel
Moves its hands in a fierce delight
    Of so, and so, and so.

## ALL LEGENDARY OBSTACLES

All legendary obstacles lay between
Us, the long imaginary plain,
The monstrous ruck of mountains
And, swinging across the night,
Flooding the Sacramento, San Joaquin,
The hissing drift of winter rain.

All day I waited, shifting
Nervously from station to bar
As I saw another train sail
By, the San Francisco Chief or
Golden Gate, water dripping
From great flanged wheels.

At midnight you came, pale
Above the negro porter's lamp.
I was too blind with rain
And doubt to speak, but
Reached from the platform
Until our chilled hands met.

You had been travelling for days
With an old lady, who marked
A neat circle on the glass
With her glove, to watch us
Move into the wet darkness
Kissing, still unable to speak.

## THAT ROOM

Side by side on the narrow bed
We lay, like chained giants,
Tasting each other's tears, in terror
Of the news which left little to hide
But our two faces that stared
To ritual masks, absurd and flayed.

Rarely in a lifetime comes such news
Shafting knowledge straight to the heart
Making shameless sorrow start—
Not childish tears, querulously vain—
But adult tears that hurt and harm,
Seeping like acid to the bone.

Sound of hooves on the midnight road
Raised a romantic image to mind:
Someone riding late to Marley?
But we must suffer the facts of self;
No one endures a similar fate
And no one will ever know

What happened in that room
But that when we came to leave
We scrubbed each other's tears
Prepared the usual show. That day
Love's claims made chains of time and place
To bind us together more: equal in adversity.

## THE ANSWER

for Christopher Ricks

How when one entered a cottage
to ask directions, the woman of the house
rose to greet you, not as a stranger
but a visitor:
                    that was the old way,
the way of courtesy.
                              Searching for Gallarus,
I crossed a half-door on the Dingle peninsula
and stood tasting the neat silence
of the swept flags, the scoured delft
on the tall dresser where even something
tinny like a two-legged, horned alarm-clock
was isolated into meaning;
                                        while friendly,
unafraid, the woman turned her face
like a wrinkled windfall, to proffer
the ritual greetings:

*Dia dhuit*
*Dia agus Muire dhuit*
*Dia agus Muire*
*agus Padraig dhuit*
invocation of powers
to cleanse the mind.
Then the question
and the answer.
"What did she say?"
I was asked when I came back to the car
but could only point the way
over the hill to where
obscured in sea
mist, the small, grey stones of the oratory
held into the Atlantic for a thousand years.

## A LOST TRADITION

All around, shards of a lost tradition:
From the Rough Field I went to school
In the Glen of the Hazels. Close by
Was the bishopric of the Golden Stone;
The cairn of Carleton's homesick poem.

Scattered over the hills, tribal
And placenames, uncultivated pearls.
No rock or ruin, dun or dolmen
But showed memory defying cruelty
Through an image-encrusted name.

The heathery gap where the Raparee,
Shane Barnagh, saw his brother die—
On a summer's day the dying sun
Stained its colours to crimson:
So breaks the heart, Brish-mo-Cree.

The whole landscape a manuscript
We had lost the skill to read,
A part of our past disinherited;
But fumbled, like a blind man,
Along the fingertips of instinct.

The last Gaelic speaker in the parish
When I stammered my school Irish
One Sunday after mass, crinkled
A rusty litany of praise:
*Tá an Ghaedilg againn arís . . .*

*Tír Eoghain*: Land of Owen,
Province of the O'Niall;
The ghostly tread of O'Hagan's
Barefoot gallowglasses marching
To merge forces in Dun Geanainn

Push southward to Kinsale!
Loudly the war-cry is swallowed
In swirls of black rain and fog
As Ulster's pride, Elizabeth's foemen,
Founder in a Munster bog.

## WITNESS

By the crumbling fire we talked
Animal-dazed by the heat
While the lawyer unhooked a lamp
From peat blackened rafters
And climbed the circle of stairs.

Without, the cattle, heavy for milking,
Shuddered and breathed in the byre.
"It falls early these nights" I said
Lifting tongs to bruise a turf

And hide the sound of argument upstairs

From an old man, hands clenched
On rosary beads, and a hawthorn stick
For hammering the floor—
A nuisance in the working daytime,
But now, signing a parchment,

Suddenly important again, as long before.
Cannily aware of his final scene too,
With bald head swinging like a stone,
In irresistible statement: "It's rightly theirs"
Or: "They'll never see stick of mine."

Down in the kitchen, husband and wife
Watched white ash form on the hearth,
Nervously sharing my cigarettes,
While the child wailed in the pram
And a slow dark overcame fields and farm.

## THE WILD DOG ROSE

### I

I go to say goodbye to the *Cailleach*
that terrible figure who haunted my childhood
but no longer harsh, a human being
merely, hurt by event.
                                        The cottage,
circled by trees, weathered to admonitory
shapes of desolation by the mountain winds,
straggles into view. The rank thistles
and leathery bracken of untilled fields
stretch behind with—a final outcrop—
the hooped figure by the roadside,

its retinue of dogs
which give tongue
as I approach, with savage, whinging cries
so that she slowly turns, a moving nest
of shawls and rags, to view, to stare
the stranger down.
And I feel again
that ancient awe, the terror of a child
before the great hooked nose, the cheeks
dewlapped with dirt, the staring blue
of the sunken eyes, the mottled claws,
clutching a stick
but now hold
and return her gaze, to greet her,
as she greets me, in friendliness.
Memories have wrought reconciliation
between us, we talk in ease at last,
like old friends, lovers almost,
sharing secrets
Of neighbours
she quarreled with, who now lie
in Garvaghey graveyard, beyond all hatred;
of my family and hers, how she never married,
though a man came asking in her youth.
"You would be loath to leave your own"
she sighs, "and go among strangers"—
his parish ten miles off.
For sixty years
since she has lived alone, in one place.
Obscurely honoured by such confidences,
I idle by the summer roadside, listening,
while the monologue falters, continues,
rehearsing the small events of her life.
The only true madness is loneliness,
the monotonous voice in the skull
that never stops
because never heard.

## II

And there
where the dog rose shines in the hedge
she tells me a story so terrible
that I try to push it away,
my bones melting.
                                        Late at night
a drunk came, beating at her door
to break it in, the bolt snapping
from the soft wood, the thin mongrels
rushing to cut, but yelping as
he whirls with his farm boots
to crush their skulls.
                                        In the darkness
they wrestle, two creatures crazed
with loneliness, the smell of the
decaying cottage in his nostrils
like a drug, his body heavy on hers,
the tasteless trunk of a seventy year
old virgin, which he rummages while
she battles for life
                                        bony fingers
reaching desperately to push
against his bull neck. "I prayed
to the Blessed Virgin herself
for help and after a time
I broke his grip."
                                        He rolls
to the floor, snores asleep,
while she cowers until dawn
and the dogs' whimpering starts
him awake, to lurch back across
the wet bog.

## III

And still
the dog rose shines in the hedge.
Petals beaten wide by rain, it
sways slightly, at the tip of a
slender, tangled, arching branch
which, with her stick, she gathers
into us.
"The wild rose
is the only rose without thorns,"
she says, holding a wet blossom
for a second, in a hand knotted
as the knob of her stick.
"Whenever I see it, I remember
the Holy Mother of God and
all she suffered."
Briefly
the air is strong with the smell
of that weak flower, offering
its crumbling yellow cup
and pale bleeding lips
fading to white
at the rim
of each bruised and heart-
shaped petal.

## THE CAGE

My father, the least happy
man I have known. His face
retained the pallor
of those who work underground:
the lost years in Brooklyn
listening to a subway
shudder the earth.

But a traditional Irishman
who (released from his grille
in the Clark Street I.R.T.)
drank neat whiskey until
he reached the only element
he felt at home in
any longer: brute oblivion.

And yet picked himself
up, most mornings,
to march down the street
extending his smile
to all sides of the good
(non negro) neighbourhood
belled by St. Teresa's church.

When he came back
we walked together
across fields of Garvaghey
to see hawthorn on the summer
hedges, as though
he had never left;
a bend of the road

which still sheltered
primroses. But we
did not smile in
the shared complicity
of a dream, for when
weary Odysseus returns
Telemachus must leave.

Often as I descend
into subway or underground
I see his bald head behind
the bars of the small booth;

the mark of an old car
accident beating on his
ghostly forehead.

## LAMENT FOR THE O'NEILLS

> This was a distinguished crew for one ship; for it is indeed certain that the sea had not supported, and the winds had not wafted from Ireland, in modern times, a party of one ship who would have been more illustrious, or noble in point of genealogy, or more renowned for deeds, valour or high achievements. . . .
>
> *Annals of the Four Masters*

The fiddler settles in
to his playing so easily;
rosewood box tucked under chin,
saw of rosined bow
& angle of elbow

that the mind elides
for a while what he plays:
hornpipe or reel to warm
us up well, heel to toecap
twitching in tune

till the sound expands
in the slow climb of a lament.
As by some forest campfire
listeners draw near, to honour
a communal loss

& a shattered procession
of anonymous suffering
files through the brain:
burnt houses, pillaged farms,
a province in flames.

> We have killed, burnt and despoiled all along the Lough to within four miles of Dungannon . . . in which journeys we have killed above a hundred of all sorts, besides such as we have burned, how many I know not. We spare none, of what quality or sex soever, and it had bred much terror in the people who heard not a drum nor saw not a fire of long time.
> *Chichester to Mountjoy, Spring 1601*

With an intricate
& mournful mastery
the thin bow glides & slides,
assuaging like a bardic poem,
our tribal pain—

*Is uaigneach Eire*

Disappearance & death
of a world, as down Lough Swilly
the great ship, encumbered with nobles,
swells its sails for Europe:

The Flight of the Earls.

JOHN MONTAGUE

## A GRAFTED TONGUE

(Dumb,
bloodied, the severed
head now chokes to
speak another tongue:—

As in
a long suppressed dream,
some stuttering garb-
led ordeal of my own)

An Irish
child weeps at school
repeating its English.
After each mistake

The master
gouges another mark
on the tally stick
hung about its neck

Like a bell
on a cow, a hobble
on a straying goat.
To slur and stumble

In shame
the altered syllables
of your own name;
to stray sadly home

and find
the turf cured width
of your parents' hearth
growing slowly alien:

In cabin
and field, they still
speak the old tongue.
You may greet no one.

To grow
a second tongue, as
harsh a humiliation
as twice to be born.

Decades later
that child's grandchild's
speech stumbles over lost
syllables of an old order.

## LAST JOURNEY

I. M. James Montague

We stand together
on the windy platform;
how crisp the rails
running out of sight
through the wet fields!

Carney, the station master,
is peering over
his frosted window:
the hand of the signal
points down.

Crowned with churns
a cart creaks up the
incline of Main Street
to the sliding doors
of the Co-Op.

A smell of coal,
the train is coming . . .
you climb slowly in,
propped by my hand to
a seat, back to the engine,

and we leave, waving
a plume of black smoke
over the rushy meadows,
small hills & hidden villages—
Beragh, Carrickmore,

Pomeroy, Fintona—
placenames that sigh
like a pressed melodeon
across this forgotten
Northern landscape.

## WINDHARP

for Patrick Collins

The sounds of Ireland,
that restless whispering
you never get away
from, seeping out of
low bushes and grass,
heatherbells and fern,
wrinkling bog pools,
scraping tree branches,
light hunting cloud,
sound hounding sight,
a hand ceaselessly
combing and stroking
the landscape, till

the valley gleams
like the pile upon
a mountain pony's coat.

## from THE LEAPING FIRE

### I

Old lady, I now celebrate
to whom I owe so much;
bending over me in darkness
a scaly tenderness of touch

skin of bony arm & elbow
sandpapered with work:
because things be to be done
and simplicity did not shirk

the helpless, hopeless task
of maintaining a family farm,
which meant, by legal fiction,
maintaining a family name.

The thongless man's boots,
the shapeless bag apron:
would your favourite saint
accept the harness of humiliation

you bore constantly until
the hiss of milk into the pail
became as lonely a prayer as
your vigil at the altar rail.

Roses showering from heaven
upon Her uncorrupted body
after death, celebrated
the Little Flower's sanctity

& through the latticed grill
of your patron's enclosed order
an old French nun once threw me
a tiny sack of lavender.

So from the pressed herbs
of your least memory, sweetness exudes:
that of the meek and the selfless,
who should be comforted.

## FALLS FUNERAL

Unmarked faces
fierce with grief

a line of children
led by a small coffin

the young
mourning the young

a sight beyond tears
beyond pious belief

David's brethren
in the Land of Goliath.

## TRACKS

### I

The vast bedroom
a hall of air,
our linked bodies
lying there.

### II

As I turn to kiss
your long, black
hair, small breasts,
heat flares from
your fragrant skin,
your eyes widen as
deeper, more certain
and often, I enter
to search possession
of where your being
hides in flesh.

### III

Behind our eyelids
a landscape opens,
a violet horizon
pilgrims labour across,
a sky of colours
that change, explode
a fantail of stars
the mental lightning
of sex illuminating
the walls of the skull;
a floating pleasure dome.

## IV

*I shall miss you*
creaks the mirror
into which the scene
shortly disappears:
the vast bedroom
a hall of air, the
tracks of our bodies
fading there, while
giggling maids push
a trolley of fresh
linen down the corridor.

# HERBERT STREET REVISITED

for Madeleine

## I

A light is burning late
in this Georgian Dublin street:
someone is leading our old lives!

And our black cat scampers again
through the wet grass of the convent garden
upon his masculine errands.

The pubs shut: a released bull,
Behan shoulders up the street,
topples into our basement, roaring "John!"

A pony and donkey cropped flank
by flank under the trees opposite;
short neck up, long neck down,

as Nurse Mullen knelt by her bedside
to pray for her lost Mayo hills,
the bruised bodies of Easter Volunteers.

Animals, neighbours, treading the pattern
of one time and place into history,
like our early marriage, while

tall windows looked down upon us
from walls flushed light pink or salmon
watching and enduring succession.

## II

As I leave, you whisper
"don't betray our truth"
and like a ghost dancer,
invoking a lost tribal strength
I halt in tree-fed darkness

to summon back our past,
and celebrate a love that eased
so kindly, the dying bone,
enabling the spirit to sing
of old happiness, when alone.

## III

So put the leaves back on the tree,
put the tree back in the ground,
let Brendan trundle his corpse down
the street singing, like Molly Malone.

Let the black cat, tiny emissary
of our happiness, streak again

through the darkness, to fall soft
clawed into a landlord's dustbin.

Let Nurse Mullen take the last
train to Westport, and die upright
in her chair, facing a window
warm with the blue slopes of Nephin.

And let the pony and donkey come—
look, someone has left the gate open—
like hobbyhorses linked in
the slow motion of a dream

parading side by side, down
the length of Herbert Street,
rising and falling, lifting
their hooves through the moonlight.

## THE SILVER FLASK

Sweet, though short, our
hours as a family together.
Driving across dark mountains
to Midnight Mass in Fivemiletown,
lights coming up in the valleys
as in the days of Carleton.

Tussocks of heather brown
in the headlights; our mother
stowed in the back, a tartan
rug wrapped round her knees,
patiently listening as father sang,
and the silver flask went round.

Chorus after chorus of the *Adoremus*
to shorten the road before us,
till *we see amidst the winter's snows*
the festive lights of the small town
and from the choirloft an organ booms
*angels we have heard on high*, with

my father joining warmly in,
his broken tenor soaring, faltering,
a legend in dim bars of Brooklyn
(that sacramental moment of stillness
among exiled, disgruntled men)
now raised vehemently once again

in the valleys he had sprung from,
startling the stiff congregation
with fierce blasts of song, while
our mother sat silent beside him,
sad but proud, an unaccustomed
blush mantling her wan countenance.

Then driving slowly home,
tongues crossed with the communion
wafer, snowflakes melting in
the car's hungry headlights,
till we reach the warm kitchen
and the spirits round again.

The family circle briefly restored
nearly twenty lonely years after
that last Christmas in Brooklyn,
under the same tinsel of decorations
so carefully hoarded by our mother
in the cabin trunk of a Cunard liner.

## PROCESS

The structure of process,
time's gullet devouring
parents whose children
are swallowed in turn,
families, houses, towns,
built or battered down,
only the earth and sky
unchanging in change,
everything else fragile
as a wild bird's wing;
bulldozer and butterfly,
dogrose and snowflake
climb the unending stair
into God's golden eye.

Each close in his own
world of sense & memory,
races, nations locked
in their dream of history,
only love or friendship,
an absorbing discipline
(the healing harmony
of music, painting, poem)
as swaying ropeladders
across fuming oblivion
while the globe turns,
and the stars turn, and
the great circles shine,
gold & silver,

sun & moon.

## A FLOWERING ABSENCE

How can one make an absence flower,
lure a desert to fragrant bloom?
Taut with terror, I rehearse a time
when I was taken from a sick room:
as before from your flayed womb.

And given away to be fostered
wherever charity could afford.
I came back, lichened with sores,
from the care of still poorer
immigrants, new washed from the hold.

I bless their unrecorded names,
whose need was greater than mine,
wet nurses from tenement darkness
giving suck for a time,
because their milk was plentiful

Or their own children gone.
They were the first to succour
that still terrible thirst of mine,
a thirst for love and knowledge,
to learn something of that time

Of confusion, poverty, absence.
Year by year, I track it down
intent for a hint of evidence,
seeking to manage the pain—
how a mother gave away her son.

I took the subway to the hospital
in darkest Brooklyn, to call
on the old nun who nursed you
through the travail of my birth
to come on another cold trail.

*Sister Virgilius, how strange!*
*She died, just before you came.*
*She was delirious, rambling of all*
*her old patients; she could well*
*have remembered your mother's name.*

Around the bulk of St. Catherine's
another wild, raunchier Brooklyn:
as tough a territory as I have known,
strutting young Puerto Rican hoods,
flash of blade, of bicycle chain.

Mother, my birth was the death
of your love life, the last man
to flutter near your tender womb:
a neonlit barsign winks off & on,
*motherfucka, thass your name.*

There is an absence, real as presence,
In the mornings I hear my daughter
chuckle, with runs of sudden joy.
Hurt, she rushes to her mother,
as I never could, a whining boy.

All roads wind backwards to it.
An unwanted child, a primal hurt.
I caught fever on the big boat
that brought us away from America
—away from my lost parents.

Surely my father loved me,
teaching me to croon, *Ragtime Cowboy*
*Joe, swaying in his saddle*
*as he sings*, as he did, drunkenly
dropping down from the speakeasy.

So I found myself shipped back
to his home, in an older country,
transported to a previous century,
where his sisters restored me,
natural love flowering around me.

And the hurt ran briefly underground
to break out in a schoolroom
where I was taunted by a mistress
who hunted me publicly down
to near speechlessness.

*So this is our brightest infant?*
*Where did he get that outlandish accent?*
*What do you expect, with no parents,*
*sent back from some American slum:*
*none of you are to speak like him!*

Stammer, impediment, stutter:
she had found my lode of shame,
and soon I could no longer utter
those magical words I had begun
to love, to dolphin delight in.

And not for two stumbling decades
would I manage to speak straight again.
Was it any remission to learn
that she drove her daughter to suicide
later, with that same lashing tongue?

None. Only bewildered compassion.
Wounded for the second time
my tongue became a rusted hinge
until the sweet oils of poetry
eased it, and light flooded in.

## SEAN LUCY

Born in Bombay, India, in 1931, Sean Lucy was brought home to Ireland in 1935. He was educated at University College, Cork, where he received a B.A. degree in history and English and an M.A. degree in English. After teaching for eight years in England, he became a lecturer at University College, Cork, in 1962, where he has taught since, and is now Professor of Modern English. He has lectured on English and Anglo-Irish literature in Ireland, the United States, Canada, Belgium, Holland, and France. He is a member of the Cultural Relations Committee of the Irish Department of Foreign Affairs. His publications include a critical study, *T. S. Eliot and the Idea of Tradition* (1960); two collections of critical essays; and two anthologies of Irish poetry, *Love Poems of the Irish* (1967), and *Five Irish Poets* (1970), which includes a selection of his own work. His first collection of poems was *Unfinished Sequence* (1979); his play, *How They Kidnapped Aoife*, was broadcast on Irish radio. Another collection of poems is forthcoming.

### SENIOR MEMBERS

Tadhg sat up on his hills
Sniping at passing Tommies from the barracks,
Growling in Gaelic,
Plowtilth on his boots.

Vincent was just a boy
Kept in at curfew by a careful Da
In a soft suburb
Of the cautious city.

Tadhg was two-and-three with Fionn the Hero
(Meaning his cousin)
And helped to shoot him
After the treaty split them.

Vincent is solid stock:
His uncle was Home Rule M.P.:
His face is sleek with merchant generation;
"Liberal plumbing makes a cultured nation."

Tadhg is a bully on the committees
As full of malice as intelligence;
His language is as hairy as his ears;
He has a drover's voice.

Vincent works mainly for the money men.
Deep in his heart he fears the tinker's shout,
The eyes of mountain goats,
The gunman's shot.

Save us Saint Patrick! Is it gin and plush,
Or the grey ash-plant that shall master us?
The bourgeois coma or the bully's push?
This is a dilemma, not a choice.

*Footnote*
*The new politico answers my sad voice*:

Vincent and Tadhg, though sadly out of date,
Each taught me in his way to rule the state,
Ruthless as mountain rocks, slick as the city street
I am the inheritor. Kneel at my feet.

## SUPERVISING EXAMINATIONS

Stuffy chill of clouded Summer, crowdsmell, booksmell;
Grey light in the tall college hall.
Hammerbeams. Dark crosswired bookshelves of dim titles.
Portraits of former presidents. Peeling walls.

Pace slowly down the rows of little tables,
Down the long rows of bowed figures from whom rise
Gentle and continuous noises:
Scribbling-scratch, shifting, clittering, rustling, sighs.

On ranked brownsquares heraldic with hands and elbows
A hundred long white papers catch the light.
Among the clumps of dark thick mensuits
The scattering of girls looks strangely bright.

Jiggling pens trail out long rows of writing—
Loose, cramped, untidy, neat—line after line.
In the westwall stainedglass windows grouped allegorical
figures
(The Arts and Sciences) enrich slightly the dull dayshine.

The peace of boredom holds the supervisors:
He swings his legs from the high table. She wonders.
Another goes up and down.
They hear, unhearing, the clicking silence,
Backed by the far traffic rumour of the town.

With faint benevolence they move among the candidates,
Handing out ink and paper; going the old rounds.
Below those heavy trees which can be seen through the
south windows
The river creeps, choked with weeds, through the lower
grounds.

## LONGSHORE INTELLECTUAL

After all, Charlie, we shall see them go,
And feel renewal with the buff sails stirring,
After this bad weather the tall fleets will embark
Leaving the women on the quayside staring.

The dark pubs at night will become old men's places
Where the wind rattles the bar-room shutters:
Knowing only in retrospect the loud voices and beery faces,
Dim as the inarticulate story the senile drinker stutters.

And after all, Charlie, they are the men of action:
We chose the shore life of the seedy dreamer,
Deliberately abandoning the ships then weighing anchor,
Deliberately ignoring the bravado recruiting drummer.

It only needles us when they come home in glory
In camaraderie and the glow of doing,
Making their memory into a mutual and lovely story,
Leaving us wordless with our book contentment dying;

They steal our women and deride our wisdom,
They drink our whiskey and borrow our possessions,
This is their ancient and abiding custom,
With uncultured voices and unbridled passions.

But after all, Charlie, we know how they end:
Their bodies washing on the beaches of far nations,
Their eye sockets empty, their mouths full of sand,
And their girl-friends lonely—we have our consolations.

## FRIDAY EVENING

Consider the case of the many-minded men
sitting stockfast round this table, all around,
talking all shit.
meanwhile my heart was almost to the ground
wishing to hell the last amen
would let me out of it

onto a road west lost in cold rain
which shall be taken in old rattletrap
when the talkball deflates:
past Dennehy's Cross, forgetting the crap,
past Minister's Cross learning to breathe again,
on miles twisting of high-hedged roads to old gates

under trees. House long and low down left
sails in snug green; family ship *en route.*
I swing round track
into the crumbling yard. I shoot
briefcase laden to where, soft,
but partly peevish, she hugs me back.

## THESE SIX

The six of them
we all meet:
Three fierce and crooked,
three bright and sweet:

The first was High Spirits,
my princess my dear,
who loved and left me
before last year;

the second Gentleness,
a generous friend,
no one brings such blessing
in the end;

the third was Passion,
loveliest of all I met,
with a force I well remember
and a face I forget;

the fourth, Fate,
that ancient blaster,
so strong a termagant
no one can master;

the fifth, Trouble
who seems to find me sweet,
clear on my shoulders
the track of her feet;

the last, Sorrow,
a diligent bore,
wrapped in a black cloak,
who told me the score.

*(translation from the Irish)*

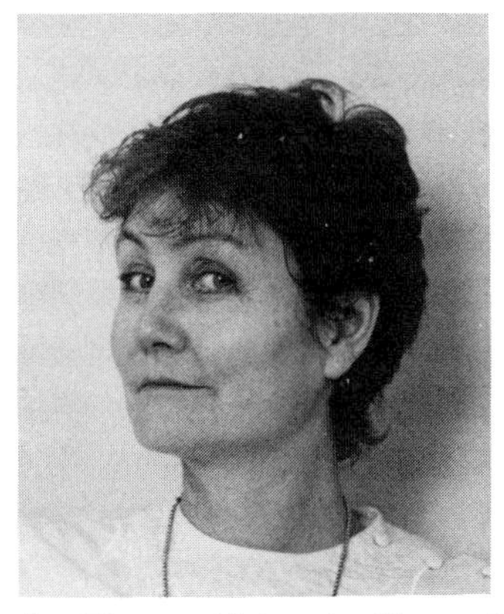

## ANNE HARTIGAN

Anne Le Marquand Hartigan was born in England in 1932 of an Irish mother and a father from the Channel Islands. She settled in Ireland in 1962 and continues to live in Dublin; she is the mother of six children. She is a painter and playwright as well as a writer: her art work has been exhibited in Ireland and England, and her plays have been produced in Ireland. Her poetry and short stories have won numerous awards. Her poems are collected in *Long Tongue* (1982) and *Return Single* (1986). A long poem, *Now is a Moveable Feast*, was broadcast on the radio in 1980. Recently she has been responsible for organizing the first series of readings by Irish women poets.

### ADVENT

Now I will make fat puddings
In the winter evenings,
Huddle home early,
Twist by the fire,
Shutting the door on the dimlight.

It is the going down time.
Curtains pull early
And I am introverted,
There are bogymen in the lane &
Moon witches in the woods.

I will make spicy cake
Pouring whiskey into its veins,
The shelves must creak with plenty
To keep out the dark &
Stop the sun slipping over the edge.

I will ladle out hot wine,
The glasses will scald your hands,
As the mists swirl up from the sea
Keep the fire higher, keep up the lights
Bring in the green branches.

Old gods are stirring under the mud,
Stir, stir, with the pudding spoon,
Muttering incantations,
Dropping the silver in,
A wish, a wish.

The house hunches her shoulders,
Wink-eyed at the ghosts,
Clasping her shirt to her knees,
Feet curled under
The cat waits at the window.

Ring out the bells in the midnight.
Blind drunk in the pub, singing loudly
To keep the spirits away.
The crackers blast, eat large
And light the flaming tree.

We drowned death in our martinis,
Set a match to the dark,
Tight bellied we laugh with the brave,
The devil is frightened of my paper hat &
The sun is an orange balloon.

## BRAZEN IMAGE

In the garden on a summer night,
A garden of Eden, when tobacco flower
And scented stock gleam unearthly,
White mouths drawing moths,
Opening delights.

I would praise Eve for raising her hand,
I would praise her; her strong teeth
Took that brazen bite;

And gates spun down
And out across the green
The brown snake moved
To race towards the light.

## ST. BRIDGET'S CROSS

The last two Februarys have passed
Without your giving a Bridget's Cross.

Mary Owens, Mary Owens,
Twist the marram into dancing forms,
Do not forget, do not forget,
The way to plait and twist it yet.

In backyard times,
The old crones
Carried the lore
In their bones,

Crooned to the young
In the cradle,
By the black pot,
By the table,

Fingering the rushes
Into whirling crosses.

Pure Saint Biddy
Out-shadowing some
Fertile deity
Or wheeling Sun.

The giddygoat sign
Abundance bring,
Nailed to the door
On the first of spring.

Look, now the arthritic apple
Blooms pink, south bent
Under overbearing beeches, last
Of the map-marked orchard . . .

O fairy tree, O fairy tree,
I turn the tale that was told to me,

Long long ago,
My mother said,
A woman in white
Bent her head

Sewing, sewing, under that tree,
Turning, smiling, then was she

Kind ghost woman
Though you have gone,
The tree still carries
The old tale on.

The last two Februarys have passed
Without your giving a Bridget's Cross.

No more the bawdy
Biddy boys bring,
The twisted cross
On the first of spring.

Mary Owens, Mary Owens,
Your bicycle wheels have turning forms,
Pedal to Mass, but do not forget
The way the bent is twisted yet.

## NO EASY HARBOUR

To put off a decision,
Penelope sat sewing a dream.
                                        Waiting for her man.
Each day she needled and knotted
Under the pungent stare of suitors,
suckers, spongers, gorged and burping.

Hot breath on her neck,
beady eyes noting the needle
pure and impervious to rust,

prising the billows of white linen.
Each rivulet of stitches,
each tuck and fold, a wave of growth.

Only to receive an early execution,
a quick pull, an easy death.
Pin prints on a bare shore.

When daylight touches dreams,
colours fade,
night's excitement twilights
with the rude stare of day.
                                        Old problems solidify.

The present
presents its pedestrian face.
Complacent, smug reality is
the rowdy diners banging goblets
on the table, hustling the servants
More, more.
                The wrecking must take place.

She knew she must unpick each stitch.
Her craft had no easy harbour, no
safe mirror, no creek to shelter.
                Cliffs, blank and dangerous.

The canvas will look back at her
empty of thought, awaiting a new charter.
She must stand feet clinging, waving
her lamp to smile, flicker and flirt
over the wine dark sea, drawing
the thread towards . . .
                A quick knife.

So as evening approaches,
her fingers wearied of pulling
neat ropes, unravelling the course,
her eye on the portents,
her eye on the stars.

With pricking fingers
came lady destroyer
mistress of birth and death.

Her small anchor weighed,
listening, whistling up the wind,
her white sails set,
for tomorrow's
homecoming.
                "A swift death
                A sorry wedding."

ANNE HARTIGAN

## SALT

I would not write a lament for you.
A requiem for you, a song for you,
I would not twine a remembrance for you,
I do not think sweetly of you, of your
Past kindness, past pleasures, past lies.

I am not biding my time for you, not repining
For you, you cause me no more the sleepless nights.
For I have killed you. I have dried you up.
Anger I have for you.
With anger I have washed out pain.
Sweet healing anger opening my eyes on you.
Seeing you, without the love blur in them.
Tears now pillars of salt.

Could call curses on you, spit on you,
Laugh at you, but I just smile at you.
Leave you alone. Climbed free of you
Away from the power of you the hold of you
The grip of you the hurt of you from
Feeding the need of you, filling you.
Bringing gifts to you. Bringing strengths
To you.

I turn my power on you,
I shine that fierce light on you, you cannot
Move or run. Caught in my full beam
Only I can unleash this moving thing.
You cannot understand it you cannot know it
But you can feel it under your brain;
Rabbit you, caught in my glare.

Clear of you clean of you
Swept of you, no more bereft of you,
My kisses not for you

No words for you
No sweet looks for you
No look over my shoulder for you,
Turn my heel on you, my back to you.
I have no lack of you. It is you
That is to be pitied now.

## TOM MACINTYRE

Tom MacIntyre was born in 1933 in County Cavan and educated at University College, Dublin. He subsequently taught at Clongowes Wood College. For some years he lived and worked on Inishbofin (an island off County Galway), occasionally teaching creative writing at American universities. He is now based in Dublin, where he is deeply involved in the theater; his recent plays include a successful dramatization of Patrick Kavanagh's poem *The Great Hunger*. He has published a volume of poems (translations from the Irish) entitled *Blood Relations* (1971), and continues to write poems as well as plays.

### ON SWEET KILLEN HILL

Flower of the flock,
Any time, any land,
Plenty your ringlets,
Plenty your hand,
Sunlight your window,
Laughter your sill,
And I must be with you
On sweet Killen Hill.

Let sleep renegue me,
Skin lap my bones,
Love and tomorrow
Can handle the reins,

You my companion
I'd never breathe ill,
And I guarantee bounty
On sweet Killen Hill.

You'll hear the pack yell
As puss devil-dances,
Hear cuckoo and thrush
Pluck song from the branches,
See fish in the pool
Doing their thing,
And the bay as God made it
From sweet Killen Hill.

Pulse of my life,
We come back to—*Mise.*
Why slave for McArdle,
That bumbailiff's issue?
I've a harp in a thousand,
Love songs at will,
And the air is cadenza
On sweet Killen Hill.

Gentle one, lovely one,
Come to me,
Now sleep the clergy,
Now sleep their care,
Sunrise will find us
But sunrise won't tell
That love lacks surveillance
On sweet Killen Hill.

(*translation from the Irish*)

## THE YELLOW BITTERN

Sickens my gut, Yellow Bittern,
To see you stretched there,
Whipped—not by starvation
But the want of a jar;
Troy's fall was skittles to this,
You flattened on bare stones,
You harmed no one, pillaged no crop,
Your preference always—the wee drop.

Sours my spit, Yellow Bittern,
Thought of you done for,
Heard your shout many's the night,
You mudlarkin'—and no want of a jar;
At that game I'll shape a coffin,
So all claim—but look at this,
A darlin' bird downed like a thistle,
*Causa mortis*: couldn't wet his whistle.

Sands my bones, Yellow Bittern, that's fact,
Your last earthlies under a bush,
Rats next—rats for the waking,
Pipes in their mouths, and them all smoking;
Christ's sake, if you'd only sent word,
Tipped me the wink you were in a bind,
Dunt of a crow-bar, the ice splitter-splatter,
Nothing to stop another week on the batter.

Heron, blackbird, thrush—they've had it too,
Sorry friends, I'm occupied,
I'm blinds down for the Yellow Bittern,
A blood relation—on the mother's side;
Whole-hog merchants, we lived it up,
*Carpe'd* our *diem*, hung out our sign,
Collared life's bottle, disregarding the label,
Angled our elbows, met under the table

While the wife moaned with the rest,
"Give it up—you're finished—a year"—
I told her she lied,
My staple and staff for the regular jar.
Now—naked proof—this lad with a gullet
Who, forced on the dry, surely prayed for a bullet.
No, men, drink it up—and piss it down,
Warm them worms waitin' undergroun'.

*(translation from the Irish)*

## DRUMLIN PRAYER

Northward bound
the ice mumbled:

thirty-mile-deep
necklace of hills,

model hills, rebel,
hasky, through-other
shite, shin-bone,
stray-sod, bare,
a load o' whins,

barm,
berry, bee-hive,
honey-flow,

sober still-
house hills,
arse-to-the-wind . . .

The rest bog,
lake, red
bog and blanket,
lakes two-a-penny
lone horizontal
constant in-
vitation.

*The soil*
*exceptionally sticky*
*water has difficulty*
*finding a way out . . .*

Therefore
forgive me,

border zone
from the year dot,
suspicion's cradle,
conspiracy's whorehouse,
ounce of blood
before the churn of butter-milk,
blood all over,

the flowers
every spring,
whitethorn
flagrant hyacinth,
a fresh
animal stir,

therefore
absolve me,

fifty-year-old child
with the killer touch,

vouchsafe my keeping,

devious watershed
wind-gall of love,
smoor of sadness,

watch over me
on the road home.

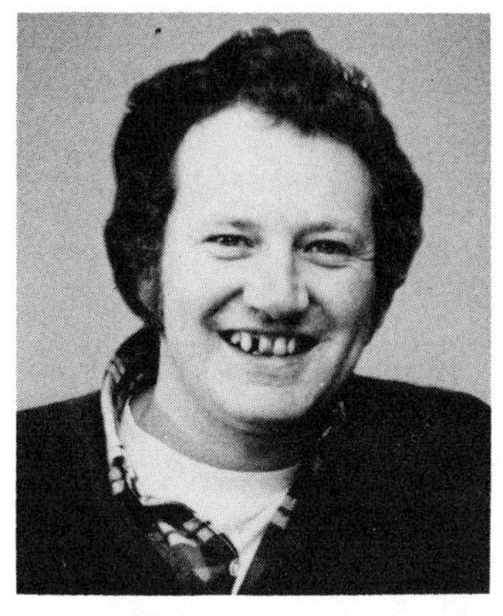

## JAMES SIMMONS

James Simmons was born in Derry, Northern Ireland, in 1933 and received a B.A. degree from Leeds University, England, in 1958. He has published widely in England and Ireland and received the Eric Gregory and the Cholmondely awards for poetry. He taught for five years at the Friends School, Northern Ireland, and for three years at Ahmadu Bello University in Nigeria. For many years he lectured in drama and Anglo-Irish literature at the New University of Ulster where he started the *Honest Ulsterman*, an influential literary magazine. Simmons is also a songwriter and performer. His collections of poetry include *Late But in Earnest* (1967), *In the Wilderness and Other Poems* (1969), *Energy to Burn* (1971), *The Long Summer Still to Come* (1973), *West Strand Visions* (1974), *Judy Garland and the Cold War* (1976), *The Selected James Simmons* (1978), *Constantly Singing* (1980), *From the Irish* (1985), and *Poems 1956–1986* (1986). He has also edited the anthology *Ten Irish Poets* (1974) and written a critical study, *Sean O'Casey* (1983).

### FEAR TEST: INTEGRITY OF HEROES

Of those rebellions that we start in jest
some must be fought out in the open street
with barricades and possible defeat.
I shake with fear, but those days are my best.

Each time a chance of love is here
it seems her kids sleep in the room below,
neighbours are going to let her husband know.
Those are my best nights when I shake with fear.

Waiting backstage to sing, hating displays
of self, yet filled with songs
that no one knows but me . . . well, pain belongs
to birth, all births. I shake on my best days.

At last asking my silly boss to take
my resignation, getting off the fence
and telling him why. Who needs a reference!
I know my best days, but I always shake.

Good risks are those you hardly dare to take.
Who has a faculty for turbulence
and storm is sick; the healthy have more sense.
They have a use for courage when they shake.

That shock of horror when the way is clear!
I wish I had more stomach for a fight.
I wish I had panache—but I'm alright.
Those are my best days when I shake with fear.

## OUTWARD BOUND

for Tony Harrison

Two campers (King Lear and his clown?)
smile to see the skies come down.
The shaken mind finds metaphors
in winds that shake the great outdoors.
As roofs and fences fall in storms
the tranquil mind's protective forms

collapse when passion, grief and fear
stir. We will spend a fortnight here.

To this small wilderness we bring
ourselves to play at suffering,
to swim in lonely bays, immerse
in the destructive elements, nurse
our bare forked bodies by wood fires
where ox-tail soup in mugs inspires
the tender flesh. By rocks we cough
and shiver in the wind, throw off
what history has lent, and lie
naked, alone, under the sky.

Of course, not one of us prefers
the cold; we are sun-worshippers,
wilderness- and storm-defiers,
neither masochists nor liars.

Cheeks whipped by freezing rain go numb.
The baffled blood is stirred, will come
again, glowing like my mind when Lear
speaks in the words of Shakespeare.
Under duress trying to sing
in tune, foretasting suffering
that we will swallow whole, the storm

endured, we hope to come to harm
at home, with better dignity
or style or courage. Anyway
I like to camp and read *King Lear.*
We had a lovely fortnight here.

## CLAUDY

for Harry Barton, a song

The Sperrins surround it, the Faughan flows by,
at each end of Main Street the hills and the sky,
the small town of Claudy at ease in the sun
last July in the morning, a new day begun.

How peaceful and pretty if the moment could stop,
McIlhenny is straightening things in his shop,
and his wife is outside serving petrol, and then
a girl takes a cloth to a big window pane.

And McCloskey is taking the weight off his feet,
and McClelland and Miller are sweeping the street,
and, delivering milk at the Beaufort Hotel,
young Temple's enjoying his first job quite well.

And Mrs McLaughlin is scrubbing her floor,
and Artie Hone's crossing the street to a door,
and Mrs Brown, looking around for her cat,
goes off up an entry—what's strange about that?

Not much—but before she comes back to the road
that strange car parked outside her house will explode,
and all of the people I've mentioned outside
will be waiting to die or already have died.

An explosion too loud for your eardrums to bear,
and young children squealing like pigs in the square,
and all faces chalk-white and streaked with bright red,
and the glass and the dust and the terrible dead.

For an old lady's legs are ripped off, and the head
of a man's hanging open, and still he's not dead.
He is screaming for mercy, and his son stands and stares
and stares, and then suddenly, quick, disappears.

And Christ, little Katherine Aiken is dead,
and Mrs McLaughlin is pierced through the head.
Meanwhile to Dungiven the killers have gone,
and they're finding it hard to get through on the phone.

## JOHN DONNE

*There's more to style than honesty.*

When you lost touch with lovers' bare skin
how could the textures not get thin
in your verse. The real blood the fleas sucked
that sang through your and her veins when you fucked
was lost for God's magic bargain drops,
and life was teasing torture, nice when it stops.
Genius is tempted to ingenious lying,
to brazening out betrayal, justifying
such acts as that old interfering king
forced you toward. *You* could do anything!

After a brave attempt to marry free,
gaoled and neglected, you chose piety,
turned an encrusted back on sweet enjoyment
and—fuck you, John—made love to your employment
improvising belief after the fact,
acting in bad faith, living the act,
faking a hot lust for the Holy Ghost!
I dare dispute because I loved you most.
They'll say I want you to write more like me,
with truly liberal consistency:

but your young self, your verse, condemns defection
from the erection to the resurrection,
bullying congregations like a bawd
for Him, then grovelling. Gawd!
It was a difficult position,
like Galileo's with the Inquisition;
but he at least had grace to stay indoors
and not make weapons for the torturers.
You, having once made such a lovely fuss
on Love's behalf, betrayed her, worse than us.

## OCTOBER IN THE COUNTRY: 1983

*What you can suffer you can sing.*

Wind shakes my window frames
with an empty afternoon roar,
and that damned born-again Christian
is out riding his lawnmower.

His garden is cluttered with Dormobiles,
powerboats of glossy fibreglass,
hedgecutters, rotavators, vans:
the expensive hobbies of a pain-in-the-ass.

And the farmer whose cowshed spoils our view,
whose poisonous leaking silage destroys
blackcurrant bushes and rhubarb clumps,
whose presence is always stink and noise,

is pumping his foul slurry and racing
backwards and forwards to his fields,
mechanically incontinent
in hot pursuit of higher yields.

We hear his crammed uneasy cattle
shifting and groaning in the barn all night
in winter, heads stuck out through bars,
up to their knees in their own shite.

This is my refuge, my countryside!
Yet, believe it or not, to speak the truth
I am happier here in my middle years
than ever I was in my Derry youth.

The only material for jokes
is annoyance. The cruel course
of our human race has been fixed for us
democratically: damned at the source

but improving, maybe. I give my vote
to reformers: but setting the cattle free
and driving them south to the Sperrins? No.
We'd be caught, and cattle frighten me.

I have lit the fire and closed the shutters
against noisy gardeners and farmers.
The votive light in my amplifier
draws me to worship great performers.

## PLAYING WITH FIRE

### I

A green garden of growing weeds
at the back of the house, a dying fall
of blown roses, half unpinned to
a brick wall. The throne I sit on
is wooden and worn grey under

the good influence of the sun.
My hand marks papers dutifully.
Wind lifts the discarded sheets
and shifts them a little on the grass.

An arm's length from me is my host's
work. That absent gardener
has mown hay and left it piled
stiff and pale to die. What I know
about dead grass is that it burns.
That possibility beside me for an hour,
it seems involuntary, my hand stretches
out to it, tiny, lively,
a lighted match.

The palest of orange flames
are tongue-shaped, not tasting the brittle
straws, then, in a wicked rush,
eating that airy pile of rubbish.
The crowded stalks writhe,
collapse, coagulating, blacken.

The walled garden hides everything
but the pillar of smoke. The aroma
of charcoal has me nostalgic for all
the fires of childhood, ritual
family picnics and solitary events
with driftwood on empty beaches
of Donegal. This old monster and I
are two connivers from way back:
I fed him dead wood and he consented
to boil kettles and take potatoes to his heart.

## II

Flame has a sort of right to dead things.
When the juice flow has dried, fruit
and blossom finished, you might think it suits you
to raise that flag of revolution,
to fasten the ghost life of fire
on dross and dry bones: rubbish to ashes.

But my hand trembled, advancing the match,
feeling my old conniver's nature.
He starts a process nothing can satisfy.
Fire can dry out ahead of it
living forests and still sigh after
every growing thing, to dry us all out
and devour us. Never mind if eventually
the greatest conflagration fizzles out
pathetically assaulting sea and sky.

Go on marking your students' papers
dutifully, grope for alternatives,
warm in a back garden, alive.
I advise wariness of callow gestures,
of bonfires, for rubbish we are,
rubbishy, that is our history,
with passing chances of felicity
you may remember as you die.

## JAMES LIDDY

James Liddy was born in 1934 in Dublin. He was educated at University College, Dublin, where he received his B.A. and M.A., and at King's Inns, Dublin, where he was barrister-at-law. From 1961 to 1966 Liddy was in practice at the Irish Bar. He has since held positions at several American and Irish universities as lecturer in English and poet-in-residence. Liddy is now coordinator of the creative writing program at the University of Wisconsin at Milwaukee. Liddy served on the editorial board of *Poetry Ireland* and was founder/editor of the Dublin magazine *Arena*. His published collections include *In a Blue Smoke* (1964), *Blue Mountain* (1968), *A Life of Stephen Dedalus* (1968), *A Munster Song of Love and War* (1969), the pamphlet *Orpheus in the Ice Cream Parlour* (1975), *Baudelaire's Bar Flowers* (a translation of *Les Fleurs du Mal,* 1975), *Corca Bascinn* (1977), and *A White Thought in a White Shade* (1987).

### THE VOICE OF AMERICA 1961

My hour switched on the cameras take.
The flash white of their advertisement roll:
beside the click faces in the colours
of the universe gaze upwards for my word.
I leave obscurity, stacking my symbols
on the shelf, Dollar, Steak, Mother (furies
of my springtime, a century and a half).

I was born in liberty and I cherish all,
so help me God, for the idealism of Lincoln,
Eisenhower, Kennedy, the kids on Main St.
At the cross bombs of history and ideology
I have prepared, the speeches typed,
and intercontinental missiles on alert;
the great heat presses: the buttons sweat.
I mount the stage to swear nuclear love,
for ever, even unto my ashes and dust.
The minute before I walk on I hesitate.
Between the wings with a book open on
his knees I catch sight of the old pioneer,
dove-eyed and his beard streaming in love.
Daddy Whitman, deployer of democracy,
serene in your chair of founder's timber,
let me steer close to touch YOUR BIG WHISKERS.

## PAEAN TO EVE'S APPLE

for Allen Ginsberg

Bud fantasies, dreams of an ear of corn,
Comas where we reduce to leaves . . .
In an orchard heady as Eden
We eat out of the way of the official keeper
Our senses exotically mutated
By transplanting and the rich hybrids,
We drop like butterflies
To the smells from psychotic flowers and grasses.

And, as the new needs words of welcome,
Pausing in our earthwatch
We pick from the windfalls under the boughs
A litany of forbidden fruit
And rechart the stars and the sins.

## HISTORY

"Tell us, streaming lady,
The cause of your wave travel
Have you left your man
You're certainly in a bad state."

"I have no husband I have
Not touched a man, Fenian
King of character, I have
The fondness only for your son."

"To which of my sons, sexual
Blossoming flower, are you giving
Passion—the opportunity
Tell us the whole story, girl."

"I'll tell you, Finn, it's that
Witty blonde son of yours
Oisin with his beautiful
Bright arms that are so long."

"You're strong for him I see,
Virgin of the unstroked hair,
Why him—there are many
Youths with wealth of skin."

"The cause is, Fenian father
I came all that distance
Because his soul's a mansion
His body has a bedroom in

Many a king's chit and courtling
Offered their brownness to get
My love—I never gave my lips
I warmly dreamed of Oisin's."

Laying my hand on you, Patrick,
It's no shame to a sensual pagan
Every inch of me was panting
For the tresses none had rifled

I clasped her soft sweating hand
Gasped in trembling sweet talk:
"I thank you for saying all that
About me, lovely little lady

You are the nicest girl I've met—
I would prefer to be marched off
By you in chains than by any
Others I've danced with."

"I have my spell on you, Oisin,
You are a hero and now my husband
Get up on my nag and we'll ride
To the cosmetic suburbs of rejuvenation."

*

On the horse's back I was put
The untouched feminine in front:
"Let us steal softly out of town,
Oisin, until we reach my place."

*(translation from the Irish)*

## THE STRAND HOTEL, ROSSLARE

for David Wall, Hotelier

I sing of great hotels and a man. In the foyer
his father's guest book lay open on a table, at
George Bernard Shaw's signature. Voluble in a
morning coat he walked from table to table of
French dishes; my sister still says, "There's
a vague cosmopolitan air about Wexford."

There was a bar on whose blue walls old fish seemed
to swim, with fleur-de-lys eyes. Counter motion in
short breaths like pub-time. When the waters were
warm, a curly-haired Jesuit in a sweater
spoke of his admiration of Joyce.
My posh Fine Gael soul went into a
swoon of blue fish heaven; my curl of
democracy, people, and song. Fleur-de-lys watched.

It was the Wexford Opera festival; we were staying in
the Strand Hotel, Rosslare. It was also the conclusion
of old God's time: Golden Razor. A telly in another
lounge screamed black smoke again and again from a
pipe in an ex-medieval sewer. Blue telly then white
and a god older than god built from wine, women, and
song. John Twenty-three, soap and water and an old cut-
throat. Opera bouffe, from now on, Lads.
Rome built in a day. Like Joyce's Dublin of a day.

Billy Kelly, proprietor, in your sartorial elegance you
were wine, woman, and song, of Paris. Your
place was Hotel Helen, not the Strand. Blue water in the
nearest distance; Nymphs with fishscales sweetly sucking.
Paris looks into Helen's eyes to drown.

I sing of hotels and of a Fine Gael man.

I sing of French dishes in Rosslare.

I sing of the white dress of a Fisherman.

Who heard the songs and nymphs? George Bernard Shaw
walking on the white strand signing GBS in the sand with
his walking stick, devising moonlight wars on
Christianity which shimmer away and turn awry.

## DESMOND O'GRADY

Desmond O'Grady was born in 1935 in Limerick, and was educated in Catholic schools in Limerick and at University College, Dublin. In 1964 he received an M.A. degree in Celtic Studies from Harvard University, where he studied with Professor John Kelleher. Since then, he has taught in Rome and Cairo. He has a permanent residence in Paros, Greece. Over the past ten years, he has given many poetry readings and public lectures both in the United States and Europe. In addition to his own poetry, which has appeared in numerous magazines and anthologies, he has translated many poems from the Irish, Italian, French, German, Armenian, Rumanian, Greek, and Russian. His major collections include *The Dark Edge of Europe* (1967), *Off License* (1968), *The Dying Gaul* (1968), *Separations* (1973), *Sing Me Creation* (1977), and *The Headgear of the Tribe* (1979). His version of the Welsh epic, *The Gododdin*, was published in 1977, and *A Limerick Rake: Versions from the Irish* in 1978.

### PROFESSOR KELLEHER AND THE CHARLES RIVER

The Charles river reaps here like a sickle. April
Light sweeps flat as ice on the inner curve
Of the living water. Overhead, far from the wave, a dove
White gull heads inland. The spring air, still
Lean from winter, thaws. Walking, John
Kelleher and I talk on the civic lawn.

West, to our left, past some trees, over the ivy walls,
The clock towers, pinnacles, the pillared university yard,
The Protestant past of Cambridge New England
    selfconsciously dead
In the thawing clay of the Old Burying Ground. Miles
East, over the godless Atlantic, our common brother,
Ploughing his myth-muddy fields, embodies our order.

But here, while the students row by eights and fours on
    the river—
As my father used to row on the Shannon when, still a
    child,
I'd cross Thomond Bridge every Sunday, my back to the
    walled
And turreted castle, listening to that uncle Mykie deliver
His version of history—I listen now to John Kelleher
Unravel the past a short generation later.

Down at the green bank's nerve ends, its roots half in the
    river,
A leafing tree gathers refuse. The secret force
Of the water worries away the live earth's under-surface.
But his words, for the moment, hold back time's being's
    destroyer,
While the falling wave on both thighs of the ocean
Erodes the coasts, at its dying conceptual motion.

Two men, one young, one old, stand stopped acrobats in
    the blue
Day, their bitch river to heel. Beyond,
Some scraper, tower or ancestral house's gable end.
Then, helplessly, as in some ancient dance, the two
Begin their ageless struggle, while the tree's shadow
With all its arms, crawls on the offal-strewn meadow.

Locked in their mute struggle there by the blood-loosed
    tide

The two abjure all innocence, tear down past order—
The one calm, dispassionate, clearsighted, the other
Wild with ecstasy, intoxicated, world mad.
Surely some new order is at hand;
Some new form emerging where they stand.

Dusk. The great dim tide of shadows from the past
Gathers for the end—the living and the dead.
All force is fruitful. All opposing powers combine.
Aristocratic privilege, divine sanction, anarchy at last
Yield the new order. The saffron sun sets.
All shadows procession in an acropolis of lights.

## IF I WENT AWAY

If I went away I should never come back
but hike the hills, sound each hollow,
tramp the stony goatherd track
and my own wild will happily follow.

My heart is as black as a burned door,
or the burnt out coal in a kitchen range,
or the stamp of a boot on a whitewashed floor
and memory makes my smile turn strange.

My heart in a thousand bits lies shattered
like broken ice on the water's face,
like a heap of stones you've knocked and scattered
or a virgin fallen in disgrace.

I shall leave this town as soon as I can
for sharp is the stone here, deep the dung;
there's nothing of value here for a man
but the heavy word from everyone's tongue.

*(translation from the Irish)*

DESMOND O'GRADY

## THE POET IN OLD AGE FISHING AT EVENING

for Ezra Pound

Comes a time
When even the old and familiar ideas
Float out of reach of the mind's hooks,
And the soul's prime
Has slipped like a fish through the once high weirs
Of an ailing confidence. O where are the books
On this kind of death?

Upright as love
Out on the tip of a tail of rock,
The sea ravelling off from the eye,
The line like the nerve
Straining the evening back from the clock,
He merges awhile into the lie
Of his own silhouette.

## from THE DYING GAUL

The day concludes burning.
The north breathes like a dragon.

Held upright by a tree-stump
he fights what cannot die
but must replace him:
sun, sea, river,
moon and marketplace.

What's forceful beyond man
mounts up in one black-crested wave
and sweeps the sod between them.

Disevaluation of all value
bartered reputation,
disdained endeavour
flood forward for the kill
upon him.

Bulls of land and sea
lock in final combat.
Black confronts white.

Over his hanging head
his seacrow circles thrice
and settling on his shoulder
folds her wings,
caws.

## IN THE GREENWOOD

### I

My darling, my love,
Together let's rove
Through the forest so fragrantly scenting.
By trout streams we'll rest,
Watch the thrush build her nest,
While the buck and the roe buck are calling.
Each ring singing bird
In the wild wind wood heard
And the cuckoo high up in the plane trees
And never will come
Death into our home
In the shade of the sweet smelling green-trees.

## II

O beautiful head
All kiss curled red,
Green and grand your eyes are;
My heart is high-strung,
Like a thread too well spun,
From loving too long from afar.

*(translation from the Irish)*

## FINN'S WISHES

Popular leader, national hero
his wishes were: praise for action,
the sounds of nature morning and evening,
rest by a waterfall, the hunt through the woods,
birdsong in the bushes, the wave's wash,
the chant of singers of stories,
the yelping of hounds at the hunt,
clatter of ravens on Skaldcrow Hill,
the stampede of venison on southern slopes,
the seagulls' glance glide off the cliffs' face,
cackle of circling crows in reply,
hauling home deer by the hind legs,
barking beagles round his knees,
and at night, round the fire, swapping stories.

*(translation from the Irish)*

## BRENDAN KENNELLY

Brendan Kennelly was born in 1936 in County Kerry. He was educated at St. Ita's College in Kerry, and at Trinity College, Dublin, where he received his Ph.D. in 1969. Kennelly is now Professor of Modern Literature at Trinity. In 1971–1972 he was a visiting professor of English at Swarthmore College in Pennsylvania. Kennelly is the editor of the *Penguin Book of Irish Verse* (1970). His numerous collections of poetry include *Collection One: Getting Up Early* (1966), *Selected Poems* (1969), *A Drinking Cup: Poems from the Irish* (1970), *Bread* (1971), *Love-Cry* (1972), *A Kind of Trust* (1975), *New and Selected Poems* (1976), *A Small Light* (1979), *The Boats are Home* (1980), *Cromwell* (1983), and *Selected Poems* (1985).

### MY DARK FATHERS

My dark fathers lived the intolerable day
Committed always to the night of wrong,
Stiffened at the hearthstone, the woman lay,
Perished feet nailed to her man's breastbone.
Grim houses beckoned in the swelling gloom
Of Munster fields where the Atlantic night
Fettered the child within the pit of doom,
And everywhere a going down of light.

And yet upon the sandy Kerry shore
The woman once had danced at ebbing tide
Because she loved flute music—and still more
Because a lady wondered at the pride
Of one so humble. That was long before
The green plant withered by an evil chance;
When winds of hunger howled at every door
She heard the music dwindle and forgot the dance.

Such mercy as the wolf receives was hers
Whose dance became a rhythm in a grave,
Achieved beneath the thorny savage furze
That yellowed fiercely in a mountain cave.
Immune to pity, she, whose crime was love,
Crouched, shivered, searched the threatening sky,
Discovered ready signs, compelled to move
Her to her innocent appalling cry.

Skeletoned in darkness, my dark fathers lay
Unknown, and could not understand
The giant grief that trampled night and day,
The awful absence moping through the land.
Upon the headland, the encroaching sea
Left sand that hardened after tides of Spring,
No dancing feet disturbed its symmetry
And those who loved good music ceased to sing.

Since every moment of the clock
Accumulates to form a final name,
Since I am come of Kerry clay and rock,
I celebrate the darkness and the shame
That could compell a man to turn his face
Against the wall, withdrawn from light so strong
And undeceiving, spancelled in a place
Of unapplauding hands and broken song.

## THE THATCHER

He whittled scallops for a hardy thatch,
His palm and fingers hard as the bog oak.
You'd see him of an evening, crouched
Under a tree, testing a branch. If it broke
He grunted in contempt and flung it away,
But if it stood the stretch, his sunken blue
Eyes briefly smiled. Then with his long knife he
Chipped, slashed, pointed. The pile of scallops grew.

Astride a house on a promised day,
He rammed and patted scallops into place
Though wind cut his eyes till he seemed to weep.
Like a god after making a world, his face
Grave with the secret, he'd stare and say—
"Let the wind rip and the rain pelt. This'll keep."

## PROOF

I would like all things to be free of me,
Never to murder the days with presupposition.
Never to feel they suffer the imposition
Of having to be this or that. How easy
It is to maim the moment
With expectation, to force it to define
Itself. Beyond all that I am, the sun
Scatters its light as though by accident.

The fox eats its own leg in the trap
To go free. As it limps through the grass
The earth itself appears to bleed.
When the morning light comes up
Who knows what suffering midnight was?
Proof is what I do not need.

## YES

I love the word
And hear its long struggle with no
Even in the bird's throat
And the budging crocus.
Some winter's night
I see it flood the faces
Of my friends, ripen their laughter
And plant early flowers in
Their conversation.

You will understand when I say
It is for me a morning word
Though it is older than the sea
And hisses in a way
That may have given
An example
To the serpent itself.
It is this ageless incipience
Whose influence is found
In the first and last pages of books,
In the grim skin of the affirmative battler
And in the voices of women
That constitutes the morning quality
Of yes.

                    We have all
Thought what it must be like
Never to grow old,
The dreams of our elders have mythic endurance
Though their hearts are stilled
But the only agelessness
Is yes.
I am always beginning to appreciate
The agony from which it is born.
Clues from here and there

Suggest such agony is hard to bear
But is the shaping God
Of the word that we
Sometimes hear, and struggle to be.

## THE HORSE'S HEAD

"Hold the horse's head" the farmer said
To the boy loitering outside the pub.
"If you're willing to hold the horse's head
You'll earn a shilling."

The boy took the reins, the farmer went inside,
The boy stood near the horse's head.

The horse's head was above the boy's head.
The boy looked up.
The sun attended the horse's head, a crown of light
Blinded the boy's eyes for a moment.

His eyes cleared and he saw the horse's head,
Eyes, ears, mane, wet
Nostrils, brown forehead splashed white,
Nervous lips,
Teeth moving on the bit.

The sun fussed over it.
The boy stared at it.
He reached up and gave the horse's head
A pat.

The horse's head shuddered, pulled on the reins,
Rasping the boy's hands, almost burning the skin,
Drawing blood to attention.
The boy's grip tightened on the reins,

Jerked the horse's head to order.
The boy was not afraid.
He would be master of the horse's head
Made of the sun
In the street outside the pub
Where the farmer stood drinking at the bar.

Daylight said the boy was praying
His head bowed before an altar.
The air itself became the prayer
Unsaid
Shared between the boy
And the horse's head.

The horse's head guarded the boy
Looking down from its great height.
If the boy should stumble
The horse's head would bear him up,
Raise him, as before,
To his human stature.

If he should lay his head against the horse's head—
Peace.

The farmer came out of the pub.
He gave the boy a shilling.
He led the horse away.
The boy stared at the horse.
He felt the reins in his hands
Now easy, now rasping,
And over his head, forever,
The horse's head
Between the earth and the sun.
He put the shilling in his pocket
And walked on.

## SEAMUS HEANEY

Seamus Heaney was born in 1939 in County Derry, Northern Ireland, where he was educated at local schools and at St. Columb's College. He received a B.A. in English from Queen's University, Belfast, and lectured there from 1966 to 1972, spending an academic year as visiting professor at the University of California, Berkeley. After moving to County Wicklow in 1972, he made his living for a time as a freelance writer, doing work for radio and television and for various journals. He has received numerous awards and prizes including the Somerset Maugham Award (1968), the Denis Devlin Award (1973), the Duff Cooper Award (1975), the W. H. Smith Literary Award (1976), and the Bennett Award (1982). Since 1975, he has taught at Carysfort College, Dublin, where he was head of the English Department and, more recently, at Harvard University, where he is Boylston Professor of Rhetoric and Oratory. He is married and has three children. His major collections of poetry are *Death of a Naturalist* (1966), *Door into the Dark* (1969), *Wintering Out* (1972), *North* (1975), *Field Work* (1979), *Poems 1965–1975* (1980), *Station Island* (1985), and *The Haw Lantern* (1987). Heaney has also published *Sweeney Astray: A Version from the Irish* (1983) and *Preoccupations: Selected Prose 1968–1978* (1980).

## DIGGING

Between my finger and my thumb
The squat pen rests; snug as a gun.

Under my window, a clean rasping sound
When the spade sinks into gravelly ground:
My father, digging. I look down

Till his straining rump among the flowerbeds
Bends low, comes up twenty years away
Stooping in rhythm through potato drills
Where he was digging.

The coarse boot nestled on the lug, the shaft
Against the inside knee was levered firmly.
He rooted out tall tops, buried the bright edge deep
To scatter new potatoes that we picked
Loving their cool hardness in our hands.

By God, the old man could handle a spade.
Just like his old man.

My grandfather cut more turf in a day
Than any other man on Toner's bog.
Once I carried him milk in a bottle
Corked sloppily with paper. He straightened up
To drink it, then fell to right away

Nicking and slicing neatly, heaving sods
Over his shoulder, going down and down
For the good turf. Digging.

The cold smell of potato mould, the squelch and slap
Of soggy peat, the curt cuts of an edge
Through living roots awaken in my head.
But I've no spade to follow men like them.

Between my finger and my thumb
The squat pen rests.
I'll dig with it.

## AT A POTATO DIGGING

### I

A mechanical digger wrecks the drill,
Spins up a dark shower of roots and mould.
Labourers swarm in behind, stoop to fill
Wicker creels. Fingers go dead in the cold.

Like crows attacking crow-black fields, they stretch
A higgledy line from hedge to headland;
Some pairs keep breaking ragged ranks to fetch
A full creel to the pit and straighten, stand

Tall for a moment but soon stumble back
To fish a new load from the crumbled surf.
Heads bow, trunks bend, hands fumble towards the black
Mother. Processional stooping through the turf

Recurs mindlessly as autumn. Centuries
Of fear and homage to the famine god
Toughen the muscles behind their humbled knees,
Make a seasonal altar of the sod.

### II

Flint-white, purple. They lie scattered
like inflated pebbles. Native
to the black hutch of clay
where the halved seed shot and clotted

these knobbed and slit-eyed tubers seem
the petrified hearts of drills. Split
by the spade, they show white as cream.

Good smells exude from crumbled earth.
The rough bark of humus erupts
knots of potatoes (a clean birth)
whose solid feel, whose wet inside
promises taste of ground and root.
To be piled in pits; live skulls, blind-eyed.

## III

Live skulls, blind-eyed, balanced on
wild higgledy skeletons
scoured the land in 'forty-five,
wolfed the blighted root and died.

The new potato, sound as stone,
putrefied when it had lain
three days in the long clay pit.
Millions rotted along with it.

Mouths tightened in, eyes died hard,
faces chilled to a plucked bird.
In a million wicker huts
beaks of famine snipped at guts.

A people hungering from birth,
grubbing, like plants, in the bitch earth,
were grafted with a great sorrow.
Hope rotted like a marrow.

Stinking potatoes fouled the land,
pits turned pus into filthy mounds:
and where potato diggers are
you still smell the running sore.

## IV

Under a gay flotilla of gulls
The rhythm deadens, the workers stop.
Brown bread and tea in bright canfuls
Are served for lunch. Dead-beat, they flop

Down in the ditch and take their fill,
Thankfully breaking timeless fasts;
Then, stretched on the faithless ground, spill
Libations of cold tea, scatter crusts.

## THE WIFE'S TALE

When I had spread it all on linen cloth
Under the hedge, I called them over.
The hum and gulp of the thresher ran down
And the big belt slewed to a standstill, straw
Hanging undelivered in the jaws.
There was such quiet that I heard their boots
Crunching the stubble twenty yards away.

He lay down and said "Give these fellows theirs.
I'm in no hurry," plucking grass in handfuls
And tossing it in the air. "That looks well."
(He nodded at my white cloth on the grass.)
"I declare a woman could lay out a field
Though boys like us have little call for cloths."
We winked, then watched me as I poured a cup
And buttered the thick slices that he likes.
"It's threshing better than I thought, and mind
It's good clean seed. Away over there and look."
Always this inspection has to be made
Even when I don't know what to look for.

But I ran my hand in the half-filled bags
Hooked to the slots. It was hard as shot,
Innumerable and cool. The bags gaped
Where the chutes ran back to the stilled drum
And forks were stuck at angles in the ground
As javelins might mark lost battlefields.
I moved between them back across the stubble.

They lay in the ring of their own crusts and dregs
Smoking and saying nothing. "There's good yield,
Isn't there?"—as proud as if he were the land itself—
"Enough for crushing and for sowing both."
And that was it. I'd come and he had shown me
So I belonged no further to the work.
I gathered cups and folded up the cloth
And went. But they still kept their ease
Spread out, unbuttoned, grateful, under the trees.

## THE OTHER SIDE

### I

Thigh-deep in sedge and marigolds
a neighbour laid his shadow
on the stream, vouching

"It's poor as Lazarus, that ground,"
and brushed away
among the shaken leafage:

I lay where his lea sloped
to meet our fallow,
nested on moss and rushes,

my ear swallowing
his fabulous, biblical dismissal,
that tongue of chosen people.

When he would stand like that
on the other side, white-haired,
swinging his blackthorn

at the marsh weeds,
he prophesied above our scraggy acres,
then turned away

towards his promised furrows
on the hill, a wake of pollen
drifting to our bank, next season's tares.

## II

For days we would rehearse
each patriarchal dictum:
Lazarus, the Pharaoh, Solomon

and David and Goliath rolled
magnificently, like loads of hay
too big for our small lanes,

or faltered on a rut—
"Your side of the house, I believe,
hardly rule by the Book at all."

His brain was a whitewashed kitchen
hung with texts, swept tidy
as the body o' the kirk.

### III

Then sometimes when the rosary was dragging
mournfully on in the kitchen
we would hear his step round the gable

though not until after the litany
would the knock come to the door
and the casual whistle strike up

on the doorstep, "A right-looking night,"
he might say, "I was dandering by
and says I, I might as well call."

But now I stand behind him
in the dark yard, in the moan of prayers.
He puts a hand in a pocket

or taps a little tune with the blackthorn
shyly, as if he were party to
lovemaking or a stranger's weeping.

Should I slip away, I wonder,
or go up and touch his shoulder
and talk about the weather

or the price of grass-seed?

## A NEW SONG

I met a girl from Derrygarve
And the name, a lost potent musk,
Recalled the river's long swerve,
A kingfisher's blue bolt at dusk

And stepping stones like black molars
Sunk in the ford, the shifty glaze
Of the whirlpool, the Moyola
Pleasuring beneath alder trees.

And Derrygarve, I thought, was just,
Vanished music, twilit water,
A smooth libation of the past
Poured by this chance vestal daughter.

But now our river tongues must rise
From licking deep in native haunts
To flood, with vowelling embrace,
Demesnes staked out in consonants.

And Castledawson we'll enlist
And Upperlands, each planted bawn—
Like bleaching-greens resumed by grass—
A vocable, as rath and bullaun.

## THE TOLLUND MAN

### I

Some day I will go to Aarhus
To see his peat-brown head,
The mild pods of his eye-lids,
His pointed skin cap.

In the flat country nearby
Where they dug him out,
His last gruel of winter seeds
Caked in his stomach,

Naked except for
The cap, noose and girdle,
I will stand a long time.
Bridegroom to the goddess,

She tightened her torc on him
And opened her fen,
Those dark juices working
Him to a saint's kept body,

Trove of the turfcutters'
Honeycombed workings.
Now his stained face
Reposes at Aarhus.

## II

I could risk blasphemy,
Consecrate the cauldron bog
Our holy ground and pray
Him to make germinate

The scattered, ambushed
Flesh of labourers,
Stockinged corpses
Laid out in the farmyards,

Tell-tale skin and teeth
Flecking the sleepers
Of four young brothers, trailed
For miles along the lines.

## III

Something of his sad freedom
As he rode the tumbril

Should come to me, driving,
Saying the names

Tollund, Grauballe, Nebelgard,
Watching the pointing hands
Of country people,
Not knowing their tongue.

Out there in Jutland
In the old man-killing parishes
I will feel lost,
Unhappy and at home.

## SUMMER 1969

While the Constabulary covered the mob
Firing into the Falls, I was suffering
Only the bullying sun of Madrid.
Each afternoon, in the casserole heat
Of the flat, as I sweated my way through
The life of Joyce, stinks from the fishmarket
Rose like the reek off a flax-dam.
At night on the balcony, gules of wine,
A sense of children in their dark corners,
Old women in black shawls near open windows,
The air a canyon rivering in Spanish.
We talked our way home over starlit plains
Where patent leather of the Guardia Civil
Gleamed like fish-bellies in flax-poisoned waters.

"Go back," one said, "try to touch the people."
Another conjured Lorca from his hill.
We sat through death counts and bullfight reports
On the television, celebrities
Arrived from where the real thing still happened.

I retreated to the cool of the Prado.
Goya's *Shootings of the Third of May*
Covered a wall—the thrown-up arms
And spasm of the rebel, the helmeted
And knapsacked military, the efficient
Rake of the fusillade. In the next room
His nightmares, grafted to the palace wall—
Dark cyclones, hosting, breaking; Saturn
Jewelled in the blood of his own children,
Gigantic Chaos turning his brute hips
Over the world. Also, that holmgang
Where two berserks club each other to death
For honour's sake, greaved in a bog, and sinking.

He painted with his fists and elbows, flourished
The stained cape of his heart as history charged.

## THE STRAND AT LOUGH BEG

In Memory of Colum McCartney

> All round this little island, on the strand
> Far down below there, where the breakers strive,
> Grow the tall rushes from the oozy sand.
> *Dante,* Purgatorio, *I, 100–103*

Leaving the white glow of filling stations
And a few lonely streetlamps among fields
You climbed the hills towards Newtownhamilton
Past the Fews Forest, out beneath the stars—
Along that road, a high, bare pilgrim's track
Where Sweeney fled before the bloodied heads,

Goat-beards and dogs' eyes in a demon pack
Blazing out of the ground, snapping and squealing.
What blazed ahead of you? A faked road block?
The red lamp swung, the sudden brakes and stalling
Engine, voices, heads hooded and the cold-nosed gun?
Or in your driving mirror, tailing headlights
That pulled out suddenly and flagged you down
Where you weren't known and far from what you knew:
The lowland clays and waters of Lough Beg,
Church Island's spire, its soft treeline of yew.

There you used hear guns fired behind the house
Long before rising time, when duck shooters
Haunted the marigolds and bulrushes,
But still were scared to find spent cartridges,
Acrid, brassy, genital, ejected,
On your way across the strand to fetch the cows.
For you and yours and yours and mine fought shy,
Spoke an old language of conspirators
And could not crack the whip or seize the day:
Big-voiced scullions, herders, feelers round
Haycocks and hindquarters, talkers in byres,
Slow arbitrators of the burial ground.

Across that strand of yours the cattle graze
Up to their bellies in an early mist
And now they turn their unbewildered gaze
To where we work our way through squeaking sedge
Drowning in dew. Like a dull blade with its edge
Honed bright, Lough Beg half shines under the haze.
I turn because the sweeping of your feet
Has stopped behind me, to find you on your knees
With blood and roadside muck in your hair and eyes,
Then kneel in front of you in brimming grass
And gather up cold handfuls of the dew
To wash you, cousin. I dab you clean with moss
Fine as the drizzle out of a low cloud.

I lift you under the arms and lay you flat.
With rushes that shoot green again, I plait
Green scapulars to wear over your shroud.

## IN MEMORIAM FRANCIS LEDWIDGE

Killed in France 31 July 1917

The bronze soldier hitches a bronze cape
That crumples stiffly in imagined wind
No matter how the real winds buff and sweep
His sudden hunkering run, forever craned

Over Flanders. Helmet and haversack,
The gun's firm slope from butt to bayonet,
The loyal, fallen names on the embossed plaque—
It all meant little to the worried pet

I was in nineteen forty-six or seven,
Gripping my Aunt Mary by the hand
Along the Portstewart prom, then round the crescent
To thread the Castle Walk out to the strand.

The pilot from Coleraine sailed to the coal-boat.
Courting couples rose out of the scooped dunes.
A farmer stripped to his studs and shiny waistcoat
Rolled the trousers down on his timid shins.

At night when coloured bulbs strung out the sea-front
Country voices rose from a cliff-top shelter
With news of a great litter—"We'll pet the runt!"—
And barbed wired that had torn a friesian's elder.

Francis Ledwidge, you courted at the seaside
Beyond Drogheda one Sunday afternoon.
Literary, sweet-talking, countrified,
You pedalled out the leafy road from Slane

Where you belonged, among the dolorous
And lovely: the May altar of wild flowers,
Easter water sprinkled in outhouses,
Mass-rocks and hill-top raths and raftered byres.

I think of you in your Tommy's uniform,
A haunted Catholic face, pallid and brave,
Ghosting the trenches with a bloom of hawthorn
Or silence cored from a Boyne passage-grave.

It's summer, nineteen-fifteen. I see the girl
My aunt was then, herding on the long acre.
Behind a low bush in the Dardanelles
You suck stones to make your dry mouth water.

It's nineteen-seventeen. She still herds cows
But a big strafe puts the candles out in Ypres:
"My soul is by the Boyne, cutting new meadows. . . .
My country wears her confirmation dress."

"To be called a British soldier while my country
Has no place among nations. . . . " You were rent
By shrapnel six weeks later. "I am sorry
That party politics should divide our tents."

In you, our dead enigma, all the strains
Criss-cross in useless equilibrium
And as the wind tunes through this vigilant bronze
I hear again the sure confusing drum

You followed from Boyne water to the Balkans
But miss the twilit note your flute should sound.
You were not keyed or pitched like these true-blue ones
Though all of you consort now underground.

## AN ULSTER TWILIGHT

The bare bulb, a scatter of nails,
Shelved timber, glinting chisels:
In a shed of corrugated iron
Eric Dawson stoops to his plane

At five o'clock on a Christmas Eve.
Carpenter's pencil next, the spoke-shave,
Fretsaw, auger, rasp and awl,
A rub with a rag of linseed oil.

A mile away it was taking shape,
The hulk of a toy battleship,
As waterbuckets iced and frost
Hardened the quiet on roof and post.

Where is he now?
There were fifteen years between us two
That night I strained to hear the bells
Of a sleigh of the mind and heard him pedal

Into our lane, get off at the gable,
Steady his Raleigh bicycle
Against the whitewash, stand to make sure
The house was quiet, knock at the door

And hand his parcel to a peering woman:
"I suppose you thought I was never coming."
Eric, tonight I saw it all
Like shadows on your workshop wall,

Smelled wood shavings under the bench,
Weighed the cold steel monkey-wrench
In my soft hand, then stood at the road
To watch your wavering tail-light fade

And knew that if we met again
In an Ulster twilight we would begin
And end whatever we might say
In a speech all toys and carpentry,

A doorstep courtesy to shun
Your father's uniform and gun,
But—now that I have said it out—
Maybe none the worse for that.

## from STATION ISLAND

### IX

"My brain dried like spread turf, my stomach
Shrank to a cinder and tightened and cracked.
Often I was dogs on my own track
Of blood on wet grass that I could have licked.
Under the prison blanket, an ambush
Stillness I felt safe in settled round me.
Street lights came on in small towns, the bomb flash
Came before the sound, I saw country
I knew from Glenshane down to Toome
And heard a car I could make out years away

With me in the back of it like a white-faced groom,
A hit-man on the brink, emptied and deadly.
When the police yielded my coffin, I was light
As my head when I took aim."
                                                  This voice from blight
And hunger died through the black dorm:
There he was, laid out with a drift of mass cards
At his shrouded feet. Then the firing party's
Volley in the yard. I saw woodworm
In gate posts and door jambs, smelt mildew
From the byre loft where he watched and hid
From fields his draped coffin would raft through.
Unquiet soul, they should have buried you
In the bog where you threw your first grenade,
Where only helicopters and curlews
Make their maimed music, and sphagnum moss
Could teach you its medicinal repose
Until, when the weasel whistles on its tail,
No other weasel will obey its call.

I dreamt and drifted. All seemed to run to waste
As down a swirl of mucky, glittering flood
Strange polyp floated like a huge corrupt
Magnolia bloom, surreal as a shed breast,
My softly awash and blanching self-disgust.
And I cried among night waters, "I repent
My unweaned life that kept me competent
To sleepwalk with connivance and mistrust."
Then, like a pistil growing from the polyp,
A lighted candle rose and steadied up
Until the whole bright-masted thing retrieved
A course and the currents it had gone with
Were what it rode and showed. No more adrift,
My feet touched bottom and my heart revived.

Then something round and clear
And mildly turbulent, like a bubbleskin

Or a moon in smoothly rippled lough water
Rose in a cobwebbed space: the molten
Inside-sheen of an instrument
Revolved its polished convexes full
Upon me, so close and brilliant
I pitched backwards in a headlong fall.
And then it was the clarity of waking
To sunlight and a bell and gushing taps
In the next cubicle. Still there for the taking!
The old brass trumpet with its valves and stops
I found once in loft thatch, a mystery
I shied from then for I thought such trove beyond me.

"I hate how quick I was to know my place.
I hate where I was born, hate everything
That made me biddable and unforthcoming,"
I mouthed at my half-composed face
In the shaving mirror, like somebody
Drunk in the bathroom during a party,
Lulled and repelled by his own reflection.
As if the cairnstone could defy the cairn.
As if the eddy could reform the pool.
As if a stone swirled under a cascade,
Eroded and eroding in its bed,
Could grind itself down to a different core.
Then I thought of the tribe whose dances never fail
For they keep dancing till they sight the deer.

## FROM THE CANTON OF EXPECTATION

### I

We lived deep in a land of optative moods,
under high, banked clouds of resignation.

A rustle of loss in the phrase *Not in our lifetime*,
the broken nerve when we prayed *Vouchsafe* or *Deign*,
were creditable, sufficient to the day.

Once a year we gathered in a field
of dance platforms and tents where children sang
songs they had learned by rote in the old language.
An auctioneer who had fought in the brotherhood
enumerated the humiliations
we always took for granted, but not even he
considered this, I think, a call to action.
Iron-mouthed loudspeakers shook the air
yet nobody felt blamed. He had confirmed us.
When our rebel anthem played the meeting shut
we turned for home and the usual harassment
by militiamen on overtime at roadblocks.

## II

And next thing, suddenly, this change of mood.
Books open in the newly-wired kitchens.
Young heads that might have dozed a life away
against the flanks of milking cows were busy
paving and pencilling their first causeways
across the prescribed texts. The paving stones
of quadrangles came next and a grammar
of imperatives, the new age of demands.
They would banish the conditional for ever,
this generation born impervious to
the triumph in our cries of *de profundis*.
Our faith in winning by enduring most
they made anathema, intelligences
brightened and unmannerly as crowbars.

### III

*What looks the strongest has outlived its term.*
*The future lies with what's affirmed from under.*
These things that corroborated us when we dwelt
under the aegis of our stealthy patron,
the guardian angel of passivity,
now sink a fang of menace in my shoulder.
I repeat the word 'stricken' to myself
and stand bareheaded under the banked clouds
edged more and more with brassy thunderlight.
I yearn for hammerblows on clinkered planks,
the uncompromised report of driven thole-pins,
to know there is one among us who never swerved
from all his instincts told him was right action,
who stood his ground in the indicative,
whose boat will lift when the cloudburst happens.

## from CLEARANCES

### III

When all the others were away at Mass
I was all hers as we peeled potatoes.
They broke the silence, let fall one by one
Like solder weeping off the soldering iron:
Cold comforts set between us, things to share
Gleaming in a bucket of clean water.
And again let fall. Little pleasant splashes
From each other's work would bring us to our senses.

So while the parish priest at her bedside
Went hammer and tongs at the prayers for the dying
And some were responding and some crying
I remembered her head bent towards my head,

Her breath in mine, our fluent dipping knives—
Never closer the whole rest of our lives.

## V

The cool that came off sheets just off the line
Made me think the damp must still be in them
But when I took my corners of the linen
And pulled against her, first straight down the hem
And then diagonally, then flapped and shook
The fabric like a sail in a cross-wind,
They made a dried-out undulating thwack.
So we'd stretch and fold and end up hand to hand
For a split second as if nothing had happened
For nothing had that had not always happened
Beforehand, day by day, just touch and go,
Coming close again by holding back
In moves where I was x and she was o
Inscribed in sheets she'd sewn from ripped-out flour sacks.

## VII

In the last minutes he said more to her
Almost than in all their life together.
"You'll be in New Row on Monday night
And I'll come up for you and you'll be glad
When I walk in the door . . . Isn't that right?"
His head was bent down to her propped-up head.
She could not hear but we were overjoyed.
He called her good and girl. Then she was dead,
The searching for a pulsebeat was abandoned
And we all knew one thing by being there.
The space we stood around had been emptied
Into us to keep, it penetrated
Clearances that suddenly stood open.
High cries were felled and a pure change happened.

## MICHAEL LONGLEY

Born in Belfast in 1939, Michael Longley was educated at the Royal Belfast Academical Institution and Trinity College, Dublin, where he read classics. After teaching for several years, he was appointed Director for Literature and the Traditional Arts on the Arts Council of Northern Ireland. He is married to the critic Edna Longley and has three children. He has edited *Causeway: The Arts in Ulster* (1971), and *Under the Moon: Over the Stars* (1971), an anthology of children's poetry. The following collections of his poetry have been published: *No Continuing City* (1969), *An Exploded View* (1973), *Man Lying on a Wall* (1976), *The Echo Gate* (1979), *Selected Poems* (1981), and *Poems 1963–1983* (1985).

## EPITHALAMION

These are the small hours when
Moths by their fatal appetite
That brings them tapping to get in,
Are steered along the night
To where our window catches light.

Who hazard all to be
Where we, the only two it seems,
Inhabit so delightfully
A room it bursts its seams
And spills on to the lawn in beams,

Such visitors as these
Reflect with eyes like frantic stars
This garden's brightest properties,
Cruising its corridors
Of light above the folded flowers,

Till our vicinity
Is rendered royal by their flight
Towards us, till more silently
The silent stars ignite,
Their aeons dwindling by a night,

And everything seems bent
On robing in this evening you
And me, all dark the element
Our light is earnest to,
All quiet gathered round us who,

When over the embankments
A train that's loudly reprobate
Shoots from silence into silence,
With ease accommodate
Its pandemonium, its freight.

I hold you close because
We have decided dark will be
For ever like this and because,
My love, already
The dark is growing elderly.

With dawn upon its way,
Punctually and as a rule,
The small hours widening into day,
Our room its vestibule
Before it fills all houses full,

We too must hazard all,
Switch off the lamp without a word
For the last of night assembled
Over it and unperturbed
By the moth that lies there littered,

And notice how the trees
Which took on anonymity
Are again in their huge histories
Displayed, that wherever we
Attempt, and as far as we can see,

The flowers everywhere
Are withering, the stars dissolved,
Amalgamated in a glare,
Which last night were revolved
Discreetly round us—and, involved,

The two of us, in these
Which early morning has deformed,
Must hope that in new properties
We'll find a uniform
To know each other truly by, or,

At the least, that these will,
When we rise, be seen with dawn
As remnant yet part raiment still,
Like flags that linger on
The sky when king and queen are gone.

## EMILY DICKINSON

Emily Dickinson, I think of you
Wakening early each morning to write,
Dressing with care for the act of poetry.

Yours is always a perfect progress through
Such cluttered rooms to eloquence, delight,
To words—your window on the mystery.

By christening the world you live and pray—
Within those lovely titles is contained
The large philosophy you tend towards:
Within your lexicon the birds that play
Beside your life, the wind that holds your hand
Are recognised. Your poems are full of words.

In your house in Amherst Massachusetts,
Though like love letters you lock them away,
The poems are ubiquitous as dust.
You sit there writing while the light permits—
While you grow older they increase each day,
Gradual as flowers, gradual as rust.

## CARAVAN

A rickety chimney suggests
The diminutive stove,
Children perhaps, the pots
And pans adding up to love—

So much concentrated under
The low roof, the windows
Shuttered against snow and wind,
That you would be magnified

(If you were there) by the dark,
Wearing it like an apron
And revolving in your hands
As weather in a glass dome,

The blizzard, the day beyond
And—tiny, barely in focus—
Me disappearing out of view
On probably the only horse,

Cantering off to the right
To collect the week's groceries,
Or to be gone for good
Having drawn across my eyes

Like a curtain all that light
And the snow, my history
Stiffening with the tea towels
Hung outside the door to dry.

## KINDERTOTENLIEDER

There can be no songs for dead children
Near the crazy circle of explosions,
The splintering tangent of the ricochet,

No songs for the children who have become
My unrestricted tenants, fingerprints
Everywhere, teethmarks on this and that.

## LETTER TO DEREK MAHON

And did we come into our own
When, minus muse and lexicon,
We traced in August sixty-nine
Our imaginary Peace Line
Around the burnt-out houses of

The Catholics we'd scarcely loved,
Two Sisyphuses come to budge
The sticks and stones of an old grudge,

Two poetic conservatives
In the city of guns and long knives,
Our ears receiving then and there
The stereophonic nightmare
Of the Shankill and the Falls,
Our matches struck on crumbling walls
To light us as we moved at last
Through the back alleys of Belfast?

Why it mattered to have you here
You who journeyed to Inisheer
With me, years back, one Easter when
With MacIntyre and the lone Dane
Our footsteps lifted up the larks,
Echoing off those western rocks
And down that darkening arcade
Hung with the failures of our trade,

Will understand. We were tongue-tied
Companions of the island's dead
In the graveyard among the dunes,
Eavesdroppers on conversations
With a Jesus who spoke Irish—
We were strangers in that parish,
Black tea with bacon and cabbage
For our sacraments and pottage,

Dank blankets making up our Lent
Till, islanders ourselves, we bent
Our knees and cut the watery sod
From the lazy-bed where slept a God
We couldn't count among our friends,

Although we'd taken in our hands
Splinters of driftwood nailed and stuck
On the rim of the Atlantic.

That was Good Friday years ago—
How persistent the undertow
Slapped by currachs ferrying stones,
Moonlight glossing the confusions
Of its each bilingual wave—yes,
We would have lingered there for less . . .
Six islanders for a ten-bob note
Rowed us out to the anchored boat.

## DESERT WARFARE

Though there are distances between us
I lean across and with my finger
Pick sleep from the corners of her eyes,
Two grains of sand. Could any soldier
Conscripted to such desert warfare
Discern more accurately than I do
The manifold hazards—a high sun,
Repetitive dunes, compasses jamming,
Delirium, death—or dare with me
During the lulls in each bombardment
To address her presence, her absence?
She might be a mirage, and my long
Soliloquies part of the action.

## FLEANCE

I entered with a torch before me
And cast my shadow on the backcloth
Momentarily: a handful of words,
One bullet with my initials on it—
And that got stuck in a property tree.

I would have caught it between my teeth
Or, a true professional, stood still
While the two poetic murderers
Pinned my silhouette to history
In a shower of accurate daggers.

But as any illusionist might
Unfasten the big sack of darkness,
The ropes and handcuffs, and emerge
Smoking a nonchalant cigarette,
I escaped—only to lose myself.

It took me a lifetime to explore
The dusty warren beneath the stage
With its trapdoor opening on to
All that had happened above my head
Like noises-off or distant weather.

In the empty auditorium I bowed
To one preoccupied caretaker
And, without removing my make-up,
Hurried back to the digs where Banquo
Sat up late with a hole in his head.

## THE LINEN WORKERS

Christ's teeth ascended with him into heaven:
Through a cavity in one of his molars
The wind whistles: he is fastened for ever
By his exposed canines to a wintry sky.

I am blinded by the blaze of that smile
And by the memory of my father's false teeth
Brimming in their tumbler: they wore bubbles
And, outside of his body, a deadly grin.

When they massacred the ten linen workers
There fell on the road beside them spectacles,
Wallets, small change, and a set of dentures:
Blood, food particles, the bread, the wine.

Before I can bury my father once again
I must polish the spectacles, balance them
Upon his nose, fill his pockets with money
And into his dead mouth slip the set of teeth.

## PEACE

after Tibullus

Who was responsible for the very first arms deal—
The man of iron who thought of marketing the sword?
Or did he intend us to use it against wild animals
Rather than ourselves? Even if he's not guilty
Murder got into the bloodstream as gene or virus
So that now we give birth to wars, short cuts to death.
Blame the affluent society: no killings when
The cup on the dinner table was made of beechwood,
And no barricades or ghettoes when the shepherd
Snoozed among sheep that weren't even thoroughbreds.

I would like to have been alive in the good old days
Before the horrors of modern warfare and warcries
Stepping up my pulse rate. Alas, as things turn out
I've been press-ganged into service, and for all I know
Someone's polishing a spear with my number on it.
God of my Fathers, look after me like a child!
And don't be embarrassed by this handmade statue
Carved out of bog oak by my great-great-grandfather
Before the mass-production of religious art
When a wooden god stood simply in a narrow shrine.

A man could worship there with bunches of early grapes,
A wreath of whiskery wheat-ears, and then say Thank you
With a wholemeal loaf delivered by him in person,
His daughter carrying the unbroken honeycomb.
Lord, if you will keep me out of the firing line
I'll pick a porker from the steamy sty and dress
In my Sunday best, a country cousin's sacrifice.
Someone else can slaughter enemy commanders
And, over a drink, rehearse with me his memoirs,
Mapping the camp in wine upon the table top.

It's crazy to beg black death to join the ranks
Who dogs our footsteps anyhow with silent feet—
No cornfields in Hell, nor cultivated vineyards,
Only yapping Cerberus and the unattractive
Oarsman of the Styx: there an anaemic crew
Sleepwalks with smoky hair and empty eye-sockets.
How much nicer to have a family and let
Lazy old age catch up on you in your retirement,
You keeping track of the sheep, your son of the lambs,
While the woman of the house puts on the kettle.

I want to live until the white hairs shine above
A pensioner's memories of better days. Meanwhile
I would like peace to be my partner on the farm,
Peace personified: oxen under the curved yoke;

Compost for the vines, grape-juice turning into wine,
Vintage years handed down from father to son;
Hoe and ploughshare gleaming, while in some dark corner
Rust keeps the soldier's grisly weapons in their place;
The labourer steering his wife and children home
In a hay cart from the fields, a trifle sozzled.

Then, if there are skirmishes, guerilla tactics,
It's only lovers quarrelling, the bedroom door
Wrenched off its hinges, a woman in hysterics,
Hair torn out, cheeks swollen with bruises and tears—
Until the bully-boy starts snivelling as well
In a pang of conscience for his battered wife:
Then sexual neurosis works them up again
And the row escalates into a war of words.
He's hard as nails, made of sticks and stones, the chap
Who beats his girlfriend up. A crime against nature.

Enough, surely, to rip from her skin the flimsiest
Of negligees, ruffle that elaborate hair-do,
Enough to be the involuntary cause of tears—
Though upsetting a sensitive girl when you sulk
Is a peculiar satisfaction. But punch-ups,
Physical violence, are out: you might as well
Pack your kit-bag, goose-step a thousand miles away
From the female sex. As for me, I want a woman
To come and fondle my ears of wheat and let apples
Overflow between her breasts. I shall call her Peace.

## THE LINEN INDUSTRY

Pulling up flax after the blue flowers have fallen
And laying our handfuls in the peaty water
To rot those grasses to the bone, or building stooks
That recall the skirts of an invisible dancer,

We become a part of the linen industry
And follow its processes to the grubby town
Where fields are compacted into window-boxes
And there is little room among the big machines.

But even in our attic under the skylight
We make love on a bleach green, the whole meadow
Draped with material turning white in the sun
As though snow reluctant to melt were our attire.

What's passion but a battering of stubborn stalks,
Then a gentle combing out of fibres like hair
And a weaving of these into christening robes,
Into garments for a marriage or funeral?

Since it's like a bereavement once the labour's done
To find ourselves last workers in a dying trade,
Let flax be our matchmaker, our undertaker,
The provider of sheets for whatever the bed—

And be shy of your breasts in the presence of death,
Say that you look more beautiful in linen
Wearing white petticoats, the bow on your bodice
A butterfly attending the embroidered flowers.

## DETOUR

I want my funeral to include this detour
Down the single street of a small market town,
On either side of the procession such names
As Philbin, O'Malley, MacNamara, Keane.
A reverent pause to let a herd of milkers pass
Will bring me face to face with grubby parsnips,
Cauliflowers that glitter after a sunshower,
Then hay rakes, broom handles, gas cylinders.

Reflected in the slow sequence of shop windows
I shall be part of the action when his wife
Draining the potatoes into a steamy sink
Calls to the butcher to get ready for dinner
And the publican descends to change a barrel.
From behind the one locked door for miles around
I shall prolong a detailed conversation
With the man in the concrete telephone kiosk
About where my funeral might be going next.

## AN AMISH RUG

As if a one-room schoolhouse were all we knew
And our clothes were black, our underclothes black,
Marriage a horse and buggy going to church
And the children silhouettes in a snowy field,

I bring you this patchwork like a smallholding
Where I served as the hired boy behind the harrow,
Its threads the colour of cantaloupe and cherry
Securing hay bales, corn cobs, tobacco leaves.

You may hang it on the wall, a cathedral window,
Or lay it out on the floor beside our bed
So that whenever we undress for sleep or love
We shall step over it as over a flowerbed.

## SEAMUS DEANE

Seamus Deane was born in Derry, Northern Ireland, in 1940. He received B.A. and M.A. degrees from Queen's University, Belfast, and a Ph.D. from Cambridge. He is Professor of Modern English and American Literature at University College, Dublin. He has been a visiting professor at Berkeley, Reed College, and Notre Dame. His first collection, *Gradual Wars* (1972), won the AE Memorial Award; *Rumours* was published in 1977, and *History Lessons* in 1983. Deane is one of Ireland's leading critics and intellectuals: his books on Irish literature are *Celtic Revivals* (1985) and *A Short History Of Irish Literature* (1986).

### A SCHOOLING

Ice in the school-room, listen,
The high authority of the cold
On some November morning
Turning to fragile crystals
In the Government milk
I was drinking and my world
All frost and snow, chalk and ice;
Quadratic equations on the board
Shining and shifting in white
Isosceles steps. In that trance
What could I know of his labour?
I, in my infinitesimally perceptive dance,

Thought nothing of the harbour
Where, in his fifth hour,
Waist-deep in water,
He laid cables, rode the dour
Iron swell between his legs
And maybe thought what kind of son,
An aesthetician of this cold,
He had, in other warmth, begot?
But there's ice in the school-room,
Father. Listen. The harbour's empty.
The Government's milk has been drunk.
It lies on the stomach yet, freezing,
Its kindness, inhuman, has sunk
In where up starts the feeling
That pitches a cold in the thought
Of authority's broken milk crystals
On the lips of the son you begot.

## DERRY

### I

The unemployment in our bones
Erupting on our hands in stones;

The thought of violence a relief,
The act of violence a grief;

Our bitterness and love
Hand in glove.

## II

At the very most
The mind's eye
Perceives the ghost
Of the hands try
To timidly knock
On the walled rock
But nothing will come
And the hands become
As they insist
Mailed fists.

## III

The Scots and English
Settling for the best.
The unfriendly natives
Ready for the worst.
It has been like this for years
Someone says,
It might be so forever, someone fears,
Or for days.

# SCHOLAR II

I remember at times
How irresponsible I have
Become. No ruling passion
Obsesses me, although passions
Are what I play among.
I'll know the library in a city
Before I know there is a slum.

I could wish the weight of
Learning would bring me down
To where things are done.

I remember the thief who fell
Half way down the wall
Of the Houghton Library because
His rope broke under the extra
Weight of the Gutenberg Bible.
Perhaps he came from a slum,
Hired to rifle the mint of published
Knowledge too. I could have told him
The difference a book would have made.

Saved him perhaps his broken leg.
Told him the new Faust stories
Of a thousand men who made
The same error and now lie
Under the weight of that beautiful,
Intransitive print. He had to fail.
And now he lies, perhaps for years,
With other slum-children in a jail,
The university of the third degree,
While in other circles move the frail
Inquirers, trailing printed liberty.

## HISTORY LESSONS

for Ronan Sheehan and Richard Kearney

"The proud and beautiful city of Moscow
Is no more." So wrote Napoleon to the Czar.
It was a November morning when we came
On this. I remember the football pitches
Beyond, stretched into wrinkles by the frost.

Someone was running across them, late for school,
His clothes scattered open by the wind.

Outside Moscow we had seen
A Napoleonic, then a Hitlerian dream
Aborted. The firegold city was burning
In the Kremlin domes, a sabred Wehrmacht
Lay opened to the bone, churches were ashen
Until heretics restored their colour
And their stone. Still that boy was running.

Fragrance of Christ, as in the whitethorn
Brightening through Lent, the stricken aroma
Of the Czars in ambered silence near Pavlovsk,
The smoking gold of icons at Zagorsk,
And this coal-smoke in the sunlight
Stealing over frost, houses huddled up in
Droves, deep drifts of lost

People. This was history, although the State
Exam confined Ireland to Grattan and allowed
Us roam from London to Moscow. I brought
Black gladioli bulbs from Samarkand
To flourish like omens in our cooler air;
Coals ripening in a light white as vodka.
Elections, hunger-strikes and shots

Greeted our return. Houses broke open
In the season's heat and the bulbs
Burned in the ground. Men on ladders
Climbed into roselight, a roof was a swarm of fireflies
At dusk. The city is no more. The lesson's learned.
I will remember it always as a burning
In the heart of winter and a boy running.

## A BURIAL

The broken sods, a whipped flag,
The broad river beyond. Gunfire;
The young graves blotted all over.

Angels of morning light dance
On the silver needles of the estuary.
The helicopter prowls, a dragonfly
Popping its shuttered eyes.

Here we have a pause before rain,
And the clatter of clay
Feet on the porch of heaven.

In the stripped rain we wonder
What is going on here.
The cloudburst seems elegy enough.
Drooked shadows raise

White cellophaned flowers
In the darkened air.
Others kneel one-kneed

On a handkerchief. Cars
Glisten. Cameras at full exposure
Click. *Zeiss* and *Leica*
Whirr like crickets. Someone folds

A pistol in waterproof.
He is about to start his dry life,
This one, under the earth roof,

Tunnelling to his companions
In the honeycomb below
That weakens, with its intricacy,
The earth we hide in now.

## MICHAEL HARTNETT

Born in County Limerick in 1941, Michael Hartnett studied at University College, Dublin, and lived for some years in London and Madrid. He was the recipient of the Irish-American Cultural Institute's Award for Irish writing in 1975 and the Arts Council of Ireland Award in the same year. A gifted translator, he has published versions of the Old Irish *Hag of Beare* (1969), Lorca's *Gypsy Ballads* (1976), the ancient Chinese classic, *Tao* (1971), and *O Bruadair* (1985). His own poetry in English is collected in *Anatomy of a Cliché* (1968), *Selected Poems* (1970), *The Retreat of Ita Cagney / Cúlú Íde*—a bilingual poem (1975), *A Farewell to English* (1975), *Poems in English 1958–1974* (1977), and *Collected Poems, Volume One* (1984), and *Volume Two* (1985). His poems in Irish are collected in *Adharca Broic* (1978), *An Phurgóid* (1983), and *DoNuala: Foighne Chrainn* (1984). *A Necklace of Wrens* (1987) consist of poems in Irish with translations by the author.

### ALL THE DEATH-ROOM NEEDS

all the death-room needs,
long hair in silver
spiralled and unbright:
shadows of the eyes,
finest lace: finest
wax and candles and
finest wax the face,

the gnarled horn beads
about the lax hand.
the priest in passion
for the dead, his soft
hands and quiet sounds
deathbed linen kept.
and the ritual
of prayer; and cries;
and Christ's chrism.

## A SMALL FARM

All the perversions of the soul
I learnt on a small farm.
How to do the neighbours harm
by magic, how to hate.
I was abandoned to their tragedies,
minor but unhealing:
bitterness over boggy land,
casual stealing of crops,
venomous cardgames
across swearing tables,
a little music on the road,
a little peace in decrepit stables.
Here were rosarybeads,
a bleeding face,
the glinting doors
that did encase
their cutler needs,
their plates, their knives,
the cracked calendars
of their lives.

I was abandoned to their tragedies
and began to count the birds,
to deduce secrets in the kitchen cold
and to avoid among my nameless weeds
the civil war of that household.

## from A FAREWELL TO ENGLISH

for Brendan Kennelly

Gaelic is the conscience of our leaders,
the memory of a mother-rape they will
not face, the heap of bloody rags they see
and scream at in their boardrooms of mock oak.
They push us towards the world of total work,
our politicians with their seedy minds
and dubious labels, Communist or
Capitalist, none wanting freedom—
only power. All that reminds us
we are human and therefore not a herd
must be concealed or killed or slowly left
to die, or microfilmed to waste no space.
For Gaelic is our final sign that
we are human, therefore not a herd.

I saw our governments the other night—
I think the scene was Leopardstown—
horribly deformed dwarfs rode the racetrack
each mounted on a horribly deformed dwarf:
greenfaced, screaming, yellow-toothed, prodding
each other with electric prods, thrashing
each others' skinny arses, dribbling snot
and smeared with their own dung, they galloped
towards the prize, a glass and concrete anus.

I think the result was a dead heat.

## DEATH OF AN IRISHWOMAN

Ignorant, in the sense
she ate monotonous food
and thought the world was flat,
and pagan, in the sense
she knew the things that moved
at night were neither dogs nor cats
but púcas and darkfaced men
she nevertheless had fierce pride.
But sentenced in the end
to eat thin diminishing porridge
in a stone-cold kitchen
she clenched her brittle hands
around a world
she could not understand.
I loved her from the day she died.
She was a summer dance at the crossroads.
She was a cardgame where a nose was broken.
She was a song that nobody sings.
She was a house ransacked by soldiers.
She was a language seldom spoken.
She was a child's purse, full of useless things.

## THE RETREAT OF ITA CAGNEY

for Liam Brady

### I

Their barbarism did not assuage the grief:
their polished boots, their Sunday clothes,
the drone of hoarse melodeons.
The smoke was like the edge of blue scythes.

The downpour smell of overcoats
made the kitchen cry for air:
snuff lashed the nose like nettles
and the toothless praising of the dead
spun on like unoiled bellows.
She could not understand her grief:
the women who had washed his corpse
were now more intimate with him
than she had ever been.
She put a square of silk upon her head
and hidden in the collars of her coat
she felt her way along the white-washed walls.
The road became a dim knife.
She had no plan
but instinct neighed around her
like a pulling horse.

## II

Moulded to a wedge of jet
by the wet night, her black hair
showed one grey rib, like a fine
steel filing on a forge floor.
One deep line, cut by silent
days of hate in the expanse
of sallow skin above her brows,
dipped down to a tragic slant.
Her eyebrows were thin penlines
finely drawn on parchment sheets,
hair after minuscule hair
a linear masterpiece.
Triangles of minute gold
broke her open blue of eyes
that had looked on bespoke love,
seeing only to despise.
Her long nose was almost bone

making her face too severe:
the tight and rose-edged nostrils
never belled into a flare.
A fine gold down above the
upper lip did not maintain
its prettiness nor lower's swell
make it less a graph of pain.
Chin and jawline delicate,
neither weak nor skeletal:
bone in definite stern mould,
small and strong like a fox-skull.
Her throat showed no signs of age.
No sinews reinforced flesh
or gathered in clenched fistfuls
to pull skin in lined mesh.

The rest was shapeless, in black woollen dress.

## III

Door opened halving darkness bronze
and half an outlined man
filled half the bronze.
Lamplight whipped upright into gold
the hairs along his nose,
flowed coils of honey
around his head.
In the centre of his throat
clipped on his blue-striped shirt
a stud briefly pierced a thorn of light.
The male smell of the kitchen
engulfed her face,
odours of lost gristle
and grease along the wall:
her headscarf laughed a challenge
its crimson wrinkles crackling.

He knuckled up the wooden latch
and closed the door for many years.

## IV

Great ceremony later causes pain:
next year in hatred and in grief, the vain
white dress, the bulging priest, the frantic dance,
the vowing and the sickening wishes, land
like careful hammers on a broken hand.
But in this house no sacred text was read.
He offered her some food: they went to bed,
his arm and side a helmet for her head.
This was no furtive country coupling: this
was the ultimate hello, kiss and kiss
exchanged and bodies introduced: their sin—
to choose so late a moment to begin
while shamefaced chalice, pyx, ciborium
clanged their giltwrapped anger in the room.

## V

The swollen leather creaks
like lost birds
and the edges of her shawl
fringe down into the dark
while glaciers of oilskins drip around her
and musical traces and chafing of harness
and tedious drumming of hooves on the gravel
make her labour pains become
the direct rebuke and pummel of the town.
Withdrawing from her pain
to the nightmare warmth
beneath her shawl
the secret meeting in the dark

becomes a public spectacle
and baleful sextons turn their heads
and sullen shadows mutter hate
and snarl and debate
and shout vague threats of hell.

The crossroads blink their headlamp warning
and break into a rainbow on the shining tar:
the new skull turns in its warm pain,
the new skull pushes towards its morning.

## VI

O my small and warm creature
with your gold hair and your skin
that smells of milk and apples,
I must always lock you in
where nothing can happen.
But you will hate these few rooms,
for a dove is bound to come
with leaves and outdoor perfumes.
Already the talons drum
a beckoning through the slates
bringing from the people words
and messages of hate.
Soon the wingbeats of this bird
will whisper down in their dive:
I dread the coming of this dove
for its beak will be a knife
and if you leave armed with my love
they will tell you what you lack:
they will make you wear my life
like a hump upon your back.

## VII

. . . each footprint being green in the wet grass
in search of mushrooms like white moons of lime,
each hazel ooze of cowdung through the toes,
being warm, and slipping like a floor of silk . . .
but all the windows are in mourning here:
the giant eye gleams like a mucous hill.
She pictured cowslips, then his farmer's face,
and waited in a patient discontent.
A heel of mud fell from his garden boots
embossed with nails and white-hilt shoots of grass:
a hive of hayseeds in the woollen grooves
of meadow coats fell golden on the floor,
and apples with medallions of rust
englobed a thickening cider on the shelf;
and holly on the varnished frames bent in
and curved its catsharp fingernails of green.
The rooms became resplendent with these signs.

## VIII

I will put purple crepe and crimson crepe
and white crepe on the shelf
and watch the candles cry
*o salutaris hostia.*
I will light the oil lamp till it burns
like a scarlet apple
and watch the candlegrease
upon the ledges interweave
to ropes of ivory.
I have not insulted God:
I have insulted
crombie coats and lace mantillas
Sunday best and church collections
and they declare my life a sinful act:

not because it hurts
the God they say they love—
not because their sins are less—
but because my happiness
is not a public fact.

## IX

In rhythmic dance the neighbours move
outside the door; become dumb dolls
as venom breaks in strident fragments
on the glass; broken insults clatter
on the slates: the pack retreats,
the instruments of siege withdraw
and skulk into the foothills to regroup.
The houses nudge and mutter through the night
and wait intently for the keep to fall.
She guards her sleeping citizen
and paces the exhausting floor;
on the speaking avenue of stones
she hears the infantry of eyes advance.

# MARBAN, A HERMIT, SPEAKS

For I inhabit a wood
    unknown but to my God
my house of hazel and ash
    as an old hut in a rath.

And my house small, not too small,
    is always accessible:
women disguised as blackbirds
    talk their words from its gable.

The stags erupt from rivers,
 brown mountains tell the distance:
I am glad as poor as this
 even in men's absence.

Death-green of yew,
huge green of oak
 sanctify,
and apples grow
close by new nuts:
 water hides.

Young of all things,
bring faith to me,
 guard my door:
the rough, unloved
wild dogs, tall deer,
 quiet does.

In small tame bands
the badgers are,
 grey, outside;
and foxes dance
before my door
 all the night.

All at evening
the day's first meal
 since dawn's bread:
trapped trout, sweet sloes
and honey, haws,
 beer and herbs.

Moans, movements of
silver-breasted
 birds rouse me:

pigeons perhaps.
And a thrush sings
    constantly.

Black winged beetles
boom, and small bees;
    November
through the lone geese
a wild winter
    music stirs.

Come fine white gulls
all sea-singing,
    and less sad,
lost in heather,
the grouses' song,
    little sad.

For music I
have pines, my tall
    music-pines:
so who can I
envy here, my
    gentle Christ?

*(translation from the Irish)*

## PITY THE MAN WHO ENGLISH LACKS

Pity the man who English lacks
    now turncoat Ormonde's made a come-back.
As I have to live here, I now wish
    to swap my poems for squeaky English.

*(translation from the Irish)*

MICHAEL HARTNETT

## ALL THE SAME, IT WOULD MAKE YOU LAUGH

All the same, it would make you laugh—
instead of the dances and games of the past
not a tittle is raised abroad in this land—
we ourselves have buried the summer at last.

Once all the girls of our world did play
mustered in companies on May Day;
now their cacophony tears my brain
as I witness their cunning, pointless games.

Our priests are scarred with greed and pride,
and all our poets are cut down to size:
but worst of all, I realise
that no one poor is considered wise.

Blast you, world, you sneaky bitch,
may your guts and liver in agony split!
What's it to you if I become rich?
You don't care when your children slip.

The once-proud men of this land have swapped
giving for gaining, culture for crap;
no tunes on the pipes, no music on harps—
we *ourselves* have buried the summer at last.

*(translation from the Irish)*

## DEREK MAHON

Derek Mahon was born in 1941 in Belfast. He was educated at the Royal Belfast Academical Institution and at Trinity College, Dublin, where he took his B.A. in 1965. In the same year he received the Eric Gregory Award for poetry. He spent two years in the United States and Canada, where he held a variety of jobs. For most of the years between 1970 and 1985, he lived and worked in London. He was features editor of *Vogue* and poetry editor of *The New Statesman*; he has also been poet-in-residence at the New University of Ulster and at Trinity. Mahon is editor of the anthology *The Sphere Book of Modern Irish Poetry* (1972), and co-editor of the forthcoming Penguin anthology of contemporary Irish poetry. He has done numerous translations from the French. His poems are collected in *Night Crossing* (1968), *Lives* (1972), *The Snow Party* (1975), *Poems 1962–1978* (1979), *The Hunt by Night* (1982), and *Antarctica* (1985). At present, he lives and works in County Cork.

## GLENGORMLEY

"Wonders are many and none is more wonderful than man"
Who has tamed the terrier, trimmed the hedge
And grasped the principle of the watering-can.
Clothes-pegs litter the window-ledge
And the long ships lie in clover. Washing lines
Shake out white linen over the chalk thanes.

Now we are safe from monsters, and the giants
Who tore up sods twelve miles by six
And hurled them out to sea to become islands
Can worry us no more. The sticks
And stones that once broke bones will not now harm
A generation of such sense and charm.

Only words hurt us now. No saint or hero,
Landing at night from the conspiring seas,
Brings dangerous tokens to the new era—
Their sad names linger in the histories.
The unreconciled, in their metaphysical pain,
Strangle on lamp-posts in the dawn rain:

And much dies with them. I should rather praise
A worldly time under this worldly sky—
The terrier-taming, garden-watering days
Those heroes pictured as they struggled through
The quick noose of their finite being. By
Necessity, if not choice, I live here too.

## IN CARROWDORE CHURCHYARD

at the grave of Louis MacNeice

Your ashes will not stir, even on this high ground,
However the wind tugs, the headstone shake.
This plot is consecrated, for your sake,
To what lies in the future tense. You lie
Past tension now, and spring is coming round
Igniting flowers on the peninsula.

Your ashes will not fly, however the rough winds burst
Through the wild brambles and the reticent trees.
All we may ask of you we have. The rest

Is not for publication, will not be heard.
Maguire, I believe, suggested a blackbird
And over your grave a phrase from Euripides.

Which suits you down to the ground, like this churchyard
With its play of shadow, its humane perspective.
Locked in the winter's fist, these hills are hard
As nails, yet soft and feminine in their turn
When fingers open and the hedges burn.
This, you implied, is how we ought to live—

The ironical, loving crush of roses against snow,
Each fragile, solving ambiguity. So
From the pneumonia of the ditch, from the ague
Of the blind poet and the bombed-out town you bring
The all-clear to the empty holes of spring;
Rinsing the choked mud, keeping the colours new.

## AFTERLIVES

for James Simmons

### I

I wake in a dark flat
To the soft roar of the world.
Pigeons neck on the white
Roofs as I draw the curtains
And look out over London
Rain-fresh in the morning light.

This is our element, the bright
Reason on which we rely
For the long-term solutions.

The orators yap, and guns
Go off in a back street;
But the faith does not die

That in our time these things
Will amaze the literate children
In their non-sectarian schools
And the dark places be
Ablaze with love and poetry
When the power of good prevails.

What middle-class cunts we are
To imagine for one second
That our privileged ideals
Are divine wisdom, and the dim
Forms that kneel at noon
In the city not ourselves.

## II

I am going home by sea
For the first time in years.
Somebody thumbs a guitar
On the dark deck, while a gull
Dreams at the masthead,
The moon-splashed waves exult.

At dawn the ship trembles, turns
In a wide arc to back
Shuddering up the grey lough
Past lightship and buoy,
Slipway and dry dock
Where a naked bulb burns;

And I step ashore in a fine rain
To a city so changed

By five years of war
I scarcely recognise
The places I grew up in,
The faces that try to explain.

But the hills are still the same
Grey-blue above Belfast.
Perhaps if I'd stayed behind
And lived it bomb by bomb
I might have grown up at last
And learnt what is meant by home.

## THE SNOW PARTY

for Louis Asekoff

Bashō, coming
To the city of Nagoya,
Is asked to a snow party.

There is a tinkling of china
And tea into china;
There are introductions.

Then everyone
Crowds to the window
To watch the falling snow.

Snow is falling on Nagoya
And farther south
On the tiles of Kyōto.

Eastward, beyond Irago,
It is falling
Like leaves on the cold sea.

Elsewhere they are burning
Witches and heretics
In the boiling squares,

Thousands have died since dawn
In the service
Of barbarous kings;

But there is silence
In the houses of Nagoya
And the hills of Ise.

## MATTHEW V. 29–30

Lord, mine eye offended, so I plucked it out.
    Imagine my chagrin
when the offence continued.
    So I plucked out
the other; but the offence continued.

In the dark now, and working by touch,
    I shaved my head.
(The offence continued.)
    Removed an ear,
another, dispatched the nose.
    The offence continued.
Imagine my chagrin.

Next, in long strips, the skin—
    razored the tongue, the toes,
the personal nitty-gritty.
    The offence continued.

But now, the thing finding its own momentum,
    the more so since

the offence continued,
I entered upon a prolonged course
of lobotomy and vivisection,
reducing the self
to a rubble of organs, a wreckage of bones
in the midst of which, somewhere,
the offence continued.

Quicklime, then, for the calcium, paraquat
for the unregenerate offal;
a spreading of topsoil,
a ploughing of this
and a sowing of it with barley.

Paraffin for the records of birth, flu
and abortive scholarship,
for the whimsical postcards, the cheques
dancing like hail,
the surviving copies of poems published
and unpublished; a scalpel
for the casual turns of phrase engraved
on the minds of others;
an aerosol for the stray thoughts
hanging in air,
for the people who breathed them in.

Sadly, therefore, deletion of the many people
from their desks, beds, breakfasts,
buses and catamarans;
deletion of their machinery and architecture,
all evidence whatever
of civility and reflection,
of laughter and tears.

Destruction of all things on which
that reflection fed,
of vegetable and bird;

erosion of all rocks
from the holiest mountain
to the least stone;
evaporation of all seas,
the extinction of heavenly bodies—
until, at last, offence
was not to be found
in that silence without bound.

Only then was I fit for human society.

## A DISUSED SHED IN CO. WEXFORD

Let them not forget us, the weak souls among the asphodels.
*Seferis*, Mythistorema

for J. G. Farrell

Even now there are places where a thought might grow—
Peruvian mines, worked out and abandoned
To a slow clock of condensation,
An echo trapped for ever, and a flutter
Of wildflowers in the lift-shaft,
Indian compounds where the wind dances
And a door bangs with diminished confidence,
Lime crevices behind rippling rainbarrels,
Dog corners for shit burials;
And in a disused shed in Co. Wexford,

Deep in the grounds of a burnt-out hotel,
Among the bathtubs and the washbasins
A thousand mushrooms crowd to a keyhole.
This is the one star in their firmament
Or frames a star within a star.
What should they do there but desire?
So many days beyond the rhododendrons

With the world waltzing in its bowl of cloud,
They have learnt patience and silence
Listening to the rooks querulous in the high wood.

They have been waiting for us in a foetor of
Vegetable sweat since civil war days,
Since the gravel-crunching, interminable departure
Of the expropriated mycologist.
He never came back, and light since then
Is a keyhole rusting gently after rain.
Spiders have spun, flies dusted to mildew,
And once a day, perhaps, they have heard something—
A trickle of masonry, a shout from the blue
Or a lorry changing gear at the end of the lane.

There have been deaths, the pale flesh flaking
Into the earth that nourished it;
And nightmares, born of these and the grim
Dominion of stale air and rank moisture.
Those nearest the door grow strong—
"Elbow room! Elbow room!"
The rest, dim in a twilight of crumbling
Utensils and broken flower-pots, groaning
For their deliverance, have been so long
Expectant that there is left only the posture.

A half century, without visitors, in the dark—
Poor preparation for the cracking lock
And creak of hinges. Magi, moonmen,
Powdery prisoners of the old regime,
Web-throated, stalked like triffids, racked by drought
And insomnia, only the ghost of a scream
At the flash-bulb firing squad we wake them with
Shows there is life yet in their feverish forms.
Grown beyond nature now, soft food for worms,
They lift frail heads in gravity and good faith.

They are begging us, you see, in their wordless way,
To do something, to speak on their behalf
Or at least not to close the door again.
Lost people of Treblinka and Pompeii!
"Save us, save us," they seem to say,
"Let the god not abandon us
Who have come so far in darkness and in pain.
We too had our lives to live.
You with your light meter and relaxed itinerary,
Let not our naive labours have been in vain!"

## CONSOLATIONS OF PHILOSOPHY

When we start breaking up in the wet darkness
And the rotten boards fall from us, and the ribs
Crack under the constriction of tree-roots
And the seasons slip from the fields unknown to us,

Oh, then there will be the querulous complaining
From citizens who had never dreamed of this—
Who, shaken to the bone in their stout boxes
By the latest bright cars, will not inspect them

And, kept awake by the tremors of new building,
Will not be there to comment. When the broken
Wreath bowls are speckled with rain-water
And the grass grows wild for want of a caretaker

Oh, then a few will remember with delight
The dust gyrating in a shaft of light;
The integrity of pebbles; a sheep's skull
Grinning its patience on a wintry sill.

## ECCLESIASTES

God, you could grow to love it, God-fearing, God-
    chosen purist little puritan that,
for all your wiles and smiles, you are (the
    dank churches, the empty streets,
the shipyard silence, the tied-up swings) and
    shelter your cold heart from the heat
of the world, from woman-inquisiton, from the
    bright eyes of children. Yes you could
wear black, drink water, nourish a fierce zeal
    with locusts and wild honey, and not
feel called upon to understand and forgive
    but only to speak with a bleak
afflatus, and love the January rains when they
    darken the dark doors and sink hard
into the Antrim hills, the bog meadows, the heaped
    graves of your fathers. Bury that red
bandana and stick, that banjo, this is your
    country, close one eye and be king.
Your people await you, their heavy washing
    flaps for you in the housing estates—
a credulous people. God, you could do it, God
    help you, stand on a corner stiff
with rhetoric, promising nothing under the sun.

## COURTYARDS IN DELFT

*Pieter de Hooch, 1659*

for Gordon Woods

Oblique light on the trite, on brick and tile—
Immaculate masonry, and everywhere that
Water tap, that broom and wooden pail

To keep it so. House-proud, the wives
Of artisans pursue their thrifty lives
Among scrubbed yards, modest but adequate.
Foliage is sparse, and clings. No breeze
Ruffles the trim composure of those trees.

No spinet-playing emblematic of
The harmonies and disharmonies of love;
No lewd fish, no fruit, no wide-eyed bird
About to fly its cage while a virgin
Listens to her seducer, mars the chaste
Precision of the thing and the thing made.
Nothing is random, nothing goes to waste:
We miss the dirty dog, the fiery gin.

That girl with her back to us who waits
For her man to come home for his tea
Will wait till the paint disintegrates
And ruined dykes admit the esurient sea;
Yet this is life too, and the cracked
Out-house door a verifiable fact
As vividly mnemonic as the sunlit
Railings that front the houses opposite.

I lived there as a boy and know the coal
Glittering in its shed, late-afternoon
Lambency informing the deal table,
The ceiling cradled in a radiant spoon.
I must be lying low in a room there,
A strange child with a taste for verse,
While my hard-nosed companions dream of war
On parched veldt and fields of rain-swept gorse;

For the pale light of that provincial town
Will spread itself, like ink or oil,
Over the not yet accurate linen
Map of the world which occúpies one wall

And punish nature in the name of God.
If only, now, the Maenads, as of right,
Came smashing crockery, with fire and sword,
We could sleep easier in our beds at night.

## ANOTHER SUNDAY MORNING

We wake and watch the sun make bright
The corners of our London flat—
No sound but the sporadic, surly
Snarl of a car making an early
Dash for the country or the coast.
This is the time I like the most
When, for an hour or two, the strife
And strain of the late bourgeois life

Let up, we lie and grin to hear
The children bickering next door—
Hilarious formulations based
On a weird logic we have lost.
Oil crises and vociferous crowds
Seem as far off as tiny clouds;
The long-range forecast prophesies
Mean temperatures and azure skies.

Out in the park where Celia's father
Died, the Sunday people gather—
Residents towed by Afghan hounds,
Rastafarians trailing 'sounds,'
Provincial tourists, Japanese
Economists, Saudi families,
Fresh-faced American college kids
Making out in the green shades.

A chiliastic prig, I prowl
Among the dog-lovers and growl;
Among the kite-fliers and fly
The private kite of poetry—
A sort of winged sandwich board
El-Grecoed to receive the Lord;
An airborne, tremulous brochure
Proclaiming that the end is near.

Black diplomats with stately wives,
Sauntering by, observe the natives
Dozing beside the palace gates—
Old ladies under wide straw-hats
Who can remember *Chu Chin Chow*
And Kitchener. Exhausted now
By decades of retrenchment, they
Wait for the rain at close of play.

So many empires come and gone—
The spear and scimitar laid down,
The long-bow and the arquebus
Adapted to domestic use.
A glimpse of George V at Cowes
Lives on behind the wrinkled brows
Of an old man in Bognor Regis
Making dreadnoughts out of matches.

Asia now for a thousand years—
A flower that blooms and disappears
In a sand-storm; every artefact
A pure, self-referential act,
That the intolerant soul may be
Retrieved from triviality
And the locked heart, so long in pawn
To steel, redeemed by wood and stone.

## EILEAN NI CHUILLEANAIN

Eiléan Ní Chuilleanáin was born in 1942 in Cork and educated at University College, Cork, and at Oxford. She lives in Dublin and teaches at Trinity College. Ní Chuilleanáin has been the recipient of various awards, including the Irish Times Award for Poetry (1966) and the Patrick Kavanagh Award (1973). She is co-editor of the literary magazine *Cyphers*. Gallery Press received the Irish Publishers Award in 1976 for her second book, *Site of Ambush*. Her major collections of poetry are *Acts and Monuments* (1972), *Site of Ambush* (1975), *The Second Voyage* (1977), and *The Rose-Geranium* (1981).

### SWINEHERD

"When all this is over," said the swineherd,
"I mean to retire, where
Nobody will have heard about my special skills
And conversation is mainly about the weather.

"I intend to learn how to make coffee at least as well
As the Portuguese lay-sister in the kitchen
And polish the brass fenders every day.
I want to lie awake at night
Listening to cream crawling to the top of the jug
And the water lying soft in the cistern.

"I want to see an orchard where the trees grow in straight
lines
And the yellow fox finds shelter between the navy-blue
trunks,
Where it gets dark early in summer
And the apple-blossom is allowed to wither on the bough."

## DEAD FLY

Sparafucile fought his peasant war
Although his grey crudely-slung chassis lacked
The jet lines of midge or mosquito,
The wasp's armour, the spider's intellectual speed;
Still the rough guerilla survived my stalking,
Until by mistake I closed a bible
And cramped his limbs to soak in his scarce blood.

A monk that read this book and lived alone
Domesticated an insect of your kind,
Taught him to stand and mark the words on the page
And live in peace inside the same stone house
With a mouse he kept to bite his ear
Whenever he winked, and a cock that blasted him
Out of his bed for matins in the dark.

Planting these three companions as watchmen
At the frontiers of his ambition, he forgot
Mortality, till death knocked them off in a row.
He complained to his friend the exile, across the profound
Indelible sea. Roused by the frosty wind
Of a friend's voice, the thought of home stinging
Fresh and sweet as the smell of oranges,

He considered the island, so far away now it shone
Bright as a theory or a stained-glass window,

Coloured and clear in the sun, his austere mind
Half sure he had invented it, and replied:
To possess is to be capable of loss
Which no possible profit can reconcile
As David, his kingdom sure, could not forget Saul.

## LUCINA SCHYNNING IN SILENCE OF THE NIGHT . . .

Moon shining in silence of the night
The heaven being all full of stars
I was reading my book in a ruin
By a sour candle, without roast meat or music
Strong drink or a shield from the air
Blowing in the crazed window, and I felt
Moonlight on my head, clear after three days' rain.

I washed in cold water; it was orange, channelled down
    bogs
Dipped between cresses.
The bats flew through my room where I slept safely;
Sheep stared at me when I woke.

Behind me the waves of darkness lay, the plague
Of mice, plague of beetles
Crawling out of the spines of books,
Plague shadowing pale faces with clay
The disease of the moon gone astray.

In the desert I relaxed, amazed
As the mosaic beasts on the chapel floor
When Cromwell had departed and they saw
The sky growing through the hole in the roof.

Sheepdogs embraced me; the grasshopper
Returned with a lark and bee.
I looked down between hedges of high thorn and saw
The hare, absorbed, sitting still
In the middle of the track; I heard
Again the chirp of the stream running.

## from SITE OF AMBUSH

### Narration

At alarming bell daybreak, before
Scraping of cats or windows creaking over the street,
Eleven miles of road between them,
The enemy commanders synchronised their heartbeats:
Seven forty-five by the sun.
At ten the soldiers were climbing into lorries
Asthmatic engines drawing breath in even shifts.
The others were fretting over guns
Counting up ammunition and money.
At eleven they lay in wait at the cross
With over an hour to go.
The pine trees looked up stiff;
At the angle of the road, polished stones
Forming a stile, a knowing path
Twisting away; the rough grass
Gripped the fragments of the wall.
A small deep stream glassily descended:
Ten minutes to the hour.
The clouds grew grey, the road grey as iron,
The hills dark, the trees deep,
The fields faded; like white mushrooms
Sheep remote under the wind.
The stream ticked and throbbed
Nearer; a boy carried a can to the well

Nearer on the dark road.
The driver saw the child's back,
Nearer; the birds shoaled off the branches in fright.

Deafly rusting in the stream
The lorry now is soft as a last night's dream.
The soldiers and the deaf child
Landed gently in the water
They were light between long weeds
Settled and lay quiet, nobody
To listen to them now.
They all looked the same face down there:
Water too thick and deep to see.
They were separated for good.
It was cold, their teeth shrilling.
They slept like falling hay in waves.
Shells candied their skin; the water
Lay heavy and they could not rise but coiled
By scythefuls limply in ranks.
A long winter stacks their bodies
And words above their stillness hang from hooks
In skeins, like dark nets drying,
Flapping against the stream.
A watch vibrates alone in the filtering light;
Flitters of hair wave at the sun.

## from THE ROSE-GERANIUM

### IV

"*A l'usage de M. et Mme van Gramberen*"
—the convent phrase (nothing is to be mine,
Everything ours) marks the small round enclosure,
Its table and bench. Distinguished

From the other old people, from the nuns' gravel
They sat in the windmill's afternoon shadow, half
Hidden by a moving carthorse's huge blond rump
And quarrelled over their sins for Saturday:
*Examination of Conscience before Confession*

Prepared and calm in case one thought
Struck them both, an attentive pose
Eluding me now, at ten in the morning, alone
With a clean college pantry: piled rings
Of glass rising, smooth as a weir.

The moment sways
Tall and soft as a poplar
Pointing into a lifetime of sky.

## V

The precious dry rose-geranium smell
Comes down with spirals of sunlit dust
From the high sill: nodding stems
Travelling out from the root
Embrace a fistful of dusk among the leaves.

The man sitting below, his head
Veiled in smoke, the face a cliff in shadow,
Waits: the sun in Scorpio climbs in
Dodging the fragrant leaves; and as subtly
As the eyes of two musicians touching
Light strokes his hair in place.

In spite of your long horizontal twilights
There is an instant when the sun meets the sea
Dividing light from dark
An hour when the shadow passes the mark on the wall
And the cloud of the rose-geranium dulls your hair.

## MICHAEL SMITH

Michael Smith was born in 1942 in Dublin. He was educated at O'Connell's School and University College, Dublin, where he received his B.A. and diploma in Education. Smith is a teacher by profession; he is also a member of the Arts Council of Ireland and editor of New Writers Press. He has published two major collections of his own poems, *Times & Locations* (1972), and *Selected Poems* (1985). He has also translated Neruda, Machado, Bécquer, Quevedo, Hernandez, and other poets from the Spanish and edited the poems of James Clarence Mangan.

### FALL

The desolate rhythm of dying recurs,
The rhythm of outgoing tides, corrosion of stone,

Fall of petal, of leaf and soft rain on empty squares,
The fading memory of song, say, in an old man's head

That never stops in a moment of time,
A rainbowed vertigo spinning beyond the nurse's cool
    hand,

Subsidence of wind and branches against a settling sky,
And stars fading at dawn, or fall of snow:

Something ordered, yet desperate and violent—
A rose, say, or an old man's humiliation.

## MITCHING

for James Liddy

Blonde hair at the edge of the pavement
caught in the sunlight like a bright leaf:
the dull classroom as far away as the heaven
of angels' white wings that never crumple.

The lorries passing the pigeons, the gulls;
the smells from the factories, soap, chocolate, timber;
and the bandy drover's shouts that rise forever
over the thousand brindled backs of the cattle . . .

How infinitely important all that was
to the wide eyes under the blonde hair.

A big stick poised to beat their backs
when the drovers turned theirs . . .

What sense of importance swelled at the smack
of the stick on the dung-caked dumb flesh.

## DINNER QUEUE

At the appointed hour they came
from who knows where, or who knew then;
from the farthest reaches of the city,
from park bench and slobland and river's edge;
from hostelries and distant places beyond time.

I can remember no details to speak of.
A queue of greasy men against the railings
moving to their own slow tempo
or the whiskered nun's brisk propriety.
I can recall the hour from the tolling of bells.

In the bushes the caterpillars ate voraciously
at the sooty leaves.
The cakeman came with trays of cakes
caught in their last act of decay,
dessert and industrial refuse.

I remember the summer as hot pavements.
The time is imprecise, but the place is there,
and the wailing of factory sirens,
and the workers' clean sweep on foot or bicycle.
In the evening the air sank with the weight of darkness.

## CITY II

Here is the abattoir where, in the old days, were heard
The ultimate cries of table beasts.

Here is the home for unfortunate women
Who launder a twelve hour day and are never cleansed.

Here is the Union, picturesque on a sunny Sunday,
In fact, stables of appalling decrepitude.

Here are the slums where life swings back and forth
With a thud like a heavy pendulum.

Here is, partly, love's ecology: occasional blue skies
And, more often, thunderous falls of black stars.

MICHAEL SMITH

## FROM THE CHINESE

for Trevor Joyce

It is not cosy to live
in an outpost
on the crumbling edge
of an empire
on the verge of collapse,
longing for old securities,
regular mail,
certain supplies,
immediate & effective
relief in emergencies.

The desire to escape the present
increases daily.
The world of one's childhood,
of one's youth and manhood,
is coming to an end.

All around
regrets are plentiful
and totally useless.

My dreams are more real to me now
than these daily routines
of habitual survival,
And to think I was once a man of action,
considered myself so
and was so judged by others.

The Emperor's envoys
have been regularly informed
of our appraisals.
Nothing, of course, is done.
Nothing can be done.

This is neither the time nor place
for writing poems.

Gamblers and prophets
are having a field day.

## AUGUSTUS YOUNG

Augustus Young, the pseudonym of James Hogan, was born in Cork in 1943. His work has appeared in various Irish and British magazines. He has published two collections of his own poetry, *Survival* (1969) and *On Loaning Hill* (1970); two pamphlets, *Rosemaries* (1976) and *Tapestry Animals* (1977); and one collection of translations, *Dánta Grádha: Love Poems from the Irish (A.D. 1350–1750)* (1975). The first part of *The Credit,* a long poem, was published in 1980, as was a second edition of *Dánta Grádha*. He has also had two of his plays performed in Ireland, *Invoices* (1972) and *The Bone in the Heart* (1976). At present Young lives and works in London. Parts two and three of *The Credit* were published in 1986.

## THE ADVICE OF AN EFFICIENCY EXPERT

Tie your own noose if you want to be
the perfect executioner. Before the event
it's important to check the scaffold
for woodworm. What would happen if
it fell through: a flop would be fatal.

Always open the tunic at the top button:
'twould never do if you had to apply
an oxygen mask to bring it off.

Just as a matter of interest, women
are preferable to men. They break
easier and beards are an inconvenience.
But don't permit cosmetics. Don't forget,
tears are the essence. But
there must be no messing
with make-up.

No drink for a week before.
A good night's rest and you are ready
as a bride to come down to mother-
earth, ring in hand, rattling the keys.

It is in your hands. Consider.
But it mustn't show. And when
the wall blood-clots, "Freedom
is the last whiff of the rose
before death," spit on it and reply,
"The only freedom that you know
is the moment when the board goes."

Tie your own noose. Be brave. Remember,
death is on your side: you can't lose.

## HERITAGE

*the verb 'to have' does not exist in Gaelic*

One cannot possess
the house until the death
of a father, until the old man,
cutting a twist by the fire,
fails to fill the bowl,
lays down the pipe
or sometimes luckily enough
shovels himself into the earth.

One must not appear to own the place
until the first grass covers the grave.

Then you have it
and the land—one acre in ten
of arable bog. But you cannot possess
a wife until your mother
accepts the death and, in many a case,
accepts her own. There is no choice.

This is being a true son.
Allow the country die for you.

## WOMAN, DON'T BE TROUBLESOME

Woman, don't be troublesome,
though your husband I may be;
our two minds were once at one,
why withdraw your hand from me.

Put your mouth of strawberry
on my mouth, cream is your cheek;
wind round white arms about me,
and do not go back to sleep.

Stay with me my flighty maid,
and be done with betrayal;
tonight this bed is wellmade,
let us toss it without fail.

Shut your eyes to other men,
no more women will I see:
the milkwhite tooth of passion
is between us—or should be.

*(translation from the Irish)*

## BALLAD OF FAT MARGOT

If I should treat my lady with aplomb
it doesn't mean I am an idiot
for she possesses all a man might want.
I am her sword and shield and all she's got.
When loose males are around I keep a stock
of peppered wine and plenty bread and cheese
to tempt them back with me. I amn't slow
to shower attentions on lone wolves who please
to put their money down and take their ease
in the doubtful joint where we've opened shop.

It's not all pleasure. Sometimes she goes out
and comes back cowlike from an empty trough
with breasts all bowed and spirits sucked quite dry;
and that's when sweetness sours and tempers fly.
I twang her sagging garters, and let a shout
I'll strip your gauds off, put them in the hock.
The pious piece comes back at me, you'll not
as sure as Christ died screaming. On the hop
I nail a notice to her nose and mouth
in the doubtful joint where we've opened shop.

Exhausted, both, there's nothing to but bed:
she, bloated like a cockroach bred on dung,
flatulent with laughter, butts my head,
and practised hands will pump my joystick numb.
Then getting sloshed, we drop off like the dead.
Til at cockcrow, I feel a belly flop
over my carcass, on a sensitive spot,
to mount me like a daffodil: I'm done
in the doubtful joint where we've opened shop.

The weather's not important: sun or rain,
I can sit pretty with my wallet fat,
the guardian of her duty and domain.
We are well-matched: I'm sewer-rat, she wild-cat.
And in the gutter stakes we will not stop
to free the filth that clogs the honest drain
in the doubtful joint where we've opened shop.

## EAVAN BOLAND

Born in Dublin in 1944, Eavan Boland was educated in London, New York, and Dublin. She received a degree in English literature from Trinity College, Dublin, and has taught in Ireland and the United States. In 1976 she was elected a member of the Irish Academy of Letters and is its honorary secretary. She lives in Dublin with her husband, Irish novelist Kevin Casey, and her daughters. Besides writing for the *Irish Times* and co-authoring, with Michael MacLiammoir, *W. B. Yeats and His World*, she has published several collections of poetry: *New Territory* (1967), which won the Macaulay Fellowship in Poetry in 1968, *The War Horse* (1975), which includes translations from Irish, Russian, and German poetry, *In Her Own Image* (1980), *Introducing Eavan Boland: Poems* (1981), *Night Feed* (1982), and *The Journey* (1987).

### IT'S A WOMAN'S WORLD

Our way of life
has hardly changed
since a wheel first
whetted a knife.

Well, maybe flame
burns more greedily
and wheels are steadier
but we're the same

who milestone
our lives
with oversights—
living by the lights

of the loaf left
by the cash register,
the washing powder
paid for and wrapped,

the wash left wet.
Like most historic peoples
we are defined
by what we forget,

by what we never will be:
star-gazers,
fire-eaters.
It's our alibi

for all time
that as far as history goes
we were never
on the scene of the crime.

So when the king's head
gored its basket—
grim harvest—
we were gristing bread

or getting the recipe
for a good soup
to appetize
our gossip.

And it's still the same:
By night our windows

moth our children
to the flame

of hearth not history.
And still no page
scores the low music
of our outrage.

But appearances
still reassure:
That woman there,
craned to the starry mystery

is merely getting a breath
of evening air,
while this one here—
her mouth

a burning plume—
she's no fire-eater,
just my frosty neighbour
coming home.

## THE GLASS KING

Isabella of Bavaria married Charles VI of France in 1385. In later years his madness took the form of believing he was made from glass.

When he is ready he is raised and carried
among his vaporish plants; the palms and ferns flex;
they almost bend; you'd almost think they were going to
    kiss him;
and so they might; but she will not, his wife,

no she can't kiss the lips in case he splinters
into a million Bourbons, mad pieces.
What can she do with him—her daft prince?
His nightmares are the Regency of France.

Yes, she's been through it all, his Bavaroise,
blub-hipped and docile, urgent to be needed—
from churching to milk fever, from tongue-tied princess
to the queen of a mulish king—and now this.

They were each other's fantasy in youth.
No splintering at all about that mouth
when they were flesh and muscle, woman and man,
fire and kindling. See that silk divan?

Enough said. Now the times themselves
are his asylum: these are the Middle Ages, sweet
and savage era of the saving grace; indulgences
are two a penny; under the stonesmith's hand

stone turns into lace. I need his hand now.
Outside my window October soaks the stone;
you can hear it; you'd almost think
the brick was drinking it; the rowan drips

and history waits. Let it wait. I want
no elsewheres: the clover-smelling, stove-warm
air of Autumn catches cold; the year turns;
the leaves fall; the poem hesitates:

If we could see ourselves, not as we do—
in mirrors, self-deceptions, self-regardings—
but as we ought to be and as we have been:
poets, lute-stringers, makyres and abettors

of our necessary art, soothsayers of the ailment
and disease of our times, sweet singers,
truth tellers, intercessors for self-knowledge—
what would we think of these fin-de-siècle

half-hearted penitents we have become
at the sick-bed of the century: hand-wringing
elegists with an ill-concealed greed
for the inheritance?
My prince, demented

in a crystal past, a lost France, I elect you emblem
and ancestor of our lyric: it fits you like a glove—
doesn't it?—the part; untouchable, outlandish,
esoteric, inarticulate and out of reach

of human love: studied every day by your wife,
an ordinary honest woman out of place
in all this, wanting nothing more than the man
she married, all her sorrows in her stolid face.

## SONG

Where in blind files
Bats outsleep the frost
Water slips through stones
Too fast, too fast
For ice; afraid he'd slip
By me I asked him first.

Round as a bracelet
Clasping the wet grass,
An adder drowsed by berries
Which change blood to cess;
Dreading delay's venom
I risked the first kiss.

My skirt in my hand,
Lifting the hem high
I forded the river there;
Drops splashed my thigh.
Ahead of me at last
He turned at my cry:

"Look how the water comes
Boldly to my side;
See the waves attempt
What you have never tried."
He late that night
Followed the leaping tide.

## LACE

Bent over
the open notebook—

light fades out
making the trees stand out
and my room
at the back
of the house, dark.

In the dusk
I am still
looking for it—
the language that is

lace:

a baroque obligation
at the wrist
of a prince

in a petty court.
Look, just look
at the way he shakes out

the thriftless phrases,
the crystal rhetoric
of bobbined knots
and bosses:
a vagrant drift
of emphasis
to wave away an argument
of frame the hand
he kisses;
which, for all that, is still

what someone
in the corner
of a room,
in the dusk,
bent over
as the light was fading

lost their sight for.

## CHILD OF OUR TIME

for Aengus

Yesterday I knew no lullaby
But you have taught me overnight to order
This song, which takes from your final cry
Its tune, from your unreasoned end its reason;
Its rhythm from the discord of your murder
Its motive from the fact you cannot listen.

We who should have known how to instruct
With rhymes for your waking, rhythms for your sleep,
Names for the animals you took to bed,
Tales to distract, legends to protect,
Later an idiom for you to keep
And living, learn, must learn from you, dead.

To make our broken images rebuild
Themselves around your limbs, your broken
Image, find for your sake whose life our idle
Talk has cost, a new language. Child
Of our time, our times have robbed your cradle.
Sleep in a world your final sleep has woken.

## AN IRISH CHILDHOOD IN ENGLAND: 1951

The bickering of vowels on the buses,
the clicking thumbs and the big hips of
the navy-skirted ticket collectors with
their crooked seams brought it home to me:
Exile. Ration-book pudding.
Bowls of dripping and the fixed smile
of the school pianist playing "Iolanthe,"
"Land of Hope and Glory" and "John Peel."

I didn't know what to hold, to keep.
At night, filled with some malaise
of love for what I'd never known I had,
I fell asleep and let the moment pass.
The passing moment has become a night
of clipped shadows, freshly painted houses,
the garden eddying in dark and heat,
my children half-awake, half-asleep.

Airless, humid dark. Leaf-noise.
The stirrings of a garden before rain.
A hint of storm behind the risen moon.
We are what we have chosen. Did I choose to?—
in a strange city, in another country,
on nights in a North-facing bedroom,
waiting for the sleep that never did
restore me as I'd hoped to what I'd lost—

let the world I knew become the space
between the words that I had by heart
and all the other speech that always was
becoming the language of the country that
I came to in nineteen fifty-one:
barely-gelled, a freckled six-year-old,
overdressed and sick on the plane
when all of England to an Irish child

was nothing more than what you'd lost and how:
was the teacher in the London convent who
when I produced "I amn't" in the classroom
turned and said—"you're not in Ireland now."

## PAUL DURCAN

Paul Durcan was born in Dublin in 1944. He attended University College, Cork, where he studied archeology and history. He won the Patrick Kavanagh Award in 1974; in 1983 he toured Russia at the invitation of the Union of Soviet Writers, and in 1985 he was resident poet at The Frost Place in New Hampshire. At present he lives in Cork. His major collections of poems are *O Westport in the Light of Asia Minor* (1975), *Teresa's Bar* (1976), *Sam's Cross* (1978), *Jesus, Break His Fall* (1980), *Ark of the North* (1982), *The Selected Paul Durcan* ed. Edna Longley (1982), *Jumping the Train Tracks with Angela* (1983), *The Berlin Wall Café* (1985), and *Going Home to Russia* (1987).

### WIFE WHO SMASHED TELEVISION GETS JAIL

"She came home, my Lord, and smashed-in the television;
Me and the kids were peaceably watching Kojak
When she marched into the living-room and declared
That if I didn't turn off the television immediately
She'd put her boot through the screen;
I didn't turn it off, so instead she turned it off
—I remember the moment exactly because Kojak
After shooting a dame with the same name as my wife
Snarled at the corpse—Goodnight, Queen Maeve—
And then she took off her boots and smashed-in the
television;
I had to bring the kids round to my mother's place;

We got there just before the finish of Kojak;
(My mother has a fondness for Kojak, my Lord);
When I returned home my wife had deposited
What was left of the television into the dustbin,
Saying—I didn't get married to a television
And I don't see why my kids or anybody else's kids
Should have a television for a father or mother,
We'd be much better off all down in the pub talking
Or playing bar-billiards—
Whereupon she disappeared off back down again to the
pub."
Justice O'Brádaigh said wives who preferred bar-billiards to
family television
Were a threat to the family which was the basic unit of
society
As indeed the television itself could be said to be a basic
unit of the family
And when as in this case wives expressed their preference
in forms of violence
Jail was the only place for them. Leave to appeal was refused.

## GOING HOME TO MAYO, WINTER, 1949

Leaving behind us the alien, foreign city of Dublin
My father drove through the night in an old Ford Anglia,
His five-year-old son in the seat beside him,
The rexine seat of red leatherette,
And a yellow moon peered in through the windscreen.
"Daddy, Daddy," I cried, "Pass out the moon,"
But no matter how hard he drove he could not pass out
the moon.
Each town we passed through was another milestone
And their names were magic passwords into eternity:
Kilcock, Kinnegad, Strokestown, Elphin,
Tarmonbarry, Tulsk, Ballaghaderreen, Ballavarry;
Now we were in Mayo and the next stop was Turlough,

The village of Turlough in the heartland of Mayo,
And my father's mother's house, all oil-lamps and women,
And my bedroom over the public bar below,
And in the morning cattle-cries and cock-crows:
Life's seemingly seamless garment gorgeously rent
By their screeches and bellowings. And in the evenings
I walked with my father in the high grass down by the river
Talking with him—an unheard-of thing in the city.

But home was not home and the moon could be no more
outflanked
Than the daylight nightmare of Dublin city:
Back down along the canal we chugged into the city
And each lock-gate tolled our mutual doom;
And railings and palings and asphalt and traffic-lights,
And blocks after blocks of so-called 'new' tenements—
Thousands of crosses of loneliness planted
In the narrowing grave of the life of the father;
In the wide, wide cemetery of the boy's childhood.

## 10.30 AM MASS, JUNE 16, 1985

When the priest made his entrance on the altar on the stroke
of 10.30
He looked like a film star at an international airport
After having flown in from the other side of the world,
As if the other side of the world was the other side of the
street;
Only, instead of an overnight bag slung over his shoulder,
He was carrying the chalice in its triangular green veil—
The way a dapper comedian cloaks a dove in a silk
handkerchief.
Having kissed the altar, he strode over to the microphone:
I'd like to say how glad I am to be here with you this
morning.

Oddly, you could see quite well that he was genuinely
glad—
As if, in fact, he had been actually looking forward to this
Sunday service,
Much the way I had been looking forward to it myself;
As if, in fact, this was the big moment of his day—of his
week,
Not merely another ritual to be sanctimoniously performed.
He was a small, stocky, handsome man in his forties
With a big mop of curly grey hair
And black, horn-rimmed, tinted spectacles.
I am sure that more than half the women in the church
Fell in love with him on the spot—
Not to mention the men.
Myself, I felt like a cuddle.
The reading from the prophet Ezekiel (17:22–24)
Was a piece about cedar trees in Israel
(It's a long way from a tin of steak-and-kidney pie
For Sunday lunch in a Dublin bedsit
To cedar trees in Israel),
But the epistle was worse—

St Paul on his high horse and, as nearly always,
Putting his hoof in it—prating about "the law court of
Christ."
With the Gospel, however, things began to look up—
The parable of the mustard seed as being the kingdom of
heaven;
Now then the Homily, at best probably inoffensively
boring.
It's Father's Day—this small, solid, serious, sexy priest
began—
And I want to tell you about my own father
Because none of you knew him.
If there was one thing he liked, it was a pint of Guinness;
If there was one thing he liked more than a pint of
Guinness

It was two pints of Guinness.
But then when he was fifty-five he gave up drink.
I never knew why, but I had my suspicions.
Long after he had died my mother told me why:
He was so proud of me when I entered the seminary
That he gave up drinking as his way of thanking God.
But he himself never said a word about it to me—
He kept his secret to the end. He died from cancer
A few weeks before I was ordained a priest.
I'd like to go to Confession—he said to me:
OK—I'll go and get a priest—I said to him:
No—don't do that—I'd prefer to talk to *you*:
Dying, he confessed to me the story of his life.
How many of you here at Mass today are fathers?
I want all of you who are fathers to stand up.

Not one male in transept or aisle or nave stood up—
It was as if all the fathers in the church had been caught
 out
In the profanity of their sanctity,
In the bodily nakedness of their fatherhood,
In the carnal deed of their fathering;
Then, in ones and twos and threes, fifty or sixty of us
 clambered to our feet
And blushed to the roots of our being.
Now—declared the priest—let the rest of us
Praise these men our fathers.
He bagan to clap hands.
Gradually the congregation began to clap hands,
Until the church was ablaze with clapping hands—
Wives vying with daughters, sons with sons,
Clapping clapping clapping clapping clapping,
While I stood there in a trance, tears streaming down my
 cheeks:
Jesus!
I want to tell you about my own father
Because none of you knew him!

## BEWLEY'S ORIENTAL CAFÉ, WESTMORELAND STREET

When she asked me to keep an eye on her things
I told her I'd be glad to keep an eye on her things.
While she breakdanced off to the ladies' loo
I concentrated on keeping an eye on her things.
What are you doing?—a Security Guard growled,
His moustache gnawing at the beak of his peaked cap.
When I told him that a young woman whom I did not know
Had asked me to keep an eye on her things, he barked:
Instead of keeping an eye on the things
Of a young woman whom you do not know,
Keep an eye on your own things.
I put my two hands on his hips and squeezed him:
Look—for me the equivalent of the Easter Rising
Is to be accosted by a woman whom I do not know
And asked by her to keep an eye on her things;
On her medieval backpack and on her spaceage Walkman;
Calm down and cast aside your peaked cap
And take down your trousers and take off your shoes
And I will keep an eye on your things also.
Do we not cherish all the children of the nation equally?
That woman does not know the joy she has given me
By asking me if I would keep an eye on her things;
I feel as if I am on a Dart to Bray,
Keeping an eye on her things;
More radical than being on the pig's back,
Keeping an eye on nothing.
The Security Guard made a heap on the floor
Of his pants and shoes,
Sailing his peaked cap across the café like a frisbee.
His moustache sipped at a glass of milk.
It is as chivalrous as it is transcendental
To be sitting in Bewley's Oriental Café
With a naked Security Guard,

Keeping an eye on his things
And on old ladies
With thousands of loaves of brown bread under their
    palaeolithic oxters.

## THE TURKISH CARPET

No man could have been more unfaithful
To his wife than me;
Scarcely a day passed
That I was not unfaithful to her.
I would be in the living-room ostensibly reading or writing
When she'd come home from work unexpectedly early
And, popping her head round the door, find me
    wrapped round
A figure of despair.
It would not have been too bad if I'd been wrapped round
Another woman—that would have been infidelity of a kind
With which my wife could have coped.
What she could not cope with, try as she did,
Was the infidelity of unhope,
The personal betrayal of universal despair.
When my wife called to me from the living-room door
Tremblingly ajar, with her head peering round it,
—The paintwork studded with head wounds and
    knuckleprints—
Called to me across the red, red grass of home
—*The Turkish Carpet*—
Which her gay mother had given us as a wedding present
(And on which our children had so often played
Dolls' Houses on their hands and knees
And headstands and cartwheels and dances,
And on which we ourselves had so often made love),

I clutched my despair to my breast
And with brutality kissed it—Sweet Despair—
Staring red-eyed down at *The Turkish Carpet*.
O my dear husband, will you not be faithful to me?
Have I not given you hope all the days of my life?

## JOHN ENNIS

John Ennis was born in County Westmeath in 1944. He attended University College, Cork, and University College, Dublin. He received the Patrick Kavanagh Award for his poems in 1975 and has since won other literary awards. His poems are collected in *Night on Hibernia* (1976), *Dolmen Hill* (1977), *A Drink of Spring* (1979), and *The Burren Days* (1985). He lives with his wife and children in Waterford, where he teaches at the Regional College.

---

### MEETING AT A SALESYARD

It was a damp mild day of clinging mists that we met
In mid-winter outside Mullingar's busy Patrick Street
    Salesyard.
Coming home for Christmas from the African seminary, I
    stood in debt
On the pavement to the warmth that gripped my pen-soft
    hand hard.

I could smell the brute fear of the farm animals even on the
    street.
You asked me how I fared at College. There was no
    December sun
To light the small traffic-soiled houses. I heard the drovers
    beat

Fat stores and yearlings into the bidding ring. Your cattle
 had done

Better than you had hoped for. A mean string of coloured
 lights
Hung across the cold thoroughfare that murky salesyard day.
Cattle bawled, cowered in pens. Shopfronts blazed with
 the terraza rites
Of a small-town Christmas. Come night, our docile stock
 would be on Dublin Bay

Shipped to Liverpool. Huddled, we passed jobbers arguing
 at the gate
As the first lorry squelched by us boatward. As it went
Out, a thin trail of falling liquid dung told of the fate
Of beasts, pure terror. O drizzly sad Christmastide of
 excrement

We must wade to our knees through you yearly and the
 nightmare.
At home in the country at Coralstown the fields were still
 green.
Back in town, at the cathedral, shoppers rosaried the
 Christ-child's gentle stare
While workers hired from the Labour Pool hosed the
 salesyard clean.

## THE YEARS

### I

Waking to the clatter of hot-plate kettle
 and pan, knives and forks on the table,
The strains of Handel's *Water Music*
 jubilant above the sizzling bacon,
The poised voice of the BBC

announcing the Store Cattle Market—
I'd hear him off down in Lethe
rattle the grate of the Auburn range
Free of ashes, top up the Winetown
fire for my college-cycling breakfast,
Switch the wavelength back to Athlone.
Then he'd move out into the darkness,
be swallowed up by the sheds.

He struggled to be himself after a stroke.
Contort eased out in his right cheek
Fifteen years ago.
I wanted for nothing
Fed on his surfeit,
opted for a novitiate
Surprising hope in the aged
cruellest of all things.

O, a son in the priesthood,
the silk-gold robes
Of some romantic dream,
after five years
A different preface
was incomprehensible, voice
Anointing him with a last selfish solace
dashed at a gate pier early in May.

As we gathered in the July firing
the final trailer-load into the turf-house
He started, "Your father and mother,
we thought that maybe you'd go back."
Letting fall the turf-fork, I stumbled
across ankle-skinning stone sods
Walked away from his quiet entreaties
and in a twilight sultry with suffocation
Boarded the train out of Mullingar,
barred him from my thought.

By the next swathe-cutting, the fact
    had healed over, no great lesion
Hurt with resentment, scar.
    At August's hot cascade
Of sunny weather, we pitched the hay
    up the creaking stairs of Tom Coyne's,
Stocked the rooms with fodder for winter.
Fattening for the Sales in autumn
    cattle came, looked in the door.
Put to flight, they snatched at wisps
    curling around tall flowering thistles.

## II

Summer struggled back to us.
    Sunk in bed, he could not lift a hand
For chronic arthritis. Raw step to step
    limbering up a few inches a day
He fought to work down in the fields:
    jolted to the tillage in his armchair
Roped fast on a tractor-drawn trailer
    creels attached to stop his falling
Or "jumping" out. Neighbours
    marvelled at the load
That lurched on ruts.

Amid potatoes and beet
    he worked in bouts
At the roots of weeds
    he'd hoed all his life,
Tethered to his chair
    as easy distance away.

Once, dropping asleep,
    he fell off his armchair

Sprawled for an hour.
    No one picked up his calls,
Heard his morse grow querulous
    fagged out in the drills.

We were busy.
    We were in a far field.
No one thought to cross to his,
    ask how the work progressed.

Cows and calves eyed him
    their familiar faces dumb
Stretched across the twined thorns
    of a barbed-wire gap.

## A DRINK OF SPRING

After the sweat of swathes and the sinking madder sun
The clean-raked fields of a polychrome twilight
With cloudlets of indigo nomadic on the sky,
"A drink of spring" was my father's preface to the night.

As the youngest, I made fast the dairy-window reins,
Sent the galvanized bucket plummeting to sink first
Time, weighted with steel washers at one frost-patterned
    side.
His request was as habitual as a creaking kitchen joist.

The rope tautened for the upward pull under the damson
Tree and back-biting thorns of a never-pruned rose.
The water, laced with lime, was glacial to the dusty throat.
Mirage of the dying, it brings relief to the lips of the
    comatose.

Cups furred with cold I handed round the open-door fireless
Kitchen. The taste on my lips was lingering like a first kiss.

## RICHARD RYAN

Richard Ryan was born in Dublin in 1946 and educated at University College, Dublin, where he received an M.A. degree in Anglo-Irish literature in 1970. He worked at a variety of jobs in Europe and traveled throughout the United States giving poetry readings and lectures. From 1972 to 1973 he taught in the English Department at University College, Dublin, and completed a study of the Irish novelist, Liam O'Flaherty. He joined the Irish foreign service in 1973 and lived for several years in Japan with his Korean wife, Hyun Heeun. He is at present attached to the Irish Embassy in London. He has two collections of poetry, *Ledges* (1970) and *Ravenswood* (1973), as well as many articles and poems in American and Irish magazines.

### IRELAND

That ragged
leaking raft held
between sea and sea

its long
forgotten cable melting
into deeper darkness where,

at the root
of it, the slow
sea circles and chews.

Nightly the dark-
ness lands like hands
to mine downwards, springing

tiny leaks
till dawn finds
field is bog, bog lake.

## FROM MY LAI THE THUNDER WENT WEST

and it all died down
to an underground
tapping and then that,
too, stopped dead.

In cornfield, wheat
field, a black
sheet of earth
was drawn neatly

across the seed
they planted.
And the fields turn
daily to the sun.

Come high Summer
and the first shoots
will appear, puzzling
the sun as, growing

through earth, growing
through grass, the
human crop they have sown—
child bone, wife

bone, man
bone will stand

wavering in the pale fields:
the silent, eye-

less army will
march west through
Autumn and Europe
until, streaked

with December rain
they will stand in
New York and Texas;
as the lights click

out across America
they will fence in
the houses, tapping
on window, tapping

on door. Till
dawn, then rain only:
from sea to sea drifting,
drops of bright ruby.

## A WET NIGHT

Panes of light cracking
Over Aran, all
Day along the cliffs
An unseasonal booming,

But the widow
Connemara with her head
In the clouds lay,
Dreaming of salvation.

An Act of God it was
Surely—all night

Splayed, trampled
She was, hair flying

In the branches, the
Brute Atlantic wave
After wave over
Her, bony legs of

Hedges unlocking,
Fields flowing
Through, a black tide
Turf and potatoes

Cows like whales
Sailing, the swaying
Churches rooted in
Bone tugging and

Straining to be
Away, graveyards
Awash, their full
Cargoes of believers

Shifting and sliding,
Crates spilling, a mess
No angel will untangle
As delirious crows

Tumbled for tit-
Bits; a last mighty
Thrust just before
Dawn, the exhausted

Ocean sliding back
To show her sleeping
Shores aglow under
Its receding inches.

## HUGH MAXTON

Hugh Maxton (the pseudonym of W. J. McCormack) was born in 1947 in Dublin. He attended Wesley College, Dublin, then worked in a city bookshop for several years before entering Trinity College, Dublin, where he read General Studies (English, history, and philosophy). After graduating from Trinity in 1971, he was appointed to a lectureship in Anglo-Irish literature at the New University of Ulster. In 1974 he moved to England, where he taught at the University of Leeds. Since then he has taught at several American universities. He now lives in Dublin with his wife and son. Maxton's published collections of poetry include *Stones* (1970), *The Noise of the Fields* (1976), a Poetry Book Society Choice, *Jubilee for Renegades* (1982), and *At the Protestant Museum* (1986). Maxton has also done translations from the Russian of Joseph Brodsky and from the German of Johannes Bobrowski. As W. J. McCormack, he is author of *Ascendancy and Tradition in Anglo-Irish Literary History from 1789 to 1939* (1985).

### CERNUNNOS

Cernunnos, gymnast or god,
crossed his side at Clonmacnois.
Insidious and slipping
from the girdle he lingers
barely.
Once he was allwhere
when he nurtured animals
from his thighs, a helpful wolf.

Fecund one, no warrior
speared so many. None could call
you a squatter for, always
agile, you peopled the first
dawning of darkness that called
you a devilish helper.
Yet undisputed master
you remained relegated
thus; antlers your emblem.

The world grew wider and slack
and your subtle potency
went out of favour falling
foul between the coarser saints.
Censured, you crept underground.

"Dance your dance now, my little
man," they cried. And you lay down
in a bog to coddle them,
curing your codpiece and ram.
Modest, impeccable you
took your serpents by the neck.
And your feet turned in, your ears
reddened with obituaries.

## WAKING

in memory of my father, died November 1960

Someone is breathing in the room
apart from me. It is my father;
I recognise the hiss of his nostrils
closing, closing. . . . It is late;
he is doing Milltown work,
we can use the extra money.

That stub in his hand is a rent book
high as a bible, thin as his widow.
Below it, in the shadow, I imagine
the soft metal of his heart
(a gold cog, slipping) finally burred,
refusing to bite. For my life
I cannot picture him; details
melt into light. The angle
of his nose, the slight furrow
of moustache escape me. All I have
is that sound fathered in darkness
carrying a reek of tobacco-y linen,
the taste of his lip.
                                        He rustles
like a curtain. Outside it is six a.m.
A sudden fleet of cars passes
drowning my breath for about the length
of a funeral. This has gone on ten years.

## AT THE PROTESTANT MUSEUM

### I

I'm getting used to not understanding.
Underpasses chorus my migration.
Words turn to music on the landing
by my room and pantry, my exotic ration.

Enough is riches. Rare beef and cabbage
translated gravely on learned menus
I take and eat. On average
I list necessity with the virtues.

Mild days mounting to become January;
the feminine rhymes distress
a calendar at once full and free.
Time passes to make the future less.

Hus and Melancthon and Luther
thumbed the pages of my testing youth.
We hardly knew them, and yet thought them blessed.
We were the chosen of a king's protest.

The kiss of privilege, favours of the poor,
jokes we could afford, all this and more
we managed faithfully. We did not hear
a travelling preacher's echo—"history stops here."

## II

"I, Dr Luther, declare
that to my dear
and faithful wife Kate,
for her own support
or (as is usual)
for her entire use and disposal
I bequeath firstly:
a small property
at Fulsdorf
which I bought and restored . . .

I have not used
legal expression
(and for good reason)
I really am
namely under heaven
and earth and even in hell,
a well-known, just
and respected judge

whose word no
notary profiscal
will budge."

## III

This is the testimony of the pastor-lieutenant:

> "He asked me to go to his wife when the situation improves, and tell her to have his corpse exhumed for burial at Tarpa in the Calvinist cemetery, there being no Lutheran.
>
> He asked for some alcohol. He mixed wine from the chalice with brandy a soldier brought. And he drank it.
>
> Then he had diarrhoea, and asked me to leave him by himself. Some minutes later, he asked me to come in again. He asked me to give an account of his last hours to his wife. At that, the soldier faltered and kissed the hand of Bajcsy-Zsilinszky.
>
> Only after it was over was I ordered to the place of execution. I wasn't allowed to bless his ashes as he was taken for burial."

## IV

History stops here.
The curator wipes up the takings
and closes the shop,
goes home and lights the stove,
smiles in the mirror
with unsuspected gold.
She is a treasure,
she is a treasure of the Lord.

History stops here.
In a back-flip the mind
reverts home
to the sheds and attics,
power drills,
and farm buildings.
Security, the home rules,
the years of promise,
the power drills,
the secret police of majesty's
Parachute Regiment
under the chairmanship of the lord
Widgery. *Fidei defensor*,
retain the tongue
proclaimed, pack the museums.

History stops here,
with the retrospective
muse of parliament.
The favours of the poor,
mild day with neighbours.

## V

Prepared now to stop in the Metro
I pray at your station, Bajcsy-Zsilinszky.
Strangeness abates strangeness, can undo
pride that speaks of death with dignity.

An abstracted sceptic weeping red tears,
caught the distance between word and image,
caught in the schism between home and fear,
caught up in the mere oneness of an age.

Pray for the soul of Bajcsy-Zsilinszky.

Pray for the soul of Lieutenant Shepherd.

Pray for the soul of Hunter Gowan who a week prior to the late insurrection cut with his sword the finger off a papish to whisk his punch as true huntsmen do with the fox's brush.

Pray for the soul of Christ in whom all things begin.

## FRANK ORMSBY

Frank Ormsby was born in County Fermanagh, Northern Ireland, in 1947 and graduated from Queen's University, Belfast, with an M.A. degree in English. He is head of the English Department at the Royal Belfast Academical Institution and lives in Belfast with his wife and two children. In 1974 he won the Eric Gregory Award for Poetry and in 1979 a prize in England's National Poetry Competition. His first volume, *A Store of Candles*, was published in 1977 and was a Poetry Book Society Choice. His second book, *A Northern Spring* (1986), is also a Poetry Book Society Choice. He is editor of *The* Honest Ulsterman, the anthology *Poets from the North of Ireland* (1979), and *Northern Windows: An Anthology of Ulster Autobiography* (1987).

---

### ORNAMENTS

My mother's Council house is occupied
By ornaments. On all flat surfaces
The delft hens roost. Hunched and malignant-eyed
The red dwarfs squat on the mantelpiece,
And panniered donkeys draw their nostrils wide
On mouths that sparkle. The brass bells increase
In cunning mirrors and glass-backed cases.

This the extravagance she must have known
And hoarded in a house where stretching legs
Was luxury, a plaster dog the lone

Flourish that space allowed her. Now she thrives
On detail. For each dog a plaster bone;
The dwarfs have Snow White sweetening their lives;
And today the delft hens have laid delft eggs.

## SPOT THE BALL

Once, with a certain pride, we kept attempts
To the minimum. Reason was all:
To trace invisibly the upraised eyes
Of backs and forwards; where the lines converged
To plant our crosses.

Later we combed the stand advertisements
For smudged lettering, or held the thin page
Up to the light to test for shadow.
Those paler patches, blotches near the goal
Could well be erasions.

And, later still, the joking nonchalance,
The stray marks in all the wrong places,
Floodlights and flags and corners that the teams
Had turned their backs on. Even the goalie's crutch
Was not immune.

Four years now and never on the right end
Of a Snowball. Thursday's edition tells
Of prizes bound for places elsewhere.
The "Belfast man who requests no publicity"
Is always another.

We persevere from habit. When we try
These days our hope's mechanical, we trust
To accident. We are selective
No longer, the full hundred crosses
Filling the sky.

FRANK ORMSBY

## INTERIM

Five years ago we knew such ecstasies
As who in half-dead countrysides find strong
The least life stirring;
We sang first lines and thought we had learned the song.

Six months of marriage sobered us. We found,
Not disenchantment, more a compromise
Charged with affection.
We settled to the limited surprise

That day-to-day insists on, brought to bear
A tact to manage by, a quiet light
That gave its own warmth,
And knew our walking grown to sudden flight

When least expected. O, I loved those years
Of unforced loving, when the urge to stray
Was lulled to sleeping,
And hearth and kitchen sink were nothing grey.

Now, once again, I notice carefree girls
In streets, on buses. Tied, I can't but see
Their untried promise,
All the lost futures catching up with me.

The nerve to be unfaithful is the lack
That curbs my yearnings. Soon again I'm sure,
And pleased to be,
Of trusting wife, my own furniture.

What binds us, love? I struggle to define
Its shifting substance. What strange seeds are met
Within us, fashion there in our despite
This hybrid, half-contentment, half-regret?

Tonight, uncertain if the dreams have cracked,
Let's seek behind the possible illusions
How much is gone, how much remains intact;
Let's talk of change and come to no conclusions.

## SURVIVORS

Sometimes they cross an avenue at dusk,
those hoarse-voiced children brashly on the move
from mews to alley.
                    Mostly they seem too young
to keep such hours and underdressed for air
that cuts its teeth on glass and barbed-wire coils,
the rusted nails of half-wrecked garages.

Rooting behind our lives for what they can find—
the bones of broken telephones, old cars
picked bare already to their oiliest springs,
dead spars along the embankment—they hug their loads
of chosen bric-à-brac and, blindly assured,
ignite with purposes: to float an ark
or point a bonfire, angle a sheet of tin
against a brick coalhouse and call it home,
or call it a tree-house.
                    As they flit from view,
their voices sack the twilight.
Their track is a littered silence where they resound.

## from A NORTHERN SPRING

Some of us stayed forever, under the lough
in the guts of a Flying Fortress,
sealed in the buckled capsule, or dispersed

with odds and ends—propellers, dogtags, wings,
a packet of Lucky Strike, the instructor's gloves—
through an old world of shells and arrowheads,
dumped furniture, a blind Viking prow.
In ten years or a hundred we will rise
to foul your nets with crushed fuselage.
Our painted stork, nosing among the reeds
with a bomb in its beak, will startle you for a day.

## AT THE JAFFÉ MEMORIAL FOUNTAIN, BOTANIC GARDENS

### I

Lipman and Cohen, butchers, Hercules Lane,
Manuel Lightfoot, Smithfield, 'taylor and Jew.'
Names in the old leases, gone to ground
since the year the first sailing ships from Europe
breezed up the lough.

Wolff, Jaffé, Weinberg, purposeful merchant Jews
of Hamburg and Jessnitz. Later the refugees
on sleepless treks from places where they had grown
and spoke the language,
who improvised a style of making do
from trunks and travelling bags and the will to prosper.

### II

What might they leave their children,
the dead Jews of Lübeck, Lublin,
packed in Antrim clay?

Faith and unhappy memories?
The desert flower that blooms after loss,
its red heart colouring obstinately against the urge,
insistent, inward, of the petals' bordering dark:
griefs not to be assuaged, the carrier blood's
murmur of vengeance?

## III

A wind off the Lagan strays across open ground
at the Jaffé Memorial Fountain.
Half summerhouse, half temple, a room without walls,
its tenants river-smells, in-transit birds,
the dung-and-sawdust ghost of the Circus Hofmann
on a European Tour,
it stands for the ones who earned their monuments
and the ones whose lives were quiet streams hidden
for centuries in the foundations.
I think of dispersals, settlings, the random inheritors
of dispossession who kept an image of home;
of Solly Lipsitz walking his labrador
in the streets of South Belfast,
Chaim Herzog's birthplace on the Cliftonville Road.

## CIARAN CARSON

Ciaran Carson was born in 1948 in Belfast. He was educated at Queen's University, Belfast; he is Traditional Arts Officer for the Arts Council of Northern Ireland. His work has been published in numerous magazines and anthologies. *The New Estate* (1976) was his first major collection of poetry, *The Irish For No* (1987) his second. He is also author of *The Pocket Guide to Irish Traditional Music* (1986).

### THE INSULAR CELTS

Having left solid ground behind
In the hardness of their place-names,
They have sailed out for an island:

As along the top of a wood
Their boats have crossed the green ridges,
So has the pale sky overhead

Appeared as a milky surface,
A white plain where the speckled fish
Drift in lamb-white clouds of fleece.

They will come back to the warm earth
And call it by possessive names—
Thorned rose, love, woman and mother;

To hard hills of stone they will give
The words for breast; to meadowland,
The soft gutturals of rivers,

Tongues of water; to firm plains, flesh,
As one day we will discover
Their way of living, in their death.

They entered their cold beds of soil
Not as graves, for this was the land
That they had fought for, loved, and killed

Each other for. They'd arrive again:
Death could be no horizon
But the shoreline of their island,

A coming and going, as flood
Comes after ebb. In the spirals
Of their brooches is seen the flight

Of one thing into the other:
As the wheels-ruts on a battle-
Plain have filled with silver water,

The confused circles of their wars,
Their cattle-raids, have worked themselves
To a laced pattern of old scars.

But their death, since it is no real
Death, will happen over again
And again, their bones will seem still

To fall in the hail beneath hooves
Of horses, their limbs will drift down
As the branches that trees have loosed.

We cannot yet say why or how
They could not take things as they were.
Some day we will learn of how

Their bronze swords took the shape of leaves,
How their gold spears are found in cornfields,
Their arrows are found in trees.

## THE CAR CEMETERY

On winter nights
the cars bring in snow from the hills,
their bonnets white
above a wide cold smile of chromium.

From miles away
I see you coming in, a distant star
gone out of line, swaying
down from the road to take the thin lane

towards the house,
till my warm light and your cold are married,
your solitary noise
is lost among the rushing of the wind.

All around the world
there is a graveyard of defunct bodies,
wide smiles curled
in sleep. The cars at every door are hushed

beneath a soft corrosion—
robed in white, these brides of silence
whose heaven
is like ours, a detritus of lights.

## IT USED TO BE

If there was a house with three girls in it,
It only took three boys to make a dance.
You'd see a glimmer where McKeown's once was
And follow it till it became a house.
But maybe they'd have gone on, up the hill
To Loughran's, or made across the grazing,
Somewhere else. All those twistings and turnings,
Crossroads and dirt roads and skittery lanes:
You'd be glad to get in from the dark.

And when you did get in, there'd be a power
Of poteen. A big tin creamery churn,
A ladle, those mugs with blue and white bars.
Oh, good and clear like the best of water.
The music would start up. This one ould boy
Would sit by the fire and rosin away,
Sawing and sawing till it fell like snow.
That poteen was quare stuff. At the end of
The night you might be fiddling with no bow.

When everyone was ready, out would come
The tin of Tate and Lyle's Golden Syrup,
A spoon or a knife, a big farl of bread.
Some of those same boys wouldn't bother with
The way you were supposed to screw it up.
There might be courting going on outside,
Whisperings and cacklings in the barnyard;
A spider thread of gold-thin syrup
Trailed out across the glowing kitchen tiles
Into the night of promises, or broken promises.

## DRESDEN

Horse Boyle was called Horse Boyle because of his brother
Mule;
Though why Mule was called Mule is anybody's guess. I
stayed there once,
Or rather, I nearly stayed there once. But that's another story.
At any rate they lived in this decrepit caravan, not two
miles out of Carrick,
Encroached upon by baroque pyramids of empty baked bean
tins, rusts
And ochres, hints of autumn merging into twilight. Horse
believed
They were as good as a watchdog, and to tell you the truth
You couldn't go near the place without something falling over:
A minor avalanche would ensue—more like a shop bell, really,

The old-fashioned ones on string, connected to the latch,
I think,
And as you entered in, the bell would tinkle in the empty
shop, a musk
Of soap and turf and sweets would hit you from the gloom.
Tobacco.
Baling wire. Twine. And, of course, shelves and pyramids
of tins.
An old woman would appear from the back—there was a
sizzling pan in there,
Somewhere, a whiff of eggs and bacon—and ask you what
you wanted;
Or rather, she wouldn't ask; she would talk about the
weather. It had rained
That day, but it was looking better. They had just put in
the spuds.
I had only come to pass the time of day, so I bought a
token packet of Gold Leaf.

All this time the fry was frying away. Maybe she'd a
daughter in there
Somewhere, though I hadn't heard the neighbours talk of
it; if anybody knew,
It would be Horse. Horse kept his ears to the ground.
And he was a great man for current affairs; he owned the
only TV in the place.
Come dusk he'd set off on his rounds, to tell the whole
townland the latest
Situation in the Middle East, a mortar bomb attack in
Mullaghbawn—
The damn things never worked, of course—and so he'd tell
the story
How in his young day it was very different. Take young Flynn,
for instance,
Who was ordered to take this bus and smuggle some
sticks of gelignite

Across the border, into Derry, when the RUC—or was it
the RIC?—
Got wind of it. The bus was stopped, the peeler stepped on.
Young Flynn
Took it like a man, of course: he owned up right away.
He opened the bag
And produced the bomb, his rank and serial number. For
all the world
Like a pound of sausages. Of course, the thing was, the
peeler's bike
Had got a puncture, and he didn't know young Flynn
from Adam. All he wanted
Was to get home for his tea. Flynn was in for seven years
and learned to speak
The best of Irish. He had thirteen words for a cow in heat;
A word for the third thwart in a boat, the wake of a boat
on the ebb tide.

He knew the extinct names of insects, flowers, why this
place was called
Whatever: *Carrick*, for example, was *a rock*. He was damn
right there—
As the man said, *When you buy meat you buy bones, when
you buy land you buy stones.*
You'd be hard put to find a square foot in the whole bloody
parish
That wasn't thick with flints and pebbles. To this day he
could hear the grate
And scrape as the spade struck home, for it reminded him
of broken bones:
Digging a graveyard, maybe—or better still, trying to dig a
reclaimed tip
Of broken delph and crockery ware—you know that sound
that sets your teeth on edge
When the chalk squeaks on the blackboard, or you shovel
ashes from the stove?

Master McGinty—he'd be on about McGinty then, and
discipline, the capitals
Of South America, Moore's *Melodies*, the Battle of
Clootarf, and
*Tell me this, an educated man like you: What goes on four
legs when it's young,*
*Two legs when it's grown up, and three legs when it's old?* I'd
pretend
I didn't know. McGinty's leather strap would come up
then, stuffed
With threepenny bits to give it weight and sting. Of course,
it never did him
Any harm: *You could take a horse to water but you couldn't
make him drink.*
He himself was nearly going on to be a priest.
*And many's the young cub left the school, as wise as when he
came.*

Carrowkeel was where McGinty came from—
*Narrow Quarter*, Flynn explained—
Back before the Troubles, a place that was so mean and crabbed,
Horse would have it, men were known to eat their dinner from a drawer.
Which they'd slide shut the minute you'd walk in.
He'd demonstrate this at the kitchen table, hunched and furtive, squinting
Out the window—past the teetering minarets of rust, down the hedge-dark aisle—
To where a stranger might appear, a passer-by, or what was maybe worse,
Someone he knew. Someone who wanted something. Someone who was hungry.
Of course who should come tottering up the lane that instant but his brother

Mule. I forgot to mention they were twins. They were as like as two—
No, not peas in a pod, for this is not the time nor the place to go into
Comparisons, and this is really Horse's story, Horse who—now I'm getting
Round to it—flew over Dresden in the war. He'd emigrated first, to
Manchester. Something to do with scrap—redundant mill machinery,
Giant flywheels, broken looms that would, eventually, be ships, or aeroplanes.
He said he wore his fingers to the bone.
And so, on impulse, he had joined the RAF. He became a rear gunner.
Of all the missions, Dresden broke his heart. It reminded him of china.

As he remembered it, long afterwards, he could hear, or
almost hear
Between the rapid desultory thunderclaps, a thousand
tinkling echoes—
All across the map of Dresden, store-rooms full of china
shivered, teetered
And collapsed, an avalanche of porcelain, slushing and
cascading: cherubs,
Shepherdesses, figurines of Hope and Peace and Victory,
delicate bone fragments.
He recalled in particular a figure from his childhood, a
milkmaid
Standing on the mantelpiece. Each night as they knelt
down for the rosary,
His eyes would wander up to where she seemed to beckon
to him, smiling,
Offering him, eternally, her pitcher of milk, her mouth of
rose and cream.

One day, reaching up to hold her yet again, his fingers
stumbled, and she fell.
He lifted down a biscuit tin, and opened it.
It breathed an antique incense: things like pencils, snuff,
tobacco.
His war medals. A broken rosary. And there, the milkmaid's
creamy hand, the outstretched
Pitcher of milk, all that survived. Outside, there was a
scraping
And a tittering; I knew Mule's step by now, his careful
drunken weaving
Through the tin-stacks. I might have stayed the night, but
there's no time
To go back to that now; I could hardly, at any rate, pick
up the thread.
I wandered out through the steeples of rust, the gate that
was a broken bed.

## BELFAST CONFETTI

Suddenly as the riot squad moved in, it was raining
exclamation marks,
Nuts, bolts, nails, car-keys. A fount of broken type.
And the explosion
Itself—an asterisk on the map. This hyphenated line, a
burst of rapid fire . . .
I was trying to complete a sentence in my head, but it
kept stuttering,
All the alleyways and side-streets blocked with stops and
colons.

I know this labyrinth so well—Balaclava, Raglan, Inkerman,
Odessa Street—
Why can't I escape? Every move is punctuated. Crimea
Street. Dead end again.
A Saracen, Kremlin-2 mesh. Makrolon face-shields.
Walkie-talkies. What is
My name? Where am I coming from? Where am I going?
A fusillade of question-marks.

## CAMPAIGN

They had questioned him for hours. Who exactly was he?
And when
He told them, they questioned him again. When they
accepted who he was, as
Someone not involved, they pulled out his fingernails.
Then
They took him to a waste-ground somewhere near the
Horseshoe Bend, and told him
What he was. They shot him nine times.

A dark umbilicus of smoke was rising from a heap of
burning tyres.
The bad smell he smelt was the smell of himself. Broken
glass and knotted Durex.
The knuckles of a face in a nylon stocking. I used to see
him in the Gladstone Bar,
Drawing pints for strangers, his almost-perfect fingers
flecked with scum.

## TOM PAULIN

Tom Paulin was born in 1949 in Leeds. He grew up in Belfast, attending secondary school there before returning to England where he went to university at Hull and Oxford. He won an Eric Gregory Award in 1976 and a Somerset Maugham Award in 1978. His collections of poetry are *A State of Justice* (1977), *The Strange Museum* (1980), *Liberty Tree* (1983), and *Fivemile Town* (1987). He is a director of the Field Day Theatre Company, which published his pamphlet *A New Look at the Language Question* (1983) and produced his play *The Riot Act* (1985), a version of Sophocles' *Antigone*. Paulin teaches English at the University of Nottingham and has been a visiting professor at the University of Virginia. He is also author of *Thomas Hardy: The Poetry of Perception* (1975), *Ireland and the English Crisis* (1985), and editor of *The Faber Book of Political Verse* (1986). (Photo by Whiteman Studios, Nottingham.)

### UNDER THE EYES

Its retributions work like clockwork
Along murdering miles of terrace-houses
Where someone is saying, "I am angry,
I am frightened, I am justified.
Every favour, I must repay with interest,
Any slight against myself, the least slip,
Must be balanced out by an exact revenge."

The city is built on mud and wrath.
Its weather is predicted; its streetlamps
Light up in the glowering, crowded evenings.
Time-switches, ripped from them, are clamped
To sticks of sweet, sweating explosive.
All the machinery of a state
Is a set of scales that squeezes out blood.

Memory is just, too. A complete system
Nothing can surprise. The dead are recalled
From schoolroom afternoons, the hill quarries
Echoing blasts over the secured city;
Or, in a private house, a Judge
Shot in his hallway before his daughter
By a boy who shut his eyes as his hand tightened.

A rain of turds; a pair of eyes; the sky and tears.

## SURVEILLANCES

In the winter dusk
You see the prison camp
With its blank watchtowers;
It is as inevitable
As the movement of equipment
Or the car that carries you
Towards a violent district.

In the violet light
You watch a helicopter
Circling above the packed houses,
A long beam of light
Probing streets and waste ground.
All this might be happening
Underwater.

And if you would swop its functions
For a culture of bungalows
And light verse,
You know this is one
Of the places you belong in,
And that its public uniform
Has claimed your service.

## THE IMPOSSIBLE PICTURES

In this parable of vengeance
There is a grey newsreel
Being shown inside my head.

What happens is that Lenin's brother
(Aleksandr Ulyanov)
Is being led to execution.

He carries a small book
Wrapped in a piece of cloth.
Is it the Bible or a text

His brother will be forced to write?
He twists it in his hands.
I think he is frightened.

I am wrong, because suddenly
He strikes an officer on the face—
His gestures now are a jerking

Clockwork anachronism.
He is goosestepped to the scaffold.
The frozen yard of the prison

Is like this dawn of rain showers
And heavy lorries, a gull mewling
In its dream of the Atlantic.

Ah, I say, this is Ireland
And my own place, myself.
I see a Georgian rectory

Square in the salt winds
Above a broken coast,
And the sea-birds scattering

Their chill cries: I know
That every revenge is nature,
Always on time, like the waves.

## AND WHERE DO YOU STAND ON THE NATIONAL QUESTION?

> Told him the shortest way to Tara
> was via Holyhead.
> *Stephen Dedalus*

Apple-blossom, a great spread of it
above our heads.
This blue morning a new visitor
is laidback on a deckchair;
he's civil and clever,
a flinty mandarin
being entertained, like an oxymoron,
in this walled garden.
*Ecco* two glasses of young wine
 . . . *et on mange des asperges.*
I imagine him
as the state's intelligence,
a lean man in a linen suit

who has come to question me
for picking up a pen
and taking myself a shade seriously.
"Paisley's plain tongue, his cult
of Bunyan and blood
in blind dumps like Doagh and Boardmills—
that's the enemy."
I've an answer ready in the sun
but my eye tines the grass
for a tiny mound of soil:
the mole works underground,
a blind glove
that gropes the earth and cannot love.
"Your Lagan Jacobins, they've gone
with *The Northern Star*. I've heard
Hewitt and Heaney trace us back
to the Antrim weavers—
I can't come from *that*."
"Why not, though? Isn't there
this local stir in us all?—
flick of the thumb, a word's relish,
the clitoral tick of an accent,
wee lick of spit or lovejuice?
I'd call that a brave kindness."
Then a journey blows back at me—
rust-orange and green,
the Enterprise scudding north
past the brown burn of whin and bracken
till it halts and waits for clearance
under the gourly vigilance
of a corrie in bandit country—
"That's where the god, Autochthon,
is crossed by the hangman's rope."
He counters with a short fiction
called *Molyneaux's Last Hope*.
"These islands are stepping-stones
to a metropolitan home,

an archipelago that's strung
between America and Europe."
"So you're a band of Orange dandies?
Oscar in Père-Lachaise with a sash on?"
"Well, not exactly . . . that's unfair—
like my saying it's a green mess you're after."
"I want a form that's classic and secular,
the risen *République*,
a new song for a new constitution—
wouldn't you rather have that
than stay loose, baggy and British?
You don't *have* to fall back
on Burke and the Cruiser,
on a batty style
and slack o'whoozy emotion."
We hit a pause like a ramp,
shrug and mark time
before we guess the design
of life after Prior:
the last civil servant
is dropping over from Whitehall.
Call him Sir Peregrine Falkland;
he's a bit thick—not a high-flyer—
but he'll do the trick.

## DESERTMARTIN

At noon, in the dead centre of a faith,
Between Draperstown and Magherafelt,
This bitter village shows the flag
In a baked absolute September light.
Here the Word has withered to a few
Parched certainties, and the charred stubble
Tightens like a black belt, a crop of Bibles.

Because this is the territory of the Law
I drive across it with a powerless knowledge—
The owl of Minerva in a hired car.
A Jock squaddy glances down the street
And grins, happy and expendable,
Like a brass cartridge. He is a useful thing,
Almost at home, and yet not quite, not quite.

It's a limed nest, this place. I see a plain
Presbyterian grace sour, then harden,
As a free strenuous spirit changes
To a servile defiance that whines and shrieks
For the bondage of the letter: it shouts
For the Big Man to lead his wee people
To a clean white prison, their scorched tomorrow.

Masculine Islam, the rule of the Just,
Egyptian sand dunes and geometry,
A theology of rifle-butts and executions:
These are the places where the spirit dies.
And now, in Desertmartin's sandy light,
I see a culture of twigs and bird-shit
Waving a gaudy flag it loves and curses.

## BLACK BREAD

for Ann Pasternak Slater

Splitting birches, spiky thicket, kinship—
this is the passionate, the phonic surface
I can take only on trust, like a character
translated to a short story whose huge language
he doesn't know. So we break black bread
in the provinces and can't be certain
what it is we're missing, or what sacrament

this might be, the loaf wrapped in a shirt-tail
like a prisoner's secret or a caked ikon,
that is sour and good, and has crossed over versts,
kilometres, miles. It's those journeys
tholed under the salt stars, in the eager wind
that starves sentries and students in their long coats.
Claudius is on the phone, hear that hard
accent scraping its boots on the threshold,
his thick acid voice in your uncle's conscience,
*I'd have known better how to defend my friend.*
Bitter! Bitter! Bitter! the wedding-guests chant
in bast sandals, the pickled cucumbers
cry out in a prickly opera and round grains
of coriander stud the desert crust.
It's a lump of northern peat, itself alone,
and kin to the black earth, to shaggy speech;
I'll taste it on my tongue next year in the holy,
freed city of gold and parchment.

## MEDBH McGUCKIAN

Medbh McGuckian was born in Belfast in 1950. She graduated from Queen's University with B.A. and M.A. degrees in English. She lives and teaches in Belfast. Her poems won the Poetry Society Competition in 1979 and the Eric Gregory Award in 1980. Her work has been published in pamphlets, in anthologies, and in several collections: *The Flower Master* (1982), which won the Poetry Society's Alice Hunt-Bartlett Award, *Venus and the Rain* (1984), and *On Ballycastle Beach* (1988). She is writer-in-residence at Queen's University.

### MR. McGREGOR'S GARDEN

Some women save their sanity with needles.
I complicate my life with studies
Of my favourite rabbit's head, his vulgar volatility,
Or a little ladylike sketching
Of my resident toad in his flannel box;
Or search for handsome fungi for my tropical
Herbarium, growing dry-rot in the garden,
And wishing that the climate were kinder,
Turning over the spiky purple heads among the moss
With my cheese-knife to view the slimy veil.

Unlike the cupboard-love of sleepers in the siding,
My hedgehog's sleep is under his control
And not the weather's; he can rouse himself
At half-an-hour's notice in the frost, or leave at will
On a wet day in August, by the hearth.
He goes by breathing slowly, after a large meal,
A lively evening, very cross if interrupted,
And returns with a hundred respirations
To the minute, weak and nervous when he wakens,
Busy with his laundry.

On sleepless nights while learning
Shakespeare off by heart,
I feel that Bunny's at my bedside
In a white cotton nightcap,
Tickling me with his whiskers.

## THE MAST YEAR

Some kinds of trees seem ever eager
To populate new ground, the oak or pine.
Though beech can thrive on many soils
And carve itself an empire, its vocation
Is gentler; it casts a shade for wildflowers
Adapted to the gloom, which feed
Like fungus on its rot of bedstraw leaves.

It makes an awkward neighbour, as the birch
Does, that lashes out in gales, and fosters
Intimacy with toadstools, till they sleep
In the benevolence of each other's smells,
Never occupying many sites for long:
The thin red roots of alder vein
The crumbled bank, the otter's ruptured door.

Bee-keepers love the windbreak sycamore,
The twill of hanging flowers that the beech
Denies the yew—its waking life so long
It lets the stylish beechwood
Have its day, as winded oaks
Lay store upon their Lammas growth,
The thickening of their dreams.

## THE FOLK MUSEUM

You would not say to children,
Arriving at "The Mother's Cottage,"
This is where the old doll
Was put to grass or left
By her family to die, and
The old boy in his official
Green blazer and tie
Had a delicate way of expressing it.
Rita however remembered
The three-bedroomed house we had just left,
And its gleaming china.
The window, he said, was small because of the taxes,
She didn't mind
The loss of space or having to make way
For the young wife, she was happy
With the wheel in the corner,
The stone before the door.
Alison fingered her bag-apron, hanging on its nail,
And Mary Rose her heavy wooden porringer:
Fionnuala tested the sagging bed in the alcove,
Her bare legs shining in the turf-fire light.
The man's eyes glinted in his smoke-brown face,
As we bustled out, and left him to his story.

MEDBH McGUCKIAN

# THE DREAM-LANGUAGE OF FERGUS

## I

Your tongue has spent the night
In its dim sack as the shape of your foot
In its cave. Not the rudiment
Of half a vanquished sound,
The excommunicated shadow of a name,
Has rumpled the sheets of your mouth.

## II

So Latin sleeps, they say, in Russian speech,
So one river inserted into another
Becomes a leaping, glistening, splashed
And scattered alphabet
Jutting out from the voice,
Till what began as a dog's bark
Ends with bronze, what began
With honey ends with ice;
As if an aeroplane in full flight
Launched a second plane,
The sky is stabbed by their exits
And the mistaken meaning of each.

## III

Conversation is as necessary
Among these families campus trees
As the apartness of torches,
And if I am a threader
Of double-stranded words, whose
Quando has grown into now,

No text can return the honey
In its path of light from a jar,
Only a seed-fund, a pendulum,
Pressing out the diasporic snow.

## COLERIDGE

In a dream he fled the house
At the Y of three streets.
To where a roof of bloom lay hidden
In the affectation of the night,
As only the future can be. Very tightly,
Like a seam, she nursed the gradients
Of his poetry in her head,
She got used to its movements like
A glass bell being struck
With a padded hammer.
It was her own fogs and fragrances
That crawled into the verse, the
Impression of cold braids finding
Radiant escape, as if each stanza
Were a lamp that burned between
Their beds, or they were writing
The poems in a place of birth together.
Quietened by drought, his breathing
Just became audible where a little
Silk-mill emptied impetuously into it,
Some word that grew with him as a child's
Arm or leg. If she stood up, easy,
Easy, it was the warmth that finally
Leaves the golden pippin for the
Cider or the sunshine of fallen trees.

## PETER FALLON

Peter Fallon was born in Germany of Irish parents in 1951. He has lived in Ireland since 1957. He grew up on a farm in County Meath. Since he graduated from Trinity College, Dublin, in 1975, he has divided his time between farming in Meath and serving as editor and publisher of the Gallery Press in Dublin. Fallon's poems have been published in *Coincidence of Flesh* (1972), *The First Affair* (1974), *The Speaking Stones* (1978), *Winter Work* (1983), and *The News and the Weather* (1987). Fallon was poet-in-residence at Deerfield Academy in Massachusetts in 1976–1977; he is co-editor (with Sean Golden) of *Soft Day: A Miscellany of Contemporary Irish Writing* (1979) and (with Derek Mahon) co-editor of the forthcoming Penguin anthology of contemporary Irish poetry.

### MY CARE

Sometimes we sit in Phil's
and watch a film, *Hill Street Blues*,
or something. But this is new—
we make a point of turning to the news.

A kidnap, check-points, searches,
killers on the run.
The peace-keeping force can't keep
the peace. The new law is the outlaw gun.

The government debates. Here and there
it seems the talk goes on forever.
Talk, talk, talk. . . . After a while
it could be a chimney fire, or bad weather.

Should I do more? Is it enough
to keep a weather eye and talk to friends?
I honestly don't know. All I ever wanted was
to make a safe house in the midlands.

"How's all your care?" I'm asked.
"Grand. And yours?" I don't repeat
my worry for my care, my country. When I go home
the animals are healthy, safe. There's that.

I go inside and stir the fire.
Soon I'm sitting by a riot
of kindling, the soft explosions of seasoned logs.
They have shaken the roots of that familiar quiet.

## SPRING SONG

It was as if
someone only had to say
*Abracadabra*
to set alight
the chestnut
candelabra.

Bloom and blossom
everywhere, on furze,
on Queen Anne's lace.
A breeze blew
cherry snows
on the common place.

Weeds on walls;
the long grass
of the long acre:
the elderberry bushes
blazing thanks
to their maker.

Loud leaves of
southside trees,
the reticent buds of ash,
the reach of undergrowth
were voices, voices,
woods' panache.

Cub foxes.
Pheasants galvanised
themselves to sing.
The white thorn flowers
were the light infantry
of Spring

marching down the headlands.
A new flock flowed
through a breach,
a makeshift gate.
And this is heaven:
sunrise through a copper beech.

## WINTER WORK

Friends are unhappy; their long night
finds no day, their lane no turn. They wait
for things to change, as if history
happens to others, elsewhere. They hibernate

in dreams and fear. And Cathryn writes from Dublin:
she lies awake at night and hears
the noise of cars on Rathgar Road,
far from where her life coheres.

I warm to winter work, its rituals
and routines, and find—indoors
and out—a deal of pleasure, alone
or going out to work with neighbours,

a *meitheal* still. All I approve persists,
is here, at home. I think it exquisite
to stand in the yard, my feet on the ground,
in cowshit and horseshit and sheepshit.

## PAUL MULDOON

Paul Muldoon was born in County Armagh, Northern Ireland, in 1951 and was educated at Queen's University, Belfast. Until recently he lived in Belfast, where he worked as a producer for BBC radio. He now lives in New York. He has taught at Cambridge, Columbia, and Princeton. In 1972 he received the Eric Gregory Award for poetry. He has published several collections of poetry: *New Weather* (1973), *Mules* (1977), *Why Brownlee Left* (1980), *Quoof* (1983)—a Poetry Book Society Choice, *The Wishbone* (1984), *Selected Poems 1968–1983* (1986), and *Meeting the British* (1987). Muldoon is also editor of *The Faber Book of Contemporary Irish Poetry* (1986).

### CLONFEACLE

It happened not far away
In this meadowland
That Patrick lost a tooth.
I translate the placename

As we walk along
The river where he washed,
That translates stone to silt.
The river would preach

As well as Patrick did.
A tongue of water passing
Between teeth of stones.
Making itself clear,

Living by what it says,
Converting meadowland to marsh.
You turn towards me,
Coming round to my way

Of thinking, holding
Your tongue between your teeth.
I turn my back on the river
And Patrick, their sermons

Ending in the air.

## CUBA

My eldest sister arrived home that morning
In her white muslin evening dress.
"Who the hell do you think you are,
Running out to dances in next to nothing?
As though we hadn't enough bother
With the world at war, if not at an end."
My father was pounding the breakfast-table.

"Those Yankees were touch and go as it was—
If you'd heard Patton in Armagh—
But this Kennedy's nearly an Irishman
So he's not much better than ourselves.
And him with only to say the word.
If you've got anything on your mind
Maybe you should make your peace with God."

I could hear May from beyond the curtain.
"Bless me, Father, for I have sinned.
I told a lie once, I was disobedient once.
And, Father, a boy touched me once."
"Tell me, child. Was this touch immodest?
Did he touch your breast, for example?"
"He brushed against me, Father. Very gently."

## ANSEO

When the Master was calling the roll
At the primary school in Collegelands,
You were meant to call back *Anseo*
And raise your hand
As your name occurred.
*Anseo*, meaning here, here and now,
All present and correct,
Was the first word of Irish I spoke.
The last name on the ledger
Belonged to Joseph Mary Plunkett Ward
And was followed, as often as not,
By silence, knowing looks,
A nod and a wink, the Master's droll
"And where's our little Ward-of-court?"

I remember the first time he came back
The Master had sent him out
Along the hedges
To weigh up for himself and cut
A stick with which he would be beaten.
After a while, nothing was spoken;
He would arrive as a matter of course
With an ash-plant, a salley-rod.
Or, finally, the hazel-wand

He had whittled down to a whip-lash,
Its twist of red and yellow lacquers
Sanded and polished,
And altogether so delicately wrought
That he had engraved his initials on it.

I last met Joseph Mary Plunkett Ward
In a pub just over the Irish border.
He was living in the open,
In a secret camp
On the other side of the mountain.
He was fighting for Ireland,
Making things happen.
And he told me, Joe Ward,
Of how he had risen through the ranks
To Quartermaster, Commandant:
How every morning at parade
His volunteers would call back *Anseo*
And raise their hands
As their names occurred.

## GATHERING MUSHROOMS

The rain comes flapping through the yard
like a tablecloth that she hand-embroidered.
My mother has left it on the line.
It is sodden with rain.
The mushroom shed is windowless, wide,
its high-stacked wooden trays
hosed down with formaldehyde.
And my father has opened the Gates of Troy
to that first load of horse manure.
Barley straw. Gypsum. Dried blood. Ammonia.
Wagon after wagon
blusters in, a self-renewing gold-black dragon

we push to the back of the mind.
We have taken our pitchforks to the wind.

All brought back to me that September evening
fifteen years on. The pair of us
tripping through Barnett's fair demesne
like girls in long dresses
after a hail-storm.
We might have been thinking of the fire-bomb
that sent Malone House sky-high
and its priceless collection of linen
sky-high.
We might have wept with Elizabeth McCrum.
We were thinking only of psilocybin.
You sang of the maid you met on the dewy grass—
*And she stooped so low gave me to know*
*it was mushrooms she was gathering* O.

He'll be wearing that same old donkey-jacket
and the sawn-off waders.
He carries a knife, two punnets, a bucket.
He reaches far into his own shadow.
We'll have taken him unawares
and stand behind him, slightly to one side.
He is one of those ancient warriors
before the rising tide.
He'll glance back from under his peaked cap
without breaking rhythm:
his coaxing a mushroom—a flat or a cup—
the nick against his right thumb;
the bucket then, the punnet to left or right,
and so on and so forth till kingdom come.

We followed the overgrown tow-path by the Lagan.
The sunset would deepen through cinnamon
to aubergine,
the wood-pigeon's concerto for oboe and strings,

allegro, blowing your mind.
And you were suddenly out of my ken, hurtling
towards the ever-receding ground,
into the maw
of a shimmering green-gold dragon.
You discovered yourself in some outbuilding
with your long-lost companion, me,
though my head had grown into the head of a horse
that shook its dirty-fair mane
and spoke this verse:

*Come back to us. However cold and raw, your feet*
*were always meant*
*to negotiate terms with bare cement.*
*Beyond this concrete wall is a wall of concrete*
*and barbed wire. Your only hope*
*is to come back. If sing you must, let your song*
*tell of treading your own dung,*
*let straw and dung give a spring to your step.*
*If we never live to see the day we leap*
*into our true domain,*
*lie down with us now and wrap*
*yourself in the soiled grey blanket of Irish rain*
*that will, one day, bleach itself white.*
*Lie down with us and wait.*

## THE MIRROR

in memory of my father

### I

He was no longer my father
but I was still his son;
I would get to grips with that cold paradox,

the remote figure in his Sunday best
who was buried the next day.

A great day for tears, snifters of sherry,
whiskey, beef sandwiches, tea
An old mate of his was recounting
their day excursion
to Youghal in the Thirties,
how he was his first partner
on the Cork/Skibbereen route
in the late Forties.
There was a splay of Mass cards
on the sitting-room mantelpiece
which formed a crescent round a glass vase,
his retirement present from C.I.E.

## II

I didn't realize till two days later
it was the mirror took his breath away.

The monstrous old Victorian mirror
with the ornate gilt frame
we had found in the three-storey house
when we moved in from the country.
I was afraid that it would sneak
down from the wall and swallow me up
in one gulp in the middle of the night.

While he was decorating the bedroom
he had taken down the mirror
without asking for help;
soon he turned the colour of terracotta
and his heart broke that night.

## III

There was nothing for it
but to set about finishing the job,
papering over the cracks,
painting the high window,
stripping the door, like the door of a crypt.
When I took hold of the mirror
I had a fright. I imagined him breathing through it.
I heard him say in a reassuring whisper:
*I'll give you a hand, here.*

And we lifted the mirror back in position
above the fireplace,
my father holding it steady
while I drove home
the two nails.

*(from the Irish of Michael Davitt)*

# THE SIGHTSEERS

My father and mother, my brother and sister
and I, with uncle Pat, our dour best-loved uncle,
had set out that Sunday afternoon in July
in his broken-down Ford

not to visit some graveyard—one died of shingles,
one of fever, another's knees turned to jelly—
but the brand-new roundabout at Ballygawley,
the first in mid-Ulster.

Uncle Pat was telling us how the B-Specials
had stopped him one night somewhere near Ballygawley
and smashed his bicycle

and made him sing the Sash and curse the Pope of Rome.
They held a pistol so hard against his forehead
there was still the mark of an O when he got home.

## MEETING THE BRITISH

We met the British in the dead of winter.
The sky was lavender

and the snow lavender-blue.
I could hear, far below,

the sound of two streams coming together
(both were frozen over)

and, no less strange,
myself calling out in French

across that forest-
clearing. Neither General Jeffrey Amherst

nor Colonel Henry Bouquet
could stomach our willow-tobacco.

As for the unusual
scent when the Colonel shook out his hand-

kerchief: *C'est la lavande,*
*une fleur mauve comme le ciel.*

They gave us six fishhooks
and two blankets embroidered with smallpox.

## THE WISHBONE

Maureen in England, Joseph in Guelph,
my mother in her grave.

*

At three o'clock in the afternoon
we watch the Queen's
message to the Commonwealth
with the sound turned off.

*

He seems to favour *Camelot*
over *To Have and Have Not.*

*

Yet we agree, my father and myself,
that here is more than enough
for two; a frozen chicken,
spuds, sprouts, Paxo sage and onion.

*

The wishbone like a rowelled spur
on the fibula of Sir —— or Sir ——.

## SUSHI

"Why do we waste so much time in arguing?"
We were sitting at the sushi-bar
drinking *Kirin* Beer
and watching the Master chef

fastidiously shave
salmon, tuna and yellowtail
while a slightly more volatile
apprentice
fanned the rice,
every grain of which was magnetized
in one direction—east.
Then came translucent strips
of octopus,
squid and conger,
pickled ginger
and pale-green horseradish . . .
"It's as if you've some kind of death-wish.
You won't even talk . . ."
On the sidewalk
a woman in a leotard
with a real leopard
in tow.
For an instant I saw beyond the roe
of sea-urchins,
the erogenous
zones of shad and sea-bream;
I saw, when the steam
cleared, how this apprentice
had scrimshandered a rose's
exquisite petals
not from some precious metal
or wood or stone
("I might just as well be eating alone.")
but the tail-end of a carrot:
how when he submitted this work of art
to the Master—
*Is it not the height of arrogance*
*to propose that God's no more arcane*
*than the smack of oregano,*
*orgone,*
*the inner organs*

*of beasts and fowls, the mines of Arigna,*
*the poems of Louis Aragon?—*
it might have been alabaster
or jade
the Master so gravely weighed
from hand to hand
with the look of a man unlikely to confound
Duns Scotus, say, with Scotus Erigena.

## CHRISTO'S

Two workmen were carrying a sheet of asbestos
down the Main Street of Dingle;
it must have been nailed, at a slight angle,
to the same-sized gap between Brandon

and whichever's the next mountain.
Nine o'clock. We watched the village dogs
take turns to spritz the hotel's refuse-sacks.
I remembered Tralee's unbiodegradable flags

from the time of the hunger-strikes.
We drove all day past mounds of sugar-beet,
hay-stacks, silage-pits, building-sites,
a thatched cottage even—

all of them draped in black polythene
and weighted against the north-east wind
by concrete blocks, old tyres; bags of sand
at a makeshift army post

across the border. By the time we got to Belfast
the whole of Ireland would be under wraps
like, as I said, "one of your man's landscapes."
"Your man's? You don't mean Christo's?"

## NUALA NI DHOMHNAILL

Nuala Ní Dhomhnaill was born in 1952 and grew up in the Dingle Gaeltacht in County Kerry. She lived in Turkey and Holland for some years; she now lives in Dublin with her husband and children. Her poems in Gaelic are published in *An Dealg Droighin* (1981) and *Féar Suaithinseach* (1984); *Selected Poems* (translations of her poems into English by Michael Hartnett and herself) was published in 1986.

### LABASHEEDY (THE SILKEN BED)

I'd make a bed for you
in Labasheedy
in the tall grass
under the wrestling trees
where your skin
would be silk upon silk
in the darkness
when the moths are coming down.

Skin which glistens
shining over your limbs
like milk being poured
from jugs at dinnertime;
your hair is a herd of goats
moving over rolling hills,
hills that have high cliffs
and two ravines.

And your damp lips
would be as sweet as sugar
at evening and we walking
by the riverside
with honeyed breezes
blowing over the Shannon
and the fuchsias bowing down to you
one by one.

The fuchsias bending low
their solemn heads
in obeisance to the beauty
in front of them
I would pick a pair of flowers
as pendant earrings
to adorn you
like a bride in shining clothes.

O I'd make a bed for you
in Labasheedy,
in the twilight hour
with evening falling slow
and what a pleasure it would be
to have our limbs entwine
wrestling
while the moths are coming down.

*(translation of her poem in Irish by the author)*

## THE SHANNON ESTUARY WELCOMING THE FISH

The leap of the salmon
in darkness,
naked blade

shield of silver.
I am welcoming, full of nets,
inveigling,
slippery with seaweed,
quiet eddies
and eel-tails.

This fish
is nothing but meat
with very few bones
and very few entrails;
twenty pounds of muscle tauted,
aimed
at its nest in the mossy place.

And I will sing a lullaby
to my love
wave on wave,
stave upon half-stave,
my phosphorescence as bed-linen under him,
my favourite, whom I, from afar have chosen.

*(translation of her poem in Irish by the author)*

## PARTHENOGENESIS

Once, a lady of the Ó Moores
(married seven years without a child)
swam in the sea in summertime.
She swam well, and the day
was fine as Ireland ever saw
not even a puff of wind in the air
all the bay calm, all the sea smooth—
a sheet of glass—supple, she struck out
with strength for the breaking waves

and frisked, elated by the world.
She ducked beneath the surface and there saw
what seemed a shadow, like a man's.
And every twist and turn she made
the shadow did the same
and came close enough to touch.
Heart jumped and sound stopped in her mouth
her pulses ran and raced, sides near burst.
The lower currents with their ice
pierced her to the bone
and the noise of the abyss numbed all her limbs
then scales grew on her skin . . .
the lure of the quiet dreamy undersea . . .
desire to escape to sea and shells . . .
the seaweed tresses where at last
her bones changed into coral
and time made atolls of her arms,
pearls of her eyes in deep long sleep,
at rest in a nest of weed,
secure as feather beds . . .
But stop!
Her heroic heritage was there,
she rose with speedy, threshing feet
and made in desperation for the beach:
with nimble supple strokes she made the sand.
Near death until the day,
some nine months later
she gave birth to a boy.
She and her husband so satisfied,
so full of love for this new son
forgot the shadow in the sea
and did not see what only the midwife saw—
stalks of sea-tangle in the boy's hair
small shellfish and sea-ribbons
and his two big eyes
as blue and limpid as lagoons.
A poor scholar passing by

who found lodging for the night
saw the boy's eyes never closed
in dark or light and when all the world slept
he asked the boy beside the fire
"Who are your people?" Came the prompt reply
"Sea People."

This same tale is told in the West
but the woman's an Ó Flaherty
and tis the same in the South
where the lady's called Ó Shea:
this tale is told on every coast.
But whoever she was I want to say
that the fear she felt
when the sea-shadow followed her
is the same fear that vexed
the young heart of the Virgin
when she heard the angels' sweet bell
and in her womb was made flesh
by all accounts
the Son of the Living God.

*(translation from the Irish by Michael Hartnett)*

## FEEDING A CHILD

From honey-dew of milking
from cloudy heat of beestings
the sun rises up the back
of bare hills,
a guinea gold
to put in your hand,
my own.

You drink your fill from my breast
and fall back asleep
into a lasting dream
laughter in your face.
What is going through your head
you who are but
a fortnight on earth?

Do you know day from night
that the great early ebb
announces spring tide?
That the boats
are on deep ocean,
where live the seals and fishes
and the great whales,
and are coming hand over hand
each by seven oars manned?
That your small boats swims
óró in the bay
with the flippered peoples
and the small sea-creatures
she slippery-sleek
from stem to bow
stirring sea-sand up
sinking sea-foam down.

Of all these things are you
ignorant?
As my breast is explored
by your small hand
you grunt with pleasure
smiling and senseless.
I look into your face child
not knowing if you know
your herd of cattle
graze in the land of giants
trespassing and thieving

and that soon you will hear
the fee-fie-fo-fum
sounding in your ear.

You are my piggy
who went to market
who stayed at home
who got bread and butter
who got none.
There's one good bite in you
but hardly two—
I like your flesh
but not the broth thereof.
And who are the original patterns
of the heroes and giants
if not you and I?

*(translation from the Irish by Michael Hartnett)*

## THE RACE

### I

Like a mad lion, like a wild bull,
a wild boar from a Fenian tale,
a hero bounding towards a giant
with a single silken crest,
I blindly drive the car
through the small towns of the west:
I drive the wind before me
and leave the wind behind.

## II

Arrow from bow, bullet from gun.
Sparrow-hawk through flock of small March birds
I scatter miles of road behind.
Figures flash on signposts—
but in kilometres or miles?
Nenagh, Roscrea, Mountmellick
(but have I travelled through these towns?)
mere things that limit speed
mere things that slow me down.

## III

Through geographic barricades
I rush and dart from the west
I gallop towards where you wait
I speed to where you stand.
Heights are hollows, hollows heights
dry land is marsh, marshland is dry,
all contours from the map are gone:
nothing but shriek of brakes and sparks of light.

## IV

Sun's in the mirror, red and gold
in the sky behind me,
one huge crimson blazing globe—
Glas Gaibhneach's heart milk through a sieve
her drops of blood strained out
like a picture of the Sacred Heart.
Three scarlet brightnesses are there
and pain so sharp, and sob so short.

## V

I stared at the drops of blood
afraid but almost unaware—
like Sleeping Beauty when she gazed
at her thumb pricked by the wheel,
she turned it over, and over once more
as if her actions were unreal.
When Deirdre saw blood on the snow
did she know the raven's name?

## VI

Then I realize I drive towards you
my dearest friend and lovely man
(may nothing keep me from your bed tonight
but miles of road and traffic lights)
and your impatience like a stone
falls upon us from the sky
and adds to our uneasiness
the awkward weight of my hurt pride.

## VII

And more great loads will fall on us
if the omen comes to pass
much greater than the great sun's globe
that lately bled into the glass.
And so, Great Mother, cave of awe—
since it's towards you we race—
is it the truth? Is your embrace
and kiss more fine
than honey, beer, or Spanish Wine?

*(translation from the Irish by Michael Hartnett)*

## AS FOR THE QUINCE

There came this bright young thing
with a Black & Decker
and cut down my quince-tree.
I stood with my mouth hanging open
while one by one
she trimmed off the branches.

When my husband got home that evening
and saw what had happened
he lost the rag,
as you might imagine.
"Why didn't you stop her?
What would she think
if I took the Black & Decker
round to her place
and cut down a quince-tree
belonging to her?
What would she make of that?"

Her ladyship came back next morning
while I was at breakfast.
She enquired about his reaction.
I told her straight
that he was wondering how she'd feel
if he took a Black & Decker
round to her house
and cut down a quince-tree of hers,
etcetera etcetera.

"O," says she, "that's very interesting."
There was a stress on the 'very.'
She lingered over the 'ing.'
She was remarkably calm and collected.

These are the times that are in it, so,
all a bit topsy-turvy.
The bottom falling out of my belly
as if I had got a kick up the arse
or a punch in the kidneys.
A fainting-fit coming over me
that took the legs from under me
and left me so zonked
I could barely lift a finger
till Wednesday.

As for the quince, it was safe and sound
and still somehow holding its ground.

*(translation from the Irish by Paul Muldoon)*

## THOMAS McCARTHY

Thomas McCarthy was born in 1954 in County Waterford. He attended University College, Cork, where he was a founder of the poetry workshop. His poems won the Patrick Kavanagh Award in 1977; he was a fellow in 1978–1979 at the International Writing Program at the University of Iowa, and received the American-Irish Foundation's literary award for 1984. McCarthy's poems have been collected in *The First Convention* (1978), *The Sorrow Garden* (1981), which was joint winner of the Poetry Society's Alice Hunt-Bartlett Award, and *The Non-Aligned Storyteller* (1984). He lives in Cork, where he works for the city library and edits *Poetry Ireland*.

## STATE FUNERAL

Parnell will never come again, he said.
He's there, all that was mortal of him.
Peace to his ashes.
*James Joyce,* Ulysses

That August afternoon the family
Gathered. There was a native *deja-vu*
Of Funeral when we settled against the couch
On our sunburnt knees. We gripped mugs of tea
Tightly and soaked the TV spectacle;
The boxed ritual in our living-room.

My father recited prayers of memory,
Of monster meetings, blazing tar-barrels
Planted outside Free-State homes, the Broy-
Harriers pushing through a crowd, Blueshirts;
And, after the war, De Valera's words
Making Churchill's imperial palette blur.

What I remember is one decade of darkness,
A mind-stifling boredom; long summers
For blackberry picking and churning cream,
Winters for saving timber or setting lines
And snares: none of the joys of here and now
With its instant jam, instant heat and cream:

It was a landscape for old men. Today
They lowered the tallest one, tidied him
Away while his people watched quietly.
In the end he had retreated to the first dream,
Caning truth. I think of his austere grandeur;
Taut sadness, like old heroes he had imagined.

## FEEDING GROUND

Snow-covered and bleeding, he came home.
Yellow slush formed a crust on the road;
the sharp sound of a gate latch opening
ran before him to our kitchen window—
his feet crunching wafer-thin ice was a
second wave of sound. I stumbled back

when the door opened. When we stood in the
warm hall, knobs of ice melted from his
leather boots, chilling my house-warm feet.
Staring into his face, I could see red trails
where tears had settled when the pains of
a thigh wound splintered through his body.

He rested for three days; three days and
nights of continuous snow that transformed
the landscape into a brilliant white glow.
He left home on the fourth day, at first light;
journeyed north again like a snow goose with
bright plumage answering the call of Spring.

He travelled north; never came home again
to hot whiskeys or the family warmth:
migrant worker transformed into a soldier,
he followed the shifting job. Answering
some gaffer's loud command, he worked the roads
away from home; beyond all human warmth.

## THE WORD 'SILK'

Through your love words became clear,
were born again with a strange vigour,
like flat lines transformed through prayer,

or the sudden uncovering of oneself in verse,
the pleasure of a consummate image
or, coming from your lips, the word 'Silk.'

The word 'Silk'; a silk scarf brought
to the surface of your mysterious person,
a cat's tail stroking my face, insistent, taut;

and the word 'Sedative' that I take from 'Silk':
it is certain that you never induced sleep
but caused an animal awakeness, a wild

muscular presence, whenever you stopped to talk
or touch. The way 'Silk' flowed from you
when you left the car, I could see my words walk

across the road, down the Institute avenue:
and like a cat, or perishable silk, you peeled
away; coming and going, gradually working loose.

Yesterday, you zoomed past in your small blue
car, waving furiously. Under the trees in the Mall
a woman fed swans: Age, Compassion. I knew

that our love would have been a pointless web
of memory had it not altered so many words,
informed by feeling; Love, Love-Touch . . . Silk.

## THE POET OF THE MOUNTAINS

Every Sunday she prepared the brown oak table
For breakfast and listened to new writers
On the wooden wireless, while she ladled
Fresh milk from the yellow stone pitchers
By the wall. The English words that broke
Across her small kitchen were seldom spoken

When she was young. Then, it was all Irish:
Those brown words had curled about her childhood
Like collies home from a long cattle-crush
Or an alphabet of trees in the Abbey wood
Where she picked bluebells with her uncle
And caught words off the air as they fell.

She had spent all her days in the company
Of women. They had churned milk in the dairy
With her, taken weak lambs across the hills,
Or spoken in black shawls as far as chapel:
All their days were taken up in a great swell
Of work. They had to wash, sew, milk and kneel.

But at night, I imagine, she would lie awake
And listen to the mountains for her own sake.
She would listen to the linen wind at night
As it flapped the wet clothes. She would steal
Into the children's room to dream and write;
To be a whole person, a picker of bluebells.

## QUESTION TIME

Question time at the end of another Election Year;
Senators and their wives dancing on the ballroom floor;
children in corners dropping crisps and cream,
their fathers ordering them home, their mothers in
    crinoline
having to put them outside to sulk in the Christmas dark.
Enmities dissolving now in a sea of drink and smoke and
    talk.

Who was Robert Emmet's mistress? Who was Kitty
    O'Shea?
Which I.R.A. man was shot on his own wedding-day?
How many death-warrants did Kevin O'Higgins sign?
So much to answer between the buffet meal and wine—
But the prize is a week in Brussels, money for two,
and kisses from two Euro-M.P.s just passing through.

## AIDAN CARL MATHEWS

Aidan Carl Mathews was born in 1956 and educated at University College and Trinity College, Dublin. He also attended Stanford University in California. His first book, *Windfalls* (1977), won him the Patrick Kavanagh Award; he was awarded the Macauley Fellowship in 1978–1979, and an Academy of American Poets Award in 1982. He has written stories and articles in addition to his poems. His second collection of poems is *Minding Ruth* (1983). He lives in Dublin with his wife.

### DESCARTES AT DAYBREAK

The light stands over me,
And my red, expensive candle
Stops short as the curtains change colour.

Crossings, crossings-out,
A slantwise second thought cancelled,
Those unruled margins! Up all night,

My body against me, my life
In my own hand. Death of cold. Twice
She begged me to bed. Twice I refused.

To be greeted now, for my pains,
By catcalls of the sun happening
Everywhere but in my head!

If you would only listen, she said,
You would doubtless hear
The good noises of life being about to:

A newspaper slithering
Under the door, or the puppyfat
Milkgirls misting the spyhole;

And the sprinklers chattering,
Going *lovely, lovely,*
On the lawn below the window.

Something to believe on,
To start from, rise to; drops
For the sty late reading brought on . . .

I exist. I breakfast.
She brings me toast, my wife does,
With one of her hairs in the butter.

World of the precious little,
Of things taken in vain yet sworn by,
Dawn on me.

## THE LIBRARY

I have been here for a half hour,
Thinking only of you. Around me,
Book-cases close upon heads tilted
Over old volumes in buff jackets.

I close my eyes to hear
A cough, somewhere, the fretting of pens,
Creak of the sole of a suede shoe.
I open them to a high ceiling,

A bevel of cherubs on pink skirting
While, higher still, the night paints over
A blue world at the window pane.
But now my paper whitens

Like a morning, my eyes drawn down
To your dear form at the desk again,
Warm pellets of light from a lamp
Like rainwater, caught in your hair.

And I watch your shoulders stir
Or, absently, your fingers loop
Hair on the collar of your cardigan.
And now you write,

Head down, hunched over paper,
Your fist clenched on a fountain pen.
I lean into your light and listen
Until, suddenly, I hear

The small voices of words
That plead in my mind like children
Whom I send out, bare-foot, wide-eyed,
To come back, speaking only of you.

## SEVERANCES

Serene and outraged in a trenchcoat,
Warding off chain-saws for two days,

You stand beneath a condemned beech,
A settlement made of brown weather

Where I can imagine you a child
In its tall storeys, making up people

Such as will never come by night
With arc-lamps in a covered lorry.

Fetching the milk this morning
Among sparrows, you cry out to see it

A hacked stump caulked with pitch,
Its lopped roots stacked. I watch you

Draw back as if struck, a flawed
Cordage of gland and tissue

No touch stanches. These matters
Are beyond my apology. Tonight,

My hamadryad in laddered stockings,
A cold sore on your normal mouth,

Must I approach no mild accomplice
But a visitant, furred and rustling?

By then I may have almost learned
Another of you to cherish differently,

One in whose dialect
Thickets turn groves, one who starts—

As I reach across to calf and buttock,
Fictions of harm and healing—

To break out in bloom and cluster,
Wet ferns from her arm-pit, clefts

Of ladysmock and maidenhair in which
Through the small hours I would occur like rain.

## AT THE WAILING WALL

*i.m. my brother John. 1945–1978*

I make free with old albums,
Photographs that show
Your good side in profile.
From them all, I would choose
Shots of the Wailing Wall
Weeks after the truce
And the fall of Jerusalem.
Because I too stand
At the blank wall of a death
Not granted or forgiven—
*Her pavilion sacked by louts,*
*Her scriptures shat upon—*
I recall you by picturing
A skull-cap and prayer-shawl,
Arms bare to the wrist
And lifted in hosanna,
Like that print of the Baptist
Wading through Jordan.

Your head is bent forward
Toward a future unheard-of,
A four-year illness;
And the lightly downed neck
That I clung to on rides,
Burnt only by sunlight:
Neither hairless nor sutured.

## MINDING RUTH

for Seamus Deane

She wreaks such havoc in my library,
It will take ages to set it right—
A Visigoth in a pinafore

Who, weakening, plonks herself
On the works of Friedrich Nietzsche,
And pines for her mother.

She's been at it all morning,
Duck-arsed in my History section
Like a refugee among rubble,

Or, fled to the toilet, calling
In a panic that the seat is cold.
But now she relents under biscuits

To extemporise grace notes,
And sketch with a blue crayon
Arrow after arrow leading nowhere.

My small surprise of language,
I cherish you like an injury
And would swear by you at this moment

For your brisk chatter brings me
Chapter and verse, you restore
The city itself, novel and humming,

Which I enter as a civilian
Who plants his landscape with place-names.
They stand an instant, and fade.

Her hands sip at my cuff. She cranes,
Perturbedly, with a book held open
At plates from Warsaw in the last war.

*Why is the man with the long beard*
*Eating his booboos?* And I stare
At the old rabbi squatting in turds

Among happy soldiers who die laughing,
The young one clapping: you can see
A wedding band flash on his finger.

# NOTES

The notes are intended to provide brief explanations of allusions and references in the poems that may not be located in a standard dictionary, and particularly of those that refer to some aspect of Irish life.

*THOMAS MacGREEVY*

## DE CIVITATE HOMINUM

The title may be loosely translated as "concerning the state of man"—probably an allusion to St. Augustine's *De Civitate Dei* (*The City of God*).

Zillebeke; Hooge; Gheluvelt: Flemish place-names belonging to the area around Ypres in Belgium, one of the major battlefields of World War I.

*nature morte*: still life.

## AODH RUADH O'DOMHNAILL

The title is Irish for Red Hugh O'Donnell (1571–1602), Ulster chieftain and a leader (with his father-in-law, Hugh O'Neill) of the rebellion of 1595–1603. After the defeat of the Irish forces and their Spanish allies at Kinsale in 1601, Red Hugh went to Spain in the hopes of mustering another Spanish force. He was poisoned in 1602 at Simancas by an agent of the English crown. He is buried in the church of San Francisco at Valladolid, although the precise resting place of his remains is no longer known.

## RECESSIONAL

The title refers to a musical piece (usually played at the end of a religious service).

Roderick Hudson: the artist hero of Henry James's novel of the same name, who dies climbing in the Swiss Alps near Engelberg.

Mal Bay: a bay on the Atlantic coast of Ireland, in County Clare.

*AUSTIN CLARKE*

## PILGRIMAGE

Ara: the Aran Islands.

by dim wells: a Celtic custom (assimilated by Christianity) of tying rags on bushes near a sacred well, still occasionally observed in Ireland—a veneration of water and fertility.

Clonmacnoise: one of the best known of the "holy schools" referred to earlier in the poem. Situated in County Offaly, on the River Shannon, it was founded by St. Ciaran in 548. The "holy schools" were not only monasteries but also seats of learning.

Cashel: the Rock of Cashel in County Tipperary, site of the finest Celtic Romanesque church in Ireland.

The holy mountain: Croagh Patrick, the hill where St. Patrick, according to one legend, spent the years of his captivity. It is still a place of annual pilgrimage.

Culdees: anchorites.

## TENEBRAE

The title refers to that part of the mass on Holy Saturday when candles are extinguished and later rekindled as a symbol of Christ's death and resurrection.

## THE STRAYING STUDENT

Inishmore: the largest of the Aran Islands.

Salamanca: site of an Irish seminary in Spain in the eighteenth century, when education in Ireland was forbidden to the native Irish. Irish youth were educated for the priesthood at this and other Continental seminaries.

## WOLFE TONE

Tone is the most famous of the founding fathers of Irish Republicanism. A Protestant lawyer, he was a leader of the Society of United Irishmen and responsible for French support of the Rebellion of 1798. When captured and tried by the British, he committed suicide to avoid the ignominy of public hanging. He formulated the major tenet of Irish Republicanism: "To break the connection with England, the never-failing source of all our political evils." The foundation stone for a monument to Tone in St. Stephen's Green was laid in 1898, but the monument was never completed. Clarke's note to the poem concludes: "I wrote these lines on the morning that the fine Gough Monument in the Phoenix Park was blown up."

## THREE POEMS ABOUT CHILDREN

Clarke tells us the poems were inspired by the statement of a local bishop after sixty children had perished in a fire in an orphanage dormitory without a fire escape.

the book against the rock: refers to the penal days in Ireland, when the practice of Catholicism was forbidden—as a consequence the priest would often use a rock as the altar on which to celebrate the mass in the open air.

## FORGET ME NOT

The occasion for the poem was the export of horses from Ireland to the Continent to be slaughtered for meat.

The place-names are almost all in Dublin and its environs.

Cormac's Chapel: a ruined Celtic Romanesque church on the Rock of Cashel, County Tipperary.

The Gray of Macha: the best-loved horse of the Irish mythological hero Cuchulainn.

Pitch-capped: this refers to a form of torture used at the time of the 1798 rebellion to punish captured rebels (called "croppies" presumably because their hair was cut short in the revolutionary style)—the victim's head was saturated with pitch and set on fire.

## INSCRIPTION FOR A HEADSTONE

Larkin: James Larkin (1876–1947), the famous labor leader; he had the reputation of being a great orator. After the police violence used on 16 August against workers in the general strike of 1913, Larkin's comrade James Connolly organized the Irish Citizen Army, a force of about two hundred men. Connolly was commander of the Irish Citizen Army in the Easter Rising of 1916.

## THE SUBJECTION OF WOMEN

The title of the poem is also the title of a famous feminist essay by John Stuart Mill, published in 1869.

Maud Gonne: the ardent and beautiful Irish Republican, born in England in 1866; her father was an army officer in the English garrison in Dublin. Champion of the Irish poor, she organized resistance to evictions in rural Ireland, founded the revolutionary women's organization Inghinidhe na hEireann (Daughters of Erin), and was committed over her long lifetime to social and political causes that ranged from providing school meals for Dublin children to advocacy of prison reform. She was also the subject of many poems by W. B. Yeats.

Peelers: policemen.

Glenmalure . . . Tudor battle: scarcely a battle, but rather a slaughter of the native inhabitants in 1572 by English soldiers, typical of the Elizabethan war of conquest in Ireland.

the Sidhe: supernatural beings.

Countess Markievicz: née Constance Gore-Booth, she was born into the Anglo-Irish Ascendancy in 1868 but espoused the causes of labor and Irish nationalism. She organized a food kitchen during the Dublin lockout of 1913; founded the Fianna (boy scouts who were given military training for the impending fight against England); was president of Cumann na mBan, the women's organization of the Irish Volunteers and later of the Irish Republican Army; and participated in the Easter Rising of 1916 as an officer of the Irish Citizen Army. For her part in the Rising, she was sentenced to death; her sentence was commuted to penal servitude for life and ultimately rescinded. While still in prison, she was elected Sinn Fein member to Westminster, thus becoming the first woman elected to the Mother of Parliaments. She was appointed Minister for Labour in the Irish Dail, fought on the Republican side in the civil war, then joined De Valera's Fianna Fail and was elected to the Dail in 1927, the year of her death. Her patriotism and advocacy for the Dublin poor were recognized at her funeral—one source estimates that a hundred thousand attended. She is the subject of several poems by Yeats that decry her political commitment.

Martin Murphy: William Martin Murphy, Dublin tycoon, owner of the Dublin Tramway Company, newspapers, stores, etc., and organizer of the Dublin employers in the lockout of 1913.

Connolly: see note to "Inscription for a Headstone," above.

Helena Moloney: close friend and ally of Maud Gonne, secretary of Inghinidhe na hEireann (Daughters of Erin) and editor of this organization's newspaper *Bean na hEireann* (*Woman of Ireland*), active in the Irish Women Workers' Union, member of the Irish Citizen Army, participant in the Easter Rising of 1916. She was jailed by the British for her role in the Rising; she later served on the executive of the Republican organization *Saor Eire* (Free Ireland).

Louie Bennett: like Helena Moloney, a committed trade-union organizer, head of the Irish Women Workers' Union.

Eva Gore-Booth: sister of Constance Markievicz, activist in the struggle for women's suffrage, she spent twenty-seven years in the mills and factories of Lancashire organizing women workers. Yeats characterizes her as pursuing "some vague utopia" in "In Memory of Eva Gore-Booth and Con Markievicz."

Mrs. [Hanna] Sheehy-Skeffington: socialist and feminist, leader of the Women's Franchise League, close friend of Maud Gonne. Her pacifist husband, Francis, was murdered by British soldiers in 1916.

Mary Wollstonecraft: English feminist (1759–1797), author of *A Vindication of the Rights of Women.*

Dr. Kathleen Lynn: medical officer in the Irish Citizen Army during the Easter Rising and close friend of Constance Markievicz. She co-founded St. Ultan's hospital for children in Dublin, for many generations the city with the highest rate of infant mortality in the British Isles; she was elected to the Dail for North Dublin and served on the executive of Sinn Fein.

## MARTHA BLAKE AT FIFTY-ONE

The character is modeled on Clarke's sister.

*FRANK O'CONNOR*

## THE END OF CLONMACNOIS

The poem refers to the destruction by the Danes in the ninth century of this monastic settlement and seat of learning. Clonmacnois and the other monastic centers were sacked repeatedly in the second half of the ninth century.

## HOPE

Tara: ancient seat of the high kings of Ireland, County Meath.

*PATRICK KAVANAGH*

## ART McCOOEY

McCooey (Mac Cumhaigh) was a South Ulster (Gaelic) poet of the eighteenth century. Like many other Irish poets of the time, he was reduced to menial labor to make a living. The story is told of his forgetting to deliver a load of dung because he was preoccupied with fashioning a poem.

*PADRAIC FALLON*

## FOR PADDY MAC

The title refers to Fallon's friend, the poet Patrick MacDonough.

Fomorian: according to legend, the Fomorians were the first inhabitants of Ireland, pushed to the western edges of the island by the conquering Firbolgs.

Bran: a hero of early medieval Irish and Welsh literature; in Welsh literature, he is a god whose severed but living head presides over feasting and singing in the otherworld; in Irish literature he is the mortal who travels across the seas to the otherworld. Fallon seems to have joined the traditions.

Lever: Charles James Lever (1806–1872), Irish novelist.

Raftery: Anthony Raftery (1784–1835), the blind Gaelic poet of the folk tradition, who was admired for his eloquent capacity for praise and blame.

## A HEDGE SCHOOLMASTER

Among other grievous restrictions, the penal laws of the eighteenth century forbade the education of Irish Catholics. Consequently the peasant institution of the hedge schools—so called because a hedge was often the only shelter against the elements—became the illicit national school system of Ireland. These schools were largely replaced by the National School system introduced by Britain in the 1830s. A hedge school is the *mise en scène* of Brian Friel's play *Translations* (1980).

## DARDANELLES 1916

The Connaught Rangers was only one of the Irish regiments in the British Army in the First World War decimated in such battles as Gallipoli (the peninsula that forms the European shore of the Dardanelles straits in Turkey). By comparison with the large numbers of Irishmen who fought in the British Army in the First World War (many on the understanding that they were consolidating home rule for Ireland), it was a very small group that attacked the British in Dublin in the Easter Rising of 1916. Ironically, Irish regiments of the British Army helped crush the Rising.

*SAMUEL BECKETT*

## MALACODA

The title refers to a demon in Dante's *Inferno*.

## ENUEG I

The title refers to a species of medieval French verse that consists of a catalog of annoyances.

Exeo: I depart (Latin).

Portobello: area on the south side of Dublin, near the Grand Canal.

Fox and Geese: southwestern suburb of Dublin.

Chapelizod: western suburb of Dublin. (The poet has obviously taken a long, despairing walk through the southern and western parts of the city.)

*JOHN HEWITT*

## IRELAND

Clontarf: site in Dublin of the decisive battle (1014) in which Brian Boru defeated the Norse. The battle marked the end of the Viking wars in Ireland, and the establishment of a relatively high degree of Irish political unity.

## AN IRISHMAN IN COVENTRY

the Book of Kells: one of the masterpieces of early Irish art, an eighth-century illuminated manuscript translation of the Gospels; the designs are intricate and complex.

Lir's children: Aoife, the second wife of the Irish deity Lir, was jealous of the children of his first marriage and had them turned into swans who could find shelter neither on land nor on the sea.

## CALLING ON PEADAR O'DONNELL AT DUNGLOE

Peadar O'Donnell: Irish man of letters, socialist, combatant in the war for independence and (on the Republican side) in the subsequent civil war.

*LOUIS MACNEICE*

## DUBLIN

O'Connell; Grattan; Moore: refers to statues in central Dublin of Daniel O'Connell (1775–1847), leader of the movement for Catholic Emancipation; Henry Grattan (1746–1820), leader of the Irish Volunteers and prime mover in the establishment of the short-lived independent Irish parliament of the eighteenth century; Thomas Moore (1779–1852), popular poet and composer, author of Irish Melodies.

Nelson: a statue of the English admiral Horatio Nelson stood atop a tall pillar in O'Connell Street, dominating the landscape of central Dublin until 1966, when it was destroyed by an explosion.

The Four Courts burnt: a reference to the attack on the Republican garrison in the Four Courts by Irish government forces in June 1922 that marked the beginning of the Irish civil war.

Fort of the Dane . . . : a summary of the various historical identities of the city of Dublin.

## from AUTUMN JOURNAL

Maud Gonne: identified in the notes to Austin Clarke's "The Subjection of Women."

Casement: Roger Casement, an Irishman of the Ascendancy class, knighted by the British for his humanitarian work in the Congo; hanged in 1916 (by the British) for attempting to supply the insurgents of the Easter Rising with German weapons.

Kathleen Ni Houlihan: romantic embodiment of Ireland in nationalist folklore and literature, especially of the late nineteenth century.

Griffith: Arthur Griffith. Irish separatist, founder of Sinn Fein, editor of the *United Irishman*, minister for Home Affairs in the first Dail; Griffith led the Irish delegation in the treaty negotiations and was first prime minister of the Irish Free State.

Collins: Michael Collins, charismatic leader in the Irish war for independence, assassinated during the civil war that followed.

Connolly: James Connolly, identified in the notes to Austin Clarke's "Inscription for a Headstone."

*Odi atque amo*: I hate and love (Latin). The most famous expression of the sentiment is in Catullus's poem that begins *odi et amo*.

*DENIS DEVLIN*

## LOUGH DERG

The title refers to the island in County Donegal's Lough Derg known as St. Patrick's Purgatory; it is still a place of pilgrimage and penance.

Merovingian centuries: the Frankish dynasty, sixth to eighth century; apparently a reference to the missionary zeal of the Irish monks of these times, who founded monasteries in France, Germany, Switzerland, and Italy.

## ANK'HOR VAT

The title refers to a holy place of Buddhism, in Cambodia.

## DAPHNE STILLORGAN

Stillorgan: a southeastern suburb of Dublin.

*DONAGH MACDONAGH*

## THE VETERANS

in the sixteenth year of the century: the Easter Rising of 1916.

*CHARLES DONNELLY*

## POEM

Parnell: Charles Stewart Parnell (1846–1891), leader of the Home Rule movement.

Pearse: Padraic Pearse (1879–1916), leader of the Irish Volunteers in the insurrection of Easter 1916, executed by the British.

Raleigh: Sir Walter Raleigh (1551–1618), Elizabethan poet, explorer, and adventurer.

Lawrence: T. E. Lawrence (1888–1935), known as Lawrence of Arabia.

Childers: Erskine Childers (1870–1922), former British civil servant, convert to the cause of Irish nationalism, active in the Irish struggle for independence, and a member of the Republican faction in the Irish civil war. He was executed by the Free State government in 1922.

*VALENTIN IREMONGER*

## HECTOR

The brave and honorable son of King Priam, husband of Andromache, Hector was Trojan champion in Troy's war with Greece; he was killed by Achilles in single combat.

## ICARUS

Son of Daedalus, Icarus flew too close to the sun on the wings his father had constructed to enable them to flee Minos; the sun melted the wax on the wings, and Icarus fell into the sea and was drowned.

## THIS HOURE HER VIGILL

The title is taken from John Donne's "A Nocturnal upon Saint Lucy's Day."

*PADRAIC FIACC*

## THE POET

chaunt-rann: apparently a neologism combining obsolete English and Irish—"verse-chanter" is approximate.

## GLOSS

Deirdre; Naisi; Conor: refers to the Irish myth in which Deirdre, the beautiful ward of the old King Conor (Conchubor) of Ulster, runs away with the young warrior Naisi. Conor relentlessly pursues them and kills Naisi. Deirdre then kills herself.

Dermot, Fionn: a variant of the above myth in which the young woman is Grainne, the older man to whom she has been promised is Fionn MacCumhaill (Finn MacCool), leader of the warriors who defend Ireland against invaders, and Dermot the handsome lover; Grainne, though heartbroken at Dermot's death, survives to become Fionn's wife.

## INTROIT; GOODBYE TO BRIGID / AN *AGNUS DEI*

The Introit and Agnus Dei are parts of the Latin mass: the Introit is a variable prayer read by the priest early in the mass; the Agnus Dei, a prayer to Christ to have mercy and grant peace, is said just before communion. Both poems are taken from a collection called *Missa Terribilis* (The Mass of Dread).

*PEARSE HUTCHINSON*

## BOXING THE FOX

The author tells us that the phrase is Dublin slang for robbing an orchard.

## MANIFEST DESTINY

Ballyporeen: reputedly the birthplace of President Reagan's ancestors.

IDA: the Irish Industrial Development Authority.

this most ardest rí: a corruption of the Irish, rendered six lines earlier by "this highest king."

the milk thief: Prime Minister Thatcher, whose government stopped the distribution of free milk in the public schools of Britain.

the Limerick pogrom: Jewish residents of the city of Limerick were subjected to persecution in 1904 by their Catholic neighbors.

the Sack of Baltimore: Algerian pirates sacked the town of Baltimore in County Cork in 1630 and abducted the townspeople, making slaves of them.

*RICHARD MURPHY*

## from THE BATTLE OF AUGHRIM

The title refers to a decisive battle in Irish history—12 July 1691, at Aughrim in County Galway. The Irish and French army supporting the Catholic cause of James II was defeated by the English and Dutch army supporting the Protestant William of Orange; the outcome of the battle had severe consequences for the Catholic population of Ireland for several centuries.

## HIGH ISLAND

The title refers to a small island off the coast of Galway, once owned by the poet.

## BEEHIVE CELL

The title refers to a small stone building shaped like a beehive, situated near the seashore, built and inhabited by early Irish anchorites.

*THOMAS KINSELLA*

## BAGGOT STREET DESERTA

Baggot Street: a residential street on the south side of Dublin.

## CLARENCE MANGAN

The title refers to James Clarence Mangan (1803–1849), Irish poet born in the Dublin slums. His work has marked affinities with that of Edgar Allen Poe. He did extensive translations from Irish and German and wrote memorable patriotic verse. He was highly praised by Yeats and Joyce.

## COVER HER FACE

The title comes from a line in John Webster's *Duchess of Malfi*: "Cover her face; mine eyes dazzle: she died young."

## A COUNTRY WALK

MacDonagh; McBride; Connolly: ironic invocation of the leaders of the Easter Rising in 1916.

## RITUAL OF DEPARTURE

Dublin under the Georges: Dublin in the early nineteenth century after the Act of Union (1800) deprived Ireland of a parliament; George III and George IV occupied the throne of England until 1830.

famine: by the middle of the nineteenth century at least a million Irish had died from starvation and another two million had emigrated, mainly to the United States.

## A HAND OF SOLO

Indian apples: pomegranates. The pomegranate is reputed to have been the apple of the tree of knowledge, eaten by Eve and Adam.

## from THE MESSENGER

Martin Murphy . . . Connolly: see notes to Austin Clarke's "The Subjection of Women" and "Inscription for a Headstone."

## MODEL SCHOOL, INCHICORE

marla: the used plasticine (akin to modeling clay).

the adding-up table in Irish . . . her name: presumably *a ceathair (agus) a naoi*—four and nine—sounds like Carney.

*JOHN MONTAGUE*

## THE ANSWER

*Dia dhuit / Dia agus Muire dhuit / Dia agus Muire agus Padraig dhuit*: God be with you / God and Mary be with you / God and Mary and Patrick be with you.

## A LOST TRADITION

*Tá an Ghaedilg againn arís*: we have the Gaelic again.

the Raparee . . . Brish-mo-Cree: Shane Barnagh was a folkloric figure in eighteenth-century Tyrone, a Robin Hood type of outlaw; Brish-mo-cree is a phonetic spelling of a Gaelic phrase translated in the poem by the phrase that precedes it—"so breaks the heart."

## LAMENT FOR THE O'NEILLS

*Annals of the Four Masters*: the Gaelic chronicle of a thousand years of Irish history compiled by four historians. The collaboration of the four authors began in 1632, in Donegal.

Mountjoy: Lord Deputy of Ireland, the leader of Elizabeth's army when it defeated the Irish and their Spanish allies at the battle of Kinsale in 1601.

Chichester: Sir Arthur, the successor to Mountjoy as Lord Deputy of Ireland from 1606–1633.

*Is uaigneach Eire*: "Ireland is desolate," the beginning of a poem by Andrais MacMarcus on the flight of Red Hugh O'Donnell in 1602.

The Flight of the Earls: the departure into exile of Hugh O'Neill and Rory O'Donnell, princes of Ulster, with their followers in 1607, in the aftermath of the unsuccessful nine years' war against Elizabeth; they sailed from Rathmullen, in Lough Swilly. Both are buried in Rome. Their departure signaled the virtual end of the Gaelic culture in Ireland and the beginning of the Ulster plantation on a vast scale.

## THE SILVER FLASK

Carleton: William Carleton (1794–1869), Irish writer from County Tyrone; an important figure for Ulster writers.

*SEAN LUCY*

## SENIOR MEMBERS

Tadhg and Vincent are representative types of Irishmen who emerged as leaders on the Irish political scene in the period following the achievement of independence. Tadhg is clearly the former I.R.A. man, a bullying countryman, and Vincent the smooth, city businessman who has inherited his uncle's conservative if nationalist politics. The "new politico" blends their outdated styles in order to keep up with the times.

*ANNE HARTIGAN*

## ST. BRIDGET'S CROSS

The author provides the following notes to the poem:

St. Bridget's Cross is a cross of reeds, or marram/bent grass, made by country people in Ireland and hung in the cowsheds to ensure plentiful yields of milk, or in houses to protect them for the year to come and to ensure abundance. A new cross is made each year for St. Bridget's Feast on 1st February, the first day of spring. This custom, now linked to St. Bridget, dates back to rites connected with a pre-Christian goddess of fertility.

The Biddy Boys were young boys who went from house to house in some parts of Ireland on the Feast of St. Bridget, singing bawdy songs. They represent another connection with pre-Christian times.

*TOM MACINTYRE*

## ON SWEET KILLEN HILL

*Mise*: Irish for me, myself.

## DRUMLIN PRAYER

Drumlins are the small, egg-shaped hills that characterize the eastern part of the political border between the Republic of Ireland and Northern Ireland.

*JAMES LIDDY*

## HISTORY

Fenian King: Finn MacCool, leader of the Fianna, a legendary band of warriors who protected Ireland's sovereignty.

Oisin: Finn's son who goes with the fairy queen Niamh to the Land of Eternal Youth.

Patrick: St. Patrick, to whom Oisin is recounting his adventures on his return to Ireland from the Land of Eternal Youth. Oisin has lived with Niamh for three hundred years and returns to find the Fianna long dead, and Ireland Christian.

*DESMOND O'GRADY*

## from THE DYING GAUL

The title of the sequence presumably refers to the famous bronze sculpture (third century B.C.) of the dying Celtic warrior found at Pergamon, although this excerpt suggests, rather, the death of Cuchulainn, the mythological hero of the Irish sagas.

## FINN'S WISHES

Finn: Finn MacCool, hero and warrior of Irish myth.

*BRENDAN KENNELLY*

## MY DARK FATHERS

Perished feet nailed to her man's breastbone: the author explains that this detail comes from a source that described the discovery of a man and a woman who had died from famine disease—the woman's husband had tried to warm her legs by putting them inside his shirt.

the pit of doom: common burial ground for victims of the Great Famine of the 1840s.

*SEAMUS HEANEY*

## THE OTHER SIDE

Lazarus: the beggar at the rich man's gate in Luke 16, not the Lazarus awakened from the dead by Jesus.

dandering: strolling.

## THE TOLLUND MAN

The Tollund Man is one of a series of Iron Age corpses (preserved by the chemistry of the Danish bogs) that are on display in various museums in Denmark. The second stanza connects these victims of ritual violence with victims of the long-standing sectarian hatred of Ulster. The laborers were young Catholics murdered by the Ulster constabulary in the 1920s.

## SUMMER 1969

the Constabulary: the Royal Ulster Constabulary, which participated in the attack on a working-class Catholic area of Belfast (the Falls Road) in 1969.

holmgang: a duel to the death.

## THE STRAND AT LOUGH BEG

Colum McCartney: a cousin of Heaney's, murdered in a sectarian attack.

## IN MEMORIAM FRANCIS LEDWIDGE

Ledwidge (1887–1917) was an Irish laborer and poet who was killed in France in the First World War. Although he joined the British Army, he had been active in the Irish labor movement and was a friend of those who took part in the Rising of 1916.

## from STATION ISLAND

The first speaker is a hunger striker, formerly a neighbor of the poet. The author provides the following note to this sequence of poems in *Station Island*:

> "Station Island" is a sequence of dream encounters with familiar ghosts, set on Station Island on Lough Derg in Co. Donegal. The island is also known as St Patrick's Purgatory because of a tradition that Patrick was the first to establish the penitential vigil of fasting and praying which still constitutes the basis of the three-day pilgrimage. Each unit of the contemporary pilgrim's exercises is called a "station," and a large part of each station involves walking barefoot and praying round the "beds," stone circles which are said to be the remains of early medieval monastic cells.

*MICHAEL LONGLEY*

## LETTER TO DEREK MAHON

August sixty-nine: when the present violence in Northern Ireland began.

the Shankill and the Falls: the neighboring, working-class Protestant and Catholic quarters of Belfast.

Inisheer: one of the Aran Islands, off the coasts of Clare and Galway, in the west of Ireland.

## FLEANCE

Fleance, Banquo: characters in Shakespeare's *Macbeth.*

## THE LINEN WORKERS

The occasion for the poem was the sectarian murder in 1976 of ten Protestant workers in South Armagh; the outrage was one in a series of reciprocating sectarian assassinations committed in Ulster at this time.

*SEAMUS DEANE*

## A SCHOOLING

the Government milk: the government of Britain and Northern Ireland used to provide free milk to schoolchildren.

## HISTORY LESSONS

Grattan: Henry Grattan, a Protestant lawyer, leader of the short-lived "Grattan's Parliament" (1782–1800), an Irish parliament that was theoretically independent of England; it was composed entirely of members of the Protestant Ascendancy.

## A BURIAL

The occasion is presumably the funeral of a member of the Irish Republican Army.

*DEREK MAHON*

## GLENGORMLEY

The title is the name of a middle-class suburb of Belfast that overlooks Belfast Lough.

*EILEAN NI CHUILLEANAIN*

## DEAD FLY

Sparafucile is the name of the hired assassin in Verdi's opera *Rigoletto.*

## LUCINA SCHYNNING IN SILENCE OF THE NIGHT . . .

This title is the first line of a poem, "The Birth of Antichrist," by William Dunbar (Scottish, fifteenth–sixteenth century). The poem is an apocalyptic dream vision; Lucina is a personification of the moon.

## from SITE OF AMBUSH

The poem refers to an incident in the Troubles of 1919–1921.

## from THE ROSE-GERANIUM

The author provides the following information: *A l'usage de . . .* : For the use of . . . . The inscription was attached to the gate of a tiny garden in an old people's home (in Belgium) that was run by a group of nuns. The phrase was in common use in convents because of the vow of poverty forbidding individuals to own property.

*MICHAEL SMITH*

## MITCHING

The title means playing hooky.

*PAUL DURCAN*

## BEWLEY'S ORIENTAL CAFÉ, WESTMORELAND STREET

Bewley's Oriental Cafés (there are three of them in the center of Dublin) are the longest-established and most popular coffee-houses in the city.

a Dart to Bray: Dart, a train (of the Dublin Area Rapid Transit system); Bray, a seaside town south of Dublin.

oxter: armpit.

*RICHARD RYAN*

## FROM MY LAI THE THUNDER WENT WEST

My Lai: village in Vietnam; site of a notorious incident in the Vietnam War in which many civilians were murdered by United States Army personnel.

## A WET NIGHT

Connemara: a mountainous coastal area of Galway.

*HUGH MAXTON*

## CERNUNNOS

The title refers to a Celtic god with chthonic powers and special affinities with animals, particularly the stag. The only image of him in Ireland is, rather incongruously, on a stone cross at the site of the monastic settlement of Clonmacnois.

## AT THE PROTESTANT MUSEUM

The title refers to Budapest's Lutheran museum.

Hus, Melancthon, Luther: the leaders of the Reformation.

Part 2 is a free version of Luther's will.

Widgery: the British judge who conducted the inquiry into the shooting deaths of fourteen Irish civilians at the hands of British paratroopers in Derry, 1972. Many consider the results of that inquiry a whitewash.

*Fidei defensor*: the Latin title ("defender of the faith") bestowed on Henry VIII by the Pope before the English Reformation (for his refutation of a treatise by Luther) and retained by English monarchs ever since.

The author has kindly supplied the following information:

(Endre) Bajcsy-Zsilinszky: a Hungarian landowner, the only member of the Hungarian parliament to oppose his country's alliance with the fascists in the Second World War; he was executed by the fascist regime in 1945.

Lieutenant Shepherd: an invented figure, an army chaplain who belongs both to the Second World War and the present Irish Troubles.

John Hunter Gowan . . . the late insurrection: the subject of the opening poem in *The Protestant Museum*, Gowan was a notorious character in Wexford at the time of the rebellion of 1798. He was the leader of a gang of Protestants, the "Black Mob," who hunted rebels; he is said to have stirred a bowl of punch with the amputated finger of one victim.

*FRANK ORMSBY*

## SPOT THE BALL

The title refers to a weekly contest in British and Irish newspapers, in which the contestant puts a cross in a photograph of a soccer match to indicate the position of the missing ball.

## from A NORTHERN SPRING

A substantial part of the American forces that would invade Normandy in the Second World War were stationed in Northern Ireland.

*CIARAN CARSON*

## THE INSULAR CELTS

The title refers to the Celts of Britain and Ireland as opposed to the Celts of the European continent.

## DRESDEN

RUC, RIC: the Royal Ulster Constabulary is the police force of Northern Ireland; before the partition of Ireland, the all-Ireland police force was the Royal Irish Constabulary.

## BELFAST CONFETTI

Balaclava . . . Crimea Street: the names of streets in the Lower Falls area of Belfast.

A Saracen: the name of an armored car used by the British Army.

## CAMPAIGN

The subject of the poem is a sectarian murder in Belfast.

*TOM PAULIN*

## AND WHERE DO YOU STAND ON THE NATIONAL QUESTION?

Paisley: Ian Paisley, fundamentalist preacher and political leader of most of Northern Ireland's Protestants.

Doagh and Boardmills: towns in County Antrim Board and County Down, respectively.

Lagan Jacobins . . . *The Northern Star*: the eighteenth-century Belfast (Protestant) radicals, members of the United Irishmen, who founded the *Northern Star* in 1792; the newspaper extolled the virtues of Republicanism.

the Enterprise: the train between Belfast and Dublin.

Molyneaux: Ulster Unionist leader.

Burke: Edmund Burke, eighteenth-century Anglo-Irish conservative political theorist, advocate of counterrevolution.

the Cruiser: Conor Cruise O'Brien, historian, journalist, and opponent of Irish Republicanism.

Prior: James Prior, a British secretary of state for Northern Ireland.

## DESERTMARTIN

Desertmartin, Draperstown, Magherafelt: towns in County Derry.

a Jock squaddy: a Scottish soldier.

*MEDBH McGUCKIAN*

## MR. McGREGOR'S GARDEN

The poem presumably refers to Beatrix Potter's life and her stories for children: Mr. McGregor's garden is a source of temptation and danger for Peter Rabbit.

## THE MAST YEAR

Mast is the covering of acorns dropped by oak trees on the ground beneath.

*PETER FALLON*

## WINTER WORK

*meitheal*: an Irish word that refers to a group of neighbors who work together in turn on one another's farms.

*PAUL MULDOON*

## CUBA

The poem refers to the Cuban missile crisis of 1962.

## ANSEO

The title is pronounced "anshaw."

## GATHERING MUSHROOMS

Barnett's . . . demesne: a park on the outskirts of Belfast, near the river Lagan.

## THE MIRROR

C.I.E.: Coras Iompair Eireann, the Irish transport system.

## THE SIGHTSEERS

The B-Specials: the exclusively Protestant special constabulary recruited by the state of Northern Ireland to maintain its security; disbanded in 1970, it was replaced by the Ulster Defence Regiment and the Reserve of the Royal Ulster Constabulary.

## MEETING THE BRITISH

The speaker is an Ottawa Indian; the incident is historical.

## THE WISHBONE

The occasion is Christmas dinner.

*NUALA NI DHOMHNAILL*

## FEEDING A CHILD

óró: a vocable in Gaelic song and poetry.

## THE RACE

Glas Gaibhneach: the wonder cow of Irish myth and folklore that produced an endless supply of milk until someone tried to milk it into a sieve.

Deirdre: heroine of the ancient "elopement tale," Deirdre and the Sons of Uisneach.

*THOMAS McCARTHY*

## STATE FUNERAL

The funeral is that of Eamon De Valera in 1975. De Valera is synonymous with the development and consolidation of Ireland (twenty-six counties of it, at least) as a sovereign political entity; critics charge that De Valera's Ireland was narrow and provincial. He was one of the leaders of the Easter Rising, president of the Dail in 1919, opponent of the Treaty, founder of the Fianna Fail party, head of the Irish government for more than twenty years and its president for fourteen years. He saw Ireland (the twenty-six counties) through an economic war with Britain in the 1930s, later broke its remaining links with Britain, and zealously maintained its neutrality during the Second World War.

Broy-Harriers . . . Blueshirts: the latter was a fascistic paramilitary organization of the 1930s, founded by General Eoin O'Duffy. The man who replaced him as commissioner of police for the Irish Free State, Eamon Broy, recruited auxiliaries (nicknamed Broy-Harriers) to prevent any attempt at a coup d'état on the part of O'Duffy and the Blueshirts. A contingent of seven hundred Irish Blueshirts fought on the side of the fascists in the Spanish Civil War.

De Valera's words: when the Second World War ended, Winston Churchill bullyingly denigrated Ireland in his victory speech for its policy of neutrality; De Valera's dignified response, in the minds of most Irishmen, gave him and Ireland a moral victory in the exchange.

the tallest one: a reference to De Valera's stature.

## QUESTION TIME

Robert Emmet: member of the United Irishmen and leader of an abortive rising in 1803, he delivered his famous speech from the dock when he was sentenced to be hanged. His sweetheart was Sarah Curran.

Kitty O'Shea: the mistress of Charles Stuart Parnell. The affair precipitated Parnell's political downfall.

Which I.R.A. man . . . : Joseph Mary Plunkett was allowed to marry his fiancée before he was executed for his role in the Easter Rising.

How many death-warrants . . . : Kevin O'Higgins was minister of justice in the Free State government during the Irish Civil War in 1922–1923; the government executed seventy-seven Republicans. O'Higgins himself was assassinated in 1927.

# ACKNOWLEDGMENTS

The editor gratefully acknowledges the permission of writers and publishers to reprint the following copyright material:

*THOMAS MACGREEVY*

"De Civitate Hominum," "Aodh Ruadh O'Domhnaill," "Recessional," "Homage to Marcel Proust," and "Nocturne of the Self-Evident Presence," from *Collected Poems*, by permission of Michael Smith and New Writers Press.

*AUSTIN CLARKE*

"Pilgrimage," "Night and Morning," "Tenebrae," "The Straying Student," "The Envy of Poor Lovers," "Wolfe Tone," "Three Poems About Children," "Forget Me Not," an extract from *Mnemosyne Lay in Dust*, "Inscription for a Headstone," "The Subjection of Women," "Martha Blake at Fifty-One," and an extract from *Tiresias*, from *Selected Poems*, by permission of the Clarke estate and Wake Forest University Press; "The Planter's Daughter," from *Later Poems*, and "Mable Kelly," from *Flight to Africa*, by permission of the Clarke estate and Dolmen Press.

*FRANK O'CONNOR*

"The End of Clonmacnois" and "Hope," from *Kings, Lords and Commons*, by permission of Joan Daves, copyright 1959 Frank O'Connor;

"On the Death of His Wife" and "The Angry Poet," from *The Little Monasteries*, by permission of Dolmen Press.

*PATRICK KAVANAGH*

"Inniskeen Road: July Evening," "Shancoduff," "Father Mat," "Art McCooey," "Stony Grey Soil," "To the Man after the Harrow," an extract from *The Great Hunger*, "Tinker's Wife," "Epic," "The Hospital," "Canal Bank Walk," "In Memory of My Mother," and "October," from *Collected Poems*, copyright Katherine B. Kavanagh, by permission of Gallery Press.

*PADRAIC FALLON*

"Odysseus," "For Paddy Mac," "Pot Shot," "Weir Bridge," and "The Head," from *Poems*, copyright Brian Fallon; "A Hedge Schoolmaster" and "Dardanelles 1916," from *Poems and Versions*, copyright Brian Fallon, by permission of Raven Arts Press.

*BRIAN COFFEY*

An extract from "Missouri Sequence" and "Headrock," from *Selected Poems,* by permission of the author and New Writers Press; an extract from *Advent,* by permission of the author and Irish University Review; "Cold," from *Chanterelles,* by permission of the author.

*SAMUEL BECKETT*

"Malacoda," "Enueg I," and "I would like my love to die," from *Poems in English*, copyright 1961 Samuel Beckett, by permission of Grove Press, Inc.

# ACKNOWLEDGMENTS


## *JOHN HEWITT*

"Ireland," "Because I Paced My Thought," "An Irishman in Coventry," and "Once Alien Here," from *Collected Poems*, by permission of the author; "The Scar," from *Out of My Time*, by permission of the author and Blackstaff Press; "St Stephen's Day" and "Calling on Peadar O'Donnell at Dungloe," from *Loose Ends*, by permission of the author and Blackstaff Press.

## *LOUIS MACNEICE*

"Dublin," "Snow," an extract from "Trilogy for X," and an extract from *Autumn Journal*, from *The Collected Poems of Louis MacNeice*, by permission of Faber and Faber Ltd.

## *DENIS DEVLIN*

"Lough Derg," "Ank'Hor Vat," "Wishes for Her," "Daphne Stillorgan," "Anteroom: Geneva," and "Renewal by her Element," from *Collected Poems*, copyright Stephen Devlin, by permission of Dolmen Press; an extract from *The Heavenly Foreigner*, copyright Stephen Devlin, by permission of Dolmen Press.

## *W. R. RODGERS*

"The Net," from *Europa and the Bull*, by permission of Martin Secker and Warburg Ltd.; "Paired Lives," copyright W. R. Rodgers 1941, and "Scapegoat," copyright W. R. Rodgers 1971, by permission of Lucy Rodgers Cohen.

# ACKNOWLEDGMENTS

## *DONAGH MacDONAGH*

"Just An Old Sweet Song," from *A Warning to Conquerors*, by permission of Iseumt McGuinness and Dolmen Press; "The Veterans" and an extract from "Charles Donnelly," from *Veterans and Other Poems*, by permission of Irish University Press.

## *CHARLES DONNELLY*

"Poem," "The Tolerance of Crows," and "The Flowering Bars," by permission of Joseph Donnelly.

## *VALENTIN IREMONGER*

"Hector," "Icarus," and "This Houre Her Vigill," from *Horan's Field and Other Reservations*, by permission of the author and Dolmen Press.

## *PADRAIC FIACC*

"Haemorrhage," from *Odour of Blood*, by permission of the author and Goldsmith Press; "The Poet" and "Gloss," from *By the Black Stream*, by permission of the author and Goldsmith Press; "Introit" and "Goodbye to Brigid / an *Agnus Dei*," from *Missa Terribilis*, by permission of the author and Blackstaff Press.

## *ANTHONY CRONIN*

"Apology," "The Man Who Went Absent from the Native Literature," and "The Middle Years," from *New and Selected Poems*, by permission of the author and Raven Arts Press.

# ACKNOWLEDGMENTS

## *PEARSE HUTCHINSON*

"Into Their True Gentleness" and "Boxing the Fox," from *Selected Poems*, by permission of Gallery Press; "Manifest Destiny" from *Climbing the Light*, by permission of Gallery Press.

## *RICHARD MURPHY*

"The Philosopher and the Birds," "The Poet on the Island," an extract from *The Battle of Aughrim*, "Seals at High Island," "High Island," "A Nest in a Wall," and "Beehive Cell," from *The Price of Stone and Earlier Poems*, by permission of the author and Wake Forest University Press.

## *THOMAS KINSELLA*

"Baggot Street Deserta," "Another September," "Clarence Mangan," "Cover Her Face," "A Country Walk," "Mirror in February," "Wormwood," "Ritual of Departure," "Hen Woman," "A Hand of Solo," and "Death Bed," from *Poems 1956–1973*, by permission of the author and Wake Forest University Press; extracts from *A Technical Supplement* and *The Messenger*, from *Peppercanister Poems 1972–1978*, by permission of the author and Wake Forest University Press; "Model School, Inchicore," from *Songs of the Psyche*, by permission of the author.

## *JOHN MONTAGUE*

"A Bright Day," "All Legendary Obstacles," "That Room," "The Answer," "A Lost Tradition," "Witness," "The Wild Dog Rose," "The Cage," "Lament for the O'Neills," "A Grafted Tongue," "Last Journey," "Windharp," an extract from "The Leaping Fire," "Tracks," "Herbert Street Revisited," and "Process," from *Selected Poems*, by permission of the author and Wake Forest University Press; "The Silver Flask" and "A Flowering Absence" from *The Dead Kingdom*, by permission of the author and Wake Forest University Press.

# ACKNOWLEDGMENTS

*SEAN LUCY*

"Senior Members," "Supervising Examinations," and "Longshore Intellectual," from *Five Irish Poets*, by permission of the author and Mercier Press; "Friday Evening" and "These Six," by permission of the author.

*ANNE HARTIGAN*

"Advent," "Brazen Image," "St. Bridget's Cross," and "No Easy Harbour," from *Long Tongue*, by permission of the author and Beaver Row Press; "Salt" by permission of the author.

*TOM MACINTYRE*

"On Sweet Killen Hill" and "The Yellow Bittern," from *Blood Relations*, by permission of the author and New Writers Press; "Drumlin Prayer" by permission of the author.

*JAMES SIMMONS*

"Fear Test: Integrity of Heroes," "Outward Bound," "Claudy," "John Donne," and "October in the Country: 1983," from *Poems 1956–1986*, by permission of the author and Gallery Press; "Playing with Fire," from *From the Irish*, by permission of the author and Blackstaff Press.

*JAMES LIDDY*

"The Voice of America 1961," from *In a Blue Smoke*, "Paean to Eve's Apple," from *Blue Mountain*, and "History," from *Corca Bascinn*, by permission of the author and Dolmen Press; "The Strand Hotel, Rosslare," from *At the Grave of Father Sweetman*, by permission of the author.

*DESMOND O'GRADY*

"Professor Kelleher and the Charles River," "The Poet in Old Age Fishing at Evening," and an extract from "The Dying Gaul," from *The Headgear of the Tribe*, by permission of Gallery Press; "If I Went Away," "In the Greenwood," and "Finn's Wishes," from *A Limerick Rake*, by permission of Gallery Press.

*BRENDAN KENNELLY*

"My Dark Fathers," "The Thatcher," and "Proof" from *New and Selected Poems*, by permission of the author and Gallery Press; "Yes" and "The Horse's Head" from *The Boats Are Home*, by permission of the author and Gallery Press.

*SEAMUS HEANEY*

"Digging," "At a Potato Digging," "The Wife's Tale," "The Other Side," "A New Song," "The Tollund Man," and "Summer 1969," from *Poems 1965–1975*, copyright Seamus Heaney 1966, 1969, 1972, 1975, 1980, by permission of Farrar, Straus, and Giroux, Inc.; "The Strand at Lough Beg" and "In Memoriam Francis Ledwidge," from *Field Work*, copyright Seamus Heaney 1976, 1979, by permission of Farrar, Straus, and Giroux, Inc.; "An Ulster Twilight" and section 9 of "Station Island," from *Station Island*, copyright Seamus Heaney 1985, by permission of Farrar, Straus, and Giroux, Inc.; "From the Canton of Expectation" and "Clearances" (3, 5, 7), from *The Haw Lantern*, copyright 1988 Seamus Heaney, by permission of Farrar, Straus, and Giroux, Inc.

*MICHAEL LONGLEY*

"Epithalamion," "Emily Dickinson," "Kindertotenlieder," and "Desert Warfare," from *Poems 1963–1983*, by permission of the author and Gallery Press; "Letter to Derek Mahon," "Caravan," "Fleance," "The Linen Workers," "The Linen Industry," and "Peace" from *Selected Poems 1963–1980*, by permission of the author and Wake Forest University Press; "Detour" and "An Amish Rug" by kind permission of the author.

*SEAMUS DEANE*

"Derry," from *Gradual Wars*, by permission of the author; "A Schooling" and "Scholar II," from *Rumours*, by permission of the author and Dolmen Press; "History Lessons" and "A Burial," from *History Lessons*, by permission of the author and Gallery Press.

*MICHAEL HARTNETT*

"All the death-room needs," "A Small Farm," and "Marban, a Hermit, Speaks," from *Selected Poems*, by permission of the author and New Writers Press; "The Retreat of Ita Cagney," from *The Retreat of Ita Cagney/Cúlú Ide*, by permission of the author and Goldsmith Press; an extract from "A Farewell to English" and "Death of an Irishwoman," from *Poems in English*, by permission of the author and Dolmen Press; "Pity the man who English lacks," and "All the same, it would make you laugh," from O *Bruadair*, by permission of the author and Gallery Press.

*DEREK MAHON*

"Glengormley," "In Carrowdore Churchyard," "Afterlives," "The Snow Party," "Matthew V. 29–30," "A Disused Shed in Co. Wexford," "Consolations of Philosophy," and "Ecclesiastes," from *Poems 1962–1978*, copyright Derek Mahon 1979, by permission of Oxford University Press; "Courtyards in Delft" and "Another Sunday Morning," from *The Hunt By Night*, copyright Derek Mahon 1983, by permission of Wake Forest University Press.

## *EILEAN NÍ CHUILLEANÁIN*

"Swineherd," "Dead Fly," "Lucina Schynning in Silence of the Night . . . ," and an extract from "Site of Ambush," from *The Second Voyage*, by permission of Wake Forest University Press; an extract from "The Rose-Geranium," from *The Rose-Geranium*, by permission of the author and Gallery Press.

## *MICHAEL SMITH*

"Fall," "Mitching," "Dinner Queue," "City II," and "From the Chinese," from *Selected Poems*, by permission of the author and Melmoth Press.

## *AUGUSTUS YOUNG*

"The Advice of an Efficiency Expert" and "Heritage," from *On Loaning Hill*, by permission of the author and New Writers Press; "Woman, don't be troublesome," from *Danta Gradha / Love Poems from the Irish*, by permission of the author and Advent Books; "Ballad of Fat Margot," by permission of the author.

## *EAVAN BOLAND*

"Song" and "Child of Our Time," from *The War Horse*, by permission of the author; "It's a Woman's World," from *Night Feed*, by permission of the author and Arlen House; "The Glass King," "Lace," and "An Irish Childhood in England: 1951," from *The Journey and Other Poems*, by permission of the author and Arlen House.

*PAUL DURCAN*

"Wife Who Smashed Television Gets Jail," from *Teresa's Bar*, by permission of the author and Gallery Press; "Going Home to Mayo, Winter, 1949" from *Sam's Cross*, by permission of the author; "10.30 am Mass, June 16, 1985," "Bewley's Oriental Café, Westmoreland Street," and "The Turkish Carpet," from *The Berlin Wall Cafe*, by permission of the author and Blackstaff Press.

*JOHN ENNIS*

"Meeting at a Salesyard," "The Years," and "A Drink of Spring," from *A Drink of Spring*, by permission of Gallery Press.

*RICHARD RYAN*

"Ireland" and "From My Lai the Thunder Went West," from *Ravenswood*, by permission of the author and Dolmen Press; "A Wet Night," by permission of the author.

*HUGH MAXTON*

"Cernunnos," from *Stones*, by permission of the author; "Waking," from *The Noise of the Fields*, by permission of the author and Dolmen Press; "At the Protestant Museum," from *At the Protestant Museum*, by permission of the author and Dolmen Press.

*FRANK ORMSBY*

"Ornaments" and "Spot the Ball," from *A Store of Candles*, by permission of the author and Gallery Press; "Interim," from *Business as Usual*, by permission of the author and Ulsterman Publications; "Survivors," an extract from "A Northern Spring," and "At the Jaffé Memorial Fountain, Botanic Gardens," from *A Northern Spring*, by permission of Gallery Press.

*CIARAN CARSON*

"The Insular Celts" and "The Car Cemetery," from *The New Estate*, by permission of Wake Forest University Press; "It Used To Be," by permission of the author; "Dresden," "Belfast Confetti," and "Campaign," from *The Irish for No*, by permission of Wake Forest University Press.

*TOM PAULIN*

"Under the Eyes," from *A State of Justice*, by permission of Faber and Faber Ltd.; "Surveillances" and "The Impossible Pictures," from *The Strange Museum*, by permission of Faber and Faber Ltd.; "And Where Do You Stand on the National Question?" "Desertmartin," and "Black Bread," from *Liberty Tree*, by permission of Faber and Faber Ltd.

*MEDBH McGUCKIAN*

"Mr. McGregor's Garden" and "The Mast Year," from *The Flower Master*, copyright Medbh McGuckian 1982, by permission of Oxford University Press; "The Folk Museum," by permission of the author; "The Dream-Language of Fergus" and "Coleridge," from *On Ballycastle Beach*, by permission of Wake Forest University Press.

*PETER FALLON*

"Winter Work," from *Winter Work*, by permission of Gallery Press; "My Care" and "Spring Song," by permission of the author.

*PAUL MULDOON*

"Clonfeacle," from *Mules and Early Poems*, by permission of Wake Forest University Press; "Cuba" and "Anseo," from *Why Brownlee Left*, by permission of Wake Forest University Press; "Gathering Mushrooms," "The Mirror," and "The Sightseers," from *Quoof*, by permission of Wake Forest University Press; "Meeting the British," "The Wishbone," "Sushi," and "Christo's," from *Meeting the British*, by permission of Wake Forest University Press.

*NUALA NÍ DHOMHNAILL*

"Labasheedy," "The Shannon Estuary Welcoming the Fish," "Parthenogenesis," "Feeding a Child," and "The Race," from *Selected Poems*, by permission of the author and Raven Arts Press; "As for the Quince," by permission of the author and the translator.

*THOMAS McCARTHY*

"State Funeral," "Feeding Ground," and "The Word 'silk,' " from *The First Convention*, by permission of the author and Dolmen Press; "The Poet of the Mountains," from *The Sorrow Garden*, by permission of the author and Anvil Press; "Question Time," from *The Non-Aligned Storyteller*, by permission of the author and Anvil Press.

# ACKNOWLEDGMENTS

*AIDAN CARL MATHEWS*

"Descartes at Daybreak," "The Library," "Severances," "At the Wailing Wall," and "Minding Ruth," from *Minding Ruth*, by permission of Gallery Press.

# INDEXES

# INDEX OF AUTHORS

## INDEX OF TITLES

## INDEX OF FIRST LINES

NEW HANOVER COUNTY PUBLIC LIBRARY
3 4200 00292 0854